International
and
European
Monetary
Systems

International and European Monetary Systems

Edited by

Emil-Maria Claassen

PRAEGER

New York
Westport, Connecticut
London

Library of Congress Cataloging-in-Publication Data

International and European monetary systems / edited by Emil-Maria
   Claassen.
        p.   cm.
   Bibliography: p.
   Includes index.
   ISBN 0–275–93284–2 (alk. paper)
      1. Money—European Economic Community countries.   2. Monetary
policy—European Economic Community countries.   3. Money.
4. Monetary policy.   5. International finance.   I. Claassen, Emil-
Maria, 1934–   .
HG930.5.I585   1990
332.4'5—dc20   89–3916

Library of Congress Catalog Card Number: 89–3916
ISBN: 0–275–93284–2

First published in 1990

Praeger Publishers, One Madison Avenue, New York, NY 10010
A division of Greenwood Press, Inc.

Printed in the United States of America

The paper used in this book complies with the
Permanent Paper Standard issued by the National
Information Standards Organization (Z39.48–1984).

10 9 8 7 6 5 4 3 2 1

Contents

Illustrations

FIGURES

Introduction

The present world monetary system could be stylized by the coexistence of three exchange rate regimes (see table I.1): managed float, adjustable peg, and fixed peg. The managed float concerns the industrialized countries relative to the United States as the center of the dollar standard. However, among the industrialized countries, the EMS countries play a particular role. The intra-EMS exchange rates follow a fixed, but adjustable peg.

When examining the behavior of interventions by EMS central banks in the foreign exchange market, one has to distinguish between those at the margin and intramarginal ones. The former are compulsory when two currencies hit the limit of the bilateral fluctuation band and they have to be pursued by the two central banks concerned in using each other's currency. The important interventions that characterize the EMS are intramarginal. In a recent paper by Francesco Giavazzi and Alberto Giovannini on "Models of the EMS: Is Europe a Greater Deutsch-Mark Area?" (1987), one obtains the interesting information that Germany never intervenes intramarginally in EMS currencies, whereas there are important inter-marginal interventions by other EMS countries. Furthermore, when Germany intervenes, it does so with respect to the U.S. dollar, and most dollar interventions within the EMS are in fact coming from Germany. Consequently, there is an evolution toward a "German Monetary Area" in the sense that Germany, representing all other EMS countries, manages the float of the DM/dollar rate whereas the other (n−1) EMS currencies (plus Austria and Switzerland) peg to the German currency and manage the intra-EMS rates with intramarginal interventions in EMS currencies.

The third block of countries are the LDCs. Even though their exchange rate regimes are very diversified as demonstrated by Bela Balassa (from float to multiple exchange rates), the predominant feature is a fixed peg in which, for instance, the francophone LDCs peg to the French franc and other LDCs (e.g., Latin American countries) peg to the U.S. dollar.

The exchange rate system of a managed float with respect to the dollar is the object of the three first papers (Williamson, Camen/Genberg, Claassen). The fundamental question raised by the authors is whether this system of the last decade has shown basic tendencies toward increasingly disequilibrated real exchange rates or, on the contrary, has conserved their equilibrium level. As one could expect, the answers provided by the authors are not at all unanimous. Williamson points out an important misalignment in real exchange rates and, hence, proposes his well-known target-zone proposal. Camen/Genberg are more eclectic, since the exchange rate can be dominated by a mix of nominal and real shocks. Claassen refers to the "turbulent" up-and-down of the real exchange rate of the dollar during the 1980s, and he interprets it partly as an equilibrium phenomenon to the extent that it reflects the huge swings in fiscal stance between the United States on the one side and Europe and Japan on the other side.

For Williamson, the "fundamental equilibrium exchange rate" (FEER) is that real exchange rate which on average in the medium run reconciles internal and external balance. Internal balance is interpreted as the lowest unemployment rate consistent with inflationary control, and external balance refers to a sustainable current account balance that takes into account thrift (savings) and productivity (investment). Consequently, first of all, targets for internal and external balance have to be fixed by international agreement, and afterwards they have to be translated into an exchange rate target via an econometric model, which is, according to Williamson, "an essentially technical exercise." His discussant,

Table I.1

The Three Dominating Exchange Rate Regimes in the Present World Monetary System

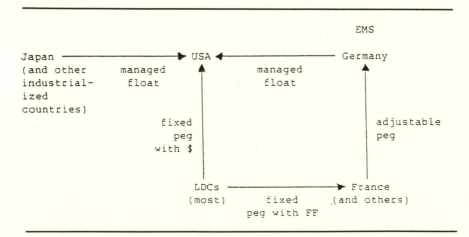

Gandolfo, casts some doubt on the existence of a generally accepted econometric model, given the existing lack of consensus among scholars concerning *the* appropriate common model. Furthermore, to the extent that there are various possible combinations of the usual policy tools to achieve internal and external balance, each of these combinations would give rise to a different FEER.

Camen and Genberg attribute changes in the real exchange rate to changes in the underlying fundamentals, or to the phenomenon of misalignment. Among the former, changing macroeconomic (fiscal or monetary) policies may be dominant; speculative bubbles may be responsible for the latter. If policies are the cause of the change in the real exchange rate, then it is not the real exchange rate but the macroeconomic policies that are "misaligned." A special merit of the Camen/Genberg paper is to have shown that one cannot draw inferences from real exchange rate movements about the nature of the disturbing (real or monetary) shock, and hence about the appropriate policy response.

The chapter by Claassen evaluates the pros and cons of exchange rate management as they are contained in the present literature, and it examines two major events since the generalized float: world inflation over the 1970s, which could have been dampened by coordinated intervention in the foreign exchange market, and the tremendous trend fluctuation in the real exchange rate of the U.S. dollar of the 1980s, which would not have been avoided by any proper exchange rate management. Real shocks affect the real fundamentals and thus the real exchange rate. Real shocks emerge in the real sector (i.e. in the goods market), and their origin can be traced to the supply side (oil price increases) or demand side (bond-financed budget deficits). The case of fiscal expansion in the United States and of (relative) fiscal contraction in Europe and Japan constitutes the major real shock of the 1980s. It raises the real world market interest and provokes a switch of savings in the world economy from Europe and Japan to the United States via capital movements. To the net capital flows must correspond net trade flows, which are brought about by a real appreciation of the U.S. dollar. Exchange rate management and, *a fortiori,* international coordination of intervention policies, would have been a nuisance to the international monetary system, and, over the long run, they would have changed only the nominal exchange rate. Only fiscal convergence would have avoided the tremendous real appreciation and the following depreciation of the U.S. dollar.

In his comment on Claassen, Douglas Purvis suggests an alternative view on the motivation of the divergent fiscal policies between the United States and Europe (including Japan) during the 1980s. To the extent that the fiscal expansion by the United States was of the Keynesian type for inducing the U.S. recovery and to the extent that European fiscal restraint occurred, there was an incentive created for an increased U.S. fiscal deficit. Thus, Europe did not react to U.S. fiscal expansion with fiscal restraint essentially for reasons of real interest rate management, as Claassen suggests, but the Americans reacted with more fiscal expansion to European fiscal restraint. According to Purvis, a more productive European response would have been fiscal expansion, which would have reduced the perceived need for U.S. deficits from the point of view of U.S. demand management. As a result, the consequences for the real interest rate would not have been as drastic as Claassen's analysis suggests, since he assumes a *given* U.S. fiscal stance.

While the first three contributions were concerned with the present and future outlook of a better managed float, the two following papers deal with an improvement of the actual role of SDRs (Jürgen Schröder) and with the appropriate exchange-rate regime for LDCs (Bela Balassa). At the moment, holdings of SDRs (20 billion) amount to approximately 5 percent of total non-gold reserves. They were first allocated in 1969, but very soon several motivations for their creation became increasingly obsolete: the suspension of convertibility of the U.S. dollar into gold in 1971; the reduced need of foreign exchange reserves in a system of flexible exchange rates; the increased access to borrowed reserves in a world of liberalized international capital movements; and the evolution of the dollar standard towards a multi-currency standard. According to Schröder one could observe, during the 1980s, an excess demand for SDR credit (i.e., the wish by deficit countries to use their allocated SDRs was larger than the supply of SDR credit by those surplus countries who were willing to hold more SDRs than their SDR allocation). Since the interest rate on SDRs is a weighted average of the three-month interest rates of the five currencies constituting the SDR basket, and since SDR credit is used very often for long-term financing, the surplus countries had no incentives to increase SDR holdings. Schröder argues that a specific long-run scenario (an increasing weakness of the U.S. dollar and the unwillingness of other countries to allow their currencies to be used as a reserve asset) could strengthen the role of the SDR.

As far as the immediate future is concerned, Schröder proposes an increase of incentives for holdings of SDRs and a decrease of incentives for using them, which could be brought about by raising the interest rate on SDR allocations and on SDR holdings. This measure could decrease, if not eliminate, the present excess demand for SDRs.

The discussion on the optimum exchange rate regime for LDCs has first of all to answer the question about the proper objectives of an exchange-rate regime. Even though the ultimate goal may be growth or growth per capita as his discussant, Marcello de Cecco, emphasizes, Bela Balassa lists four "intermediate" objectives:

1. For reasons of an efficient allocation of resources, foreign exchange restrictions should be avoided. Under exchange restrictions, the "objective" rationing by the market is replaced by the "subjective" rationing of an administrative authority, often involving bribery and rent-seeking.

2. Overevaluation of currencies—a common fact of most LDCs—should also be avoided, since it discriminates against the production of traded goods (less exports and more imports) in favor of non-traded goods. A "realistic" exchange rate should be maintained that realizes a continuing net capital inflow (in order to finance a current account deficit) that is limited by considerations of credit-worthiness.

3. Fluctuations in the exchange rates should be avoided in order to limit uncertainty for business decisions.

4. Fluctuations in macroeconomic relationships should be avoided that would require large holdings of foreign exchange reserves.

Balassa's preference for the optimal exchange rate regime for LDCs seems to lean toward the option of freely floating exchange rates. This is the more astonishing when one considers that the traditional literature has always pointed out their destabilizing effect because of limited capital flows and of the lack of sufficient reserves in case of a managed float. However, Balassa points out that recently twelve LDCs have opted for an independently floating system. A second-best choice would be a multi-currency peg, which is superior to a single-currency peg, except for the case when the bulk of a country's trade is carried out with a single currency.

The remaining four chapters are concerned with the EMS and the present and future role of the ECU. The common objectives for the creation of the EMS in 1979 and for the early 1980s was the reduction of inflation, in particular for those countries with a high inflation rate, like France and Italy. The problem was that monetary authorities in the inflation-prone countries lacked credibility. Their credibility gains by joining and staying within the EMS had to be purchased by an extra penalty to inflation in terms of competitiveness losses relative to Germany. This "discipline" approach to the EMS, formalized by F. Giavazzi and M. Pagano in 1987 ("The Advantage of Tying One's Hands: EMS Discipline and Central Bank Credibility," *European Economic Review*), has two implications, which Susan Collins tries to test in her chapter.

On one hand, one should observe not only convergence of inflation rates, but, in particular, greater and/or more rapid convergence inside the EMS than outside—or, as Giavazzi remarks in his comment, one should test whether the average inflation inside the system was lower than the inflation rate that would have prevailed in a floating exchange rate system, a task he considers to be almost impossible. By comparing the pre-EMS period with the EMS period and by comparing the EMS members with the non-member group, Collins comes to the conclusion that it remains difficult to claim that the EMS has reduced inflation rates and narrowed inflation differentials.

On the other hand, the second implication of the disciplinary model is that inflation-prone countries accept a penalty in terms of a real appreciation, which constitutes an incentive for policy convergence to narrow inflation differentials between member countries. However, according to Collins, the data do not provide strong support for this view, since another view (i.e., that of the "competitive" approach) is also observable, according to which realignments have been used to keep bilateral rates fluctuating around PPP. The particular aspect of the competitiveness model is that a competitiveness bonus must be granted to the inflation-prone countries just after the first realignment that is large enough to compensate for the competitiveness loss that they suffer before the second re-alignment takes place

Another issue treated by Collins concerns the so-called peso problem, accord-ing to which market participants anticipate realignments and where the anticipa-tions are disruptive. There is clear evidence that realignments have been antici-pated *and* that the shifts in expectations reflected changes in the fundamentals. However, the timing of exchange rate adjustments was in conflict with the former depletion of foreign exchange reserves, which can create a balance-of-payments crisis, even though this would be less pronounced for weak currencies (French franc, Italian lira), which are subject to capital controls.

In his analysis on "Fiscal Policies in the EMS," Paul De Grauwe begins his argument by pointing out the unfavourable macroeconomic performance (in terms of growth rates and inflation rates) since 1979 of the EMS countries compared with the rest of the industrialized world. The relatively lower growth performance is explained by excessively deflationary fiscal policies within the EMS since 1982. Negative outside balance-of-payments disturbances (second oil shock or the real depreciation of the U.S. dollar) led to an overreaction by certain EMS countries, since their national authorities were not only concerned by output fluctuations, but also by current account objectives. Cooperation between EMS members with less contractionary fiscal policies would have been more welfare-increasing, as he shows in a lengthy two-country model of the Mundell-Fleming type and within a game-theoretic framework. The reasons why the EMS countries adopted the Nash solution are various, among which De Grauwe em-phasizes two. We know from game theory that cooperation will not be forthcom-ing if the game (i.e., cooperation) is not played repeatedly. A major problem with fiscal policies that the national (fiscal) players do not meet frequently, in contrast to monetary policy whose agents (who stay in power longer than a typical government) are likely to meet much more often in the international arena. A second major obstacle to cooperation may lie in the uncertainty of the underlying macroeconomic model used for evaluating fiscal policy as a stimulat-ing measure (Keynesian framework) or as a neutral measure (new classical framework).

The two last chapters deal with the increasing role of private ECUs. It is a fact that the ECU deposit and loan markets have grown considerably over the last years. Tullio and Contesso provide a useful framework for the reasons why private ECUs have developed so much. It is surprising that one does not find any other private currency baskets (not even private SDRs), but only private ECUs. In the view of the two authors, the private ECU has profited from the official ECU since the latter serves as a pivot of the EMS exchange-rate regime and, thus, increased the confidence in the private ECU. Furthermore, the low risk/high return characteristics of the private ECU (in terms of more stable exchange rates and less volatile interest rates than any individual component currency) have been a cause of its development. However, as Tullio and Contesso also emphasize, the risk diversification function of the ECU is reduced as the

EMS becomes more coordinated and the exchange-rate mechanism moves more towards a system of fixed exchange rates. But even with fixed exchange rates, the interest rate on the ECU will possess a greater stability than interest rates on any individual currency. The controversial issue of whether capital controls in the weak-currency countries like France and Italy have encouraged or hindered the growth of private ECUs is also fully discussed by the two authors.

In their empirical evidence, Tullio and Contesso present the computed spreads between the interest rates of ECU deposits (for various maturities) and the corresponding combined Eurocurrency rates. They observe negative spreads until the end of 1983 and positive ones afterward. Their explanation is put in terms of expectations of realignments and of redefinitions of the ECU basket, whereas their discussant, Manfred Neumann, sees the specific behaviour of interest rate spreads as a "statistical artefact." Another controversy between the authors and the discussant concerns the market efficiency test, which is satisfactory for Tullio and Contesso, but which is defective according to Neumann.

The "Second Thoughts" by Roland Vaubel on currency unification (or currency union, which means the existence of a single currency) remain eclectic since, as he argues, there is no operational scientific method to compare the benefits of currency unification (e.g., elimination of information costs about current exchange rates and exchange controls; elimination of transaction costs of converting one money into another; elimination of exchange rate risks) with its costs (the price level risk of a unique currency), the latter being due to the weakening of currency competition. Vaubel used to believe that currency competition within Europe would merely show us the optimal path to the desirable end of currency unification. However, in the present chapter, he admits that currency competition (within a regime of flexible exchange rates) is also the optimal procedure of finding out whether a currency union is desirable. Formerly, perfect monetary integration was usually considered as a case of a single currency. However, perfect monetary integration is also conceivable with the existence of several currencies, to the extent that individuals have differences in taste with respect to currency risks.

A second-best solution of currency competition is the parallel currency approach. Instead of choosing the parallel currency among all existing EC currencies, each money user would be free to choose between his national currency and the common European currency. A possible candidate for the latter could be the private ECU, provided that the current weight structure of the ECU basket would be reformed. According to Vaubel, the ECU currency weights should be equal to the share that each member currency occupies in the EC money supply at market exchange rates, reflecting the currency preferences of European money holders. This proposal leads his discussant, Peter Kenen, to the comment that the reformed ECU would be an instrument for fostering Darwinian competition among the central banks until only one of them remained, and its national currency would become indistinguishable from the ECU—a proposal that should persuade the Bundesbank to look with more favor upon the private ECU.

PART I

THE INTERNATIONAL MONETARY SYSTEM

1

Target Zones and Monetary Stability

John Williamson

The target zone proposal for exchange rate management seeks to combine the real social benefits that exchange rate flexibility can bring while overcoming the weaknesses of unmanaged floating. Ideally it would be one element in a set of comprehensive principles for policy coordination. While the principles that I am currently suggesting for this purpose are not yet necessarily in their steady-state form, I believe they offer a more hopeful framework for monetary and macroeconomic stability than any of their traditional competitors (the gold standard, dollar standard, floating rates with fixed monetary growth rules, Bretton Woods, or McKinnon).

Section 1 of this chapter explains why I judge the performance of unmanaged floating to have been unsatisfactory. Section 2 lists the real social benefits that exchange rate flexibility can afford, which should be preserved by any reformed system. Section 3 describes the target zone proposal and explains why it would preserve the real benefits of flexibility while overcoming the weaknesses of unmanaged floating. Section 4 sketches a set of comprehensive principles for policy coordination, of which target zones would be one natural element. Section 5 explains what I perceive to be the advantages of these principles as against their principal traditional competitors.

1. THE FAILURES OF FLOATING

Unmanaged floating has proved unsatisfactory in two key respects. First, failure to factor exchange rate implications into the process of policy choice led to recurring, and at times massive, currency misalignments.[1] Misalignments can arise as a rational market response to international differences in real interest rates; in my judgment this explains, for example, much of the initial overvaluation of the dollar in 1981–83, although even here the rise of the dollar during 1982 appears paradoxical. They can also arise as a result of bandwagon effects leading to bubbles in the foreign exchange market—I can, for example, find no other explanation for the continued rise of the dollar from mid-1984 to February 1985, since this was a period when the dollar was already far above any estimate of a sustainable level, and interest rate differentials were narrowing (on every plausible basis of measurement).

The second major failure of unmanaged floating is the lack of pressure that it places on countries to coordinate their economic policies. When exchange rates were first allowed to float, most economists regarded the additional independence this afforded economic policy, notably monetary policy, as an advantage. But in retrospect it is far from clear that policy coordination was the irrelevance that this view assumed it to be. The poor performance of the world economy since 1973, including especially the extent of cyclical synchronization and the severity of the debt crisis, is in my judgment partly attributable to the virtual absence of policy coordination.

Admittedly, the costs of failing to coordinate policies are still conjectural rather than firmly established. In contrast, the costs of misalignments are glaringly apparent: massive payments imbalances, consequential international investment flows that bear no relationship to the real scarcity of capital, distortions to the optimal time pattern of consumption, unnecessary adjustment costs as resources are shifted back and forth between the tradable and nontradable sectors, the destruction of productive capacity, possible ratchet effects on inflation, and protectionist pressures (Williamson 1985a; 38–45; Bergsten 1986). Indeed, Baldwin and Krugman (1986) argue persuasively that the costs of misalignments have probably been significantly underestimated in the past because of the failure to take account of hysteresis. That is, once a company has abandoned an export market or established itself in an import market, a reversion of the real exchange rate to its initial level will not suffice to restore trade flows to their previous patterns, because of the significant overhead costs frequently involved in entering or re-entering a market. Adjusting trade flows back after a severe misalignment will therefore tend to be more difficult and costly than traditional econometric estimates suggest.

2. THE SOCIAL FUNCTIONS OF EXCHANGE FLEXIBILITY

The failure of unmanaged floating should not blind one to the fact that fixed exchange rates were abandoned for good reasons. The exchange rate debate has for too long been stilted by excessive emphasis on the textbook cases of fixed and floating rates to the neglect of intermediate regimes, which are motivated by recognition of the weaknesses in both extremes.

A first important function of exchange rate flexibility is that of reconciling differential inflation. Obviously a decision to accommodate inflation through depreciation implies that the exchange rate is not going to be used as a "nominal anchor."[2] There are other and better policies to control inflation; whether anti-inflation policy proves more or less effective than in other countries, appreciation or depreciation is needed respectively to prevent success being undermined by imported inflation or to prevent overvaluation.

A second function is that of facilitating payments adjustment when this proves necessary, by changing the incentives to export and import. It is well known that an exchange rate change is rarely sufficient to accomplish adjustment, but, except where disequilibrium is due purely to excess or deficient demand, an attempted adjustment that does not include a change in the exchange rate will involve unnecessarily high unemployment or inflation.

A third function of exchange rate flexibility is that of liberating monetary policy to pursue interest rate targets at variance with those in the rest of the world. If one country is suffering a deeper recession than its partners, it may legitimately wish to ease monetary policy relative to other countries, and that will be feasible only if its currency can depreciate so as to create an expectation of a subsequent rebound that will compensate investors for the temporarily low interest rates. Conversely, a country with abnormally severe inflation may legitimately seek to raise interest rates temporarily, which will require an appreciation. A wide band within which exchange rates are allowed to move around parity provides scope for such temporary variations in monetary policy to pursue anti-cyclical objectives.

The final legitimate function of exchange rate flexibility is that of absorbing a part of speculative pressures. Instead of requiring that every change in speculative sentiment lead to a change in international reserves and/or interest rates, one can allow changes in the exchange rate to take the strain. Provided these changes do not lead to the prolonged and substantial movements away from equilibrium that constitute misalignments, they do little harm.

3. THE TARGET ZONE PROPOSAL

The target zone proposal envisages a limited number of the major countries negotiating a set of mutually consistent targets for their effective exchange rates. The minimum number of countries needed for a meaningful system would be the three biggest: the United States, Germany, and Japan. Current proposals for policy coordination involve rather more countries; the Group of Five includes the two other countries with currencies in the SDR, namely France and Britain, while the Group of Seven also adds Canada and Italy.

The aim would be to set exchange rate targets at "fundamental equilibrium exchange rates," that is, at the real values that on average in the medium term are expected to reconcile internal and external balance. This will require agreed interpretations of internal balance (the lowest unemployment rate consistent with the control of inflation) and external balance (a current account balance that is both sustainable and appropriate in the light of thrift and productivity). Both concepts involve an element of subjective judgment and will therefore permit obfuscation by recalcitrant governments, but both provide sufficiently well-defined criteria to form a basis for the sort of technocratic argument that can ultimately lead to international agreement, given a modicum of political goodwill. Targets for internal and external balance would then have to be translated into exchange rate targets via some econometric model, which is an essentially technical exercise.

The nominal exchange rate targets corresponding to the agreed real targets should be regularly updated in the light of new data on differential inflation between countries. The real targets should be revised to accommodate both secular trends, such as superior productivity growth in the tradable sector (Balassa 1964), and real shocks or new information.

The participating countries would be expected to conduct their macroeconomic policies with a view to limiting deviations of their exchange rates from the agreed targets, and particularly with a view to preventing exchange rates going outside a broad zone of perhaps ±10 percent around the target. The principal instrument to be used for that purpose would be monetary (interest rate) policy. Provided that the market knew that the authorities were prepared to alter interest rates with a view to managing the exchange rate, there is good reason to believe that jawboning and intervention can also be useful supplementary instruments. If the necessary changes in monetary policy threatened internal balance, it would be necessary to make a compensatory adjustment in fiscal policy.

A country participating in the target zone system need not accept an absolute obligation to keep its exchange rate within the target zone. There are, in my view, two good reasons for endowing target zones with "soft buffers," which would give a country the right to argue before its peers that it not be required to prevent a breach of the zone. One such circumstance arises where some major shock (such as an oil price change) occurs. Rather than forcing the authorities to decide immediately whether to adjust the zone (as might be appropriate if the shock is permanent) or to adjust their policies to push the rate back into the zone, it may be preferable to allow a period for assessment of the magnitude and probable permanence of the shock. This could avoid the danger of countries committing themselves to defense of a disequilibrium rate, as used to happen under Bretton Woods.

The second circumstance arises where political cowardice prevents a government taking the fiscal action needed to complement the monetary measures that would be necessary to keep the exchange rate in its target zone. For example, when the dollar first became seriously overvalued in late 1981, the first-best policy would have been monetary relaxation accompanied by fiscal contraction; but had that combination been precluded by political hang-ups, it is arguable that it would have been advisable to maintain monetary discipline in the interests of ensuring success in the battle against inflation, even at the cost of the dollar rising temporarily above its target zone.[3] Maintaining the zone under those conditions would nevertheless have warned the market of an official judgment that the rate was overvalued and that policy would in due course have sought a correction, which might at least have avoided the speculative bubble of 1984–85.

A target zone system with these characteristics would in my view provide a viable alternative to both fixed and floating exchange rates, limit misalignments, and provide a spur to policy coordination (since it would require agreement on target zones, which would in turn need a degree of mutual understanding on policy objectives). It would nevertheless permit exchange rate flexibility to fulfill all four of its genuine social functions: of reconciling differential inflation (by virtue of the provision for automatic adjustment of the nominal target to maintain the target zone constant in real terms); of facilitating payments adjustment (by changing the real zone in response to permanent real shocks); of permitting a degree of independence for anticyclical monetary policy (by virtue of the wide band); and of absorbing speculative shocks (through the wide band and soft buffers).

4. POLICY COORDINATION

In the spring of 1986 the IMF Interim Committee, and subsequently the Tokyo Summit, expressed interest in using "indicators" to achieve a more comprehensive framework for policy coordination than that embodied in the target zone proposal. Since I have in part defended that proposal on the basis of the pressure it would create to improve policy coordination, it is natural to lay out my current views on the desirable content of a comprehensive set of rules for coordinated policies.

Incidentally, I do not perceive the choice facing the international community as one of target zones versus indicators. The set of rules suggested below embody target zones. Conversely, when I attempted to ask how a presumptive set of rules for policy coordination might be fashioned out of the Tokyo indicators, I ended up with an extended target zone system (Williamson 1986).

The rules developed in Edison, Miller and Williamson (1987) make use of two intermediate targets, the growth of nominal income and the (real effective) exchange rate. Expressing the internal balance objective in terms of nominal income growth has its disadvantages, notably that the lag before nominal income can be observed, but nevertheless appears preferable to alternative specifications such as the Keynesian choice of growth or output (with its danger of accelerating inflation), the monetarist choice of a monetary aggregate (an idea that at one time looked promising but in fact led to fiasco), or the New McKinnon choice of the price level (McKinnon 1986), which suffers both from the lag problem and from its disregard of the state of the real economy. A target for nominal income growth need not, however, take the naive form of a *constant* growth rate. A sensible formula, which seemed to perform acceptably in our simulations, is to choose a target growth rate of nominal income equal to the sum of the estimated rate of growth of productive potential, plus some fraction of the inherited rate of inflation (to implement a gradualist disinflation strategy), plus a positive function of the deflationary gap.

The exchange rate is a natural intermediate target since the real exchange rate is the dominant medium-run determinant of current account balances apart from income levels, which will presumably beat a reasonably constant relation to capacity in the medium run. (The lag of current balances behind exchange rates is far too long, however, to make it sensible to treat the current balance itself as an intermediate target.)

The assignment rules that we suggest to achieve these intermediate targets are the following:

1. The *average* level of world real interest rates should be revised up (down) if aggregate growth of nominal income is threatening to exceed (fall short of) the sum of the target growth of nominal income for the participating countries.[4]
2. *Differences* in interest rates among countries should be revised when necessary to limit the deviations of currencies from their target levels.
3. National *fiscal policies* should be revised with a view to achieving national target rates of growth of nominal income.

Rule 1 deals with the (n−1) problem in a McKinnonesque way ("McKinnon without the monetarism"). Rule 2 embodies the essence of the target zone system. Rule 3 endorses Keynesian fiscal policy.

Practical implementation of policy coordination would doubtless be less stark than this summary might suggest. In particular, the guidance to expectations provided by credible target zones plus exchange market intervention plus the wide band will allow significant scope for interest rate differentials to fluctuate with regard to the needs of domestic stabilization. That may well be sufficient to avoid the anticyclical fiscal policy called for by Rule 3 requiring the reinstatement of "fine tuning"; avoidance of gross mistuning plus the automatic fiscal stabilizers may well suffice. But there is no point in pretending that the world economy can perform satisfactorily irrespective of the fiscal policies pursued by the major powers. Neither can markets by expected to achieve sensibly aligned and reasonably stable exchange rates without the official sector explicitly asking itself what those rates are and being willing to adjust monetary policy to achieve them. Something in the family of target zone ideas is an essential ingredient of any coherent policy coordination program.

5. COMPARISON WITH SOME TRADITIONAL RULES

The traditional rules that will be compared with the extended target zone system described in the previous section are as follows:

Gold standard. A system of fixed exchange rates in which the world monetary base is determined by the stock of gold. That stock is redistributed by payments surpluses and deficits, and countries allow the changes in their money supplies to be determined by gold movements.

Dollar standard. A system in which the United States selects its monetary policy with a view to domestic stability and other countries peg to the dollar, with the right to change their peg at their unilateral discretion.

Floating with fixed monetary growth. A system of floating exchange rates in which each country seeks to maintain a constant growth rate of the money supply.

Bretton Woods. A gold-exchange standard with fixed but adjustable exchange rates in which countries had a commitment to the pursuit of internal balance.

McKinnon Mach I. Fixed exchange rates with a zone of moderate width among the three major powers, supported by unsterilized intervention to maintain a fixed growth rate of their collective money supply (McKinnon 1984).

McKinnon Mach II. Fixed exchange rates with a zone of moderate width among the three major powers, with their collective monetary growth devoted to the pursuit of price stability and the distribution of monetary growth determined by the aim of preserving exchange stability (McKinnon 1986).

A number of criteria seem to be relevant in an assessment of these rules. I tend to evaluate such rules in terms of the following six criteria:

Inflation control. A system has a mechanism for inflation control if adherence to the system's rules guarantees that a spontaneous burst of cost inflation will be terminated. Most of the systems possess this property, although under both the dollar standard and Bretton Woods it can be overridden, and in addition the dollar standard relies on the United States being spontaneously noninflationary. The extended target zone system brings inflation under control through pursuit of the nominal income target (rather than through an exchange rate anchor); faster inflation is only partially accommodated through a higher target growth rate of nominal income, which pushes unemployment up, which curbs inflation.

Dampens world cycle. A system has the property of dampening the world business cycle if adherence to its rules ensures that a boom or recession will bring into play built-in stabilizers that will limit cyclical movement at the world level. The gold standard had this property to the extent that a surplus (and thus monetary expansion) in one area had a counterpart deficit (thus contraction) elsewhere. I have argued that the same mechanism operated under Bretton Woods (Williamson 1985b), as it would under both McKinnon's schemes and, by virtue of the rule for the average world interest rate, under the extended target zone scheme.

Internal balance. A system allows countries to pursue internal balance if its rules permit them to direct fiscal or monetary policy toward a domestic stabilization objective when their conjunctural situation differs from the world average. Bretton Woods, extended target zones, and—especially for the United States— the dollar standard, satisfy this criterion. Monetarists believe that a constant growth rate of the money supply is *ipso facto* the best possible policy for domestic stabilization, but this claim is controversial.

Control of misalignment. A system allows the control of misalignments if its rules encourage countries to limit the deviation of exchange rates from medium-term equilibrium levels. This is true of the target zone system and, except for the United States, of the dollar standard. Bretton Woods in principle permitted devaluation or revaluation to eliminate a misalignment, but the adjustable peg discouraged exercise of this option. McKinnon would claim that misalignments could not arise under his proposals, but those who believe that misalignments can arise from differential inflation under fixed exchange rates would contest this.

Exchange rate changes as an adjustment tool. A system allows the use of exchange rate changes as a weapon of the adjustment process if its rules permit a devaluation or revaluation to help adjust away a deficit or surplus. This is true of the target zone system, except for the United States under the dollar standard, and possible but difficult under Bretton Woods.

Symmetry. A system is symmetrical if the rights and obligations of all the participants are similar. This is conspicuously untrue of a dollar standard and was *de facto* untrue of Bretton Woods. Symmetry is restricted to the three major countries under McKinnon's proposals.

The various results suggested above are summarized in Table 1.1 where an additional row ventures similar judgments regarding the EMS. Inspection reveals that the extended target zone system (alone) satisfies all six of my criteria. Since I regard these characteristics as highly desirable features of a monetary system, this may help explain my enthusiasm for the proposal. Skeptics will presumably explain why my criteria are erroneous or incomplete, or why I have mislabelled some of the cells in the table.

NOTES

1. A misalignment is defined as a persistent deviation of the real effective exchange rate from the "fundamental equilibrium exchange rate" (FEER), the level that can be expected in the medium term to reconcile internal and external balance. These concepts are sketched in Section 3.

2. I see two decisive objections to the proposal to use a fixed exchange rate as a mechanism for inflation control. The first is that it risks destruction of the tradable goods sector, since the strategy relies on the currency becoming overvalued. The second is that it has a poor track record (cf. Britain and France in the 1960s or the Southern Cone in the late 1970s).

3. However, simulations undertaken by Edison, Miller, and Williamson (1987) cast some doubt on whether a monetary relaxation inspired by an attempt to keep the dollar in a target zone would in fact have been very damaging to the cause of inflation control.

4. One possible objection to this rule is that it could perpetuate a biased monetary/fiscal mix. If the world had excessively high interest rates and loose fiscal policies when the system started operating, world interest rates might fluctuate around too high a

Table 1.1
Summary Comparison of Properties of International Monetary Systems

System / Property:	Inflation control	Dampens world cycle	Internal balance	Control of misalignments	Exchange rate changes as adjustment tool	Symmetry
Gold standard	Yes	Yes	No	No	No	Yes
Dollar standard	Relies on United States	No	Yes for United States permits for ROW	Permits, except United States	Permits, except United States	No
Floating with fixed monetary growth	Yes	No	Contested	No	Yes	Yes
Bretton Woods	Weak	Yes	Yes	Poor	Difficult	In principle
McKinnon mach I	Yes	Yes	No	Contested	No	Among troika
McKinnon mach II	Yes	Yes	No	Contested	No	Among troika
Extended target zone system	Yes	Yes	Yes	Yes	Yes	Yes
EMS	Relies on Germany	Permits	Constrained	Permits	Yes	Yes de jure No de facto

level and the system would lack any corrective mechanism requiring a tightening of fiscal policy. However, it seems unreasonable to expect rules to take care of all contingencies. This is the sort of circumstance that surveillance should identify, whereupon countries could negotiate an *ad hoc* general tightening of fiscal policy.

COMMENT BY

Giancarlo Gandolfo

I have one general observation and a few specific comments. The general observation is that the target zone proposal seems to me fairly similar to the band proposal set forth 22 years ago by George Halm (1965), but it goes back much earlier, as Halm himself shows. The main difference seems to be that in the Halm proposal the limits of the band were rigid, whereas in the Williamson proposal they are "soft." At any rate, it is interesting to note that the band proposal grew out of dissatisfaction with the then existing fixed exchange rate regime of Bretton Woods, and that the target zone proposal has grown out of dissatisfaction with the current unmanaged float. So it seems that there is a tendency to converge from both extremes toward an intermediate regime. Personally I agree with this tendency, because I believe that neither fixed nor flexible exchange rates would be the optimum, and that the future of the international monetary system lies in some form of limited-flexibility regime. But I have some reservations about the target zone proposal.

The first concerns the determination of the "fundamental equilibrium exchange rate" (FEER). According to Williamson's definition, one should first determine an agreed interpretation of internal and external balance and then translate targets for internal and external balance into exchange rate targets via some econometric model. Unfortunately this is not just "an essentially technical exercise." Econometric models are not mechanical devices, but have a probabilistic nature. There is, therefore, the risk that the *estimated* value of the FEER is so inexact that the *true* FEER may well lie outside the target zone of 10 percent built around the estimated FEER. To put it in slightly more technical terms, if the confidence interval (at the chosen probability level) built around the estimated FEER is, say, 20 percent, then there is no reason why the true FEER should lie within the target zone. But there is more to it than that, I am afraid, and to illustrate my point I borrow a similitude from Cooper (1986). If one looks at the problem of epidemic diseases (such as smallpox, cholera, yellow fever, etc.) in the nineteenth century, one is struck by the fact that it took over seventy years to reach an international agreement on the common action to fight these diseases, despite the fact that all countries firmly agreed about the need for some kind of common action. The explanation of this apparent paradox is that at the time no generally accepted model of the propagation of epidemic diseases existed, so it took all that time to agree on the model. It is sufficient to change a few words and we have the same situation here: most countries agree about the need for some form of policy coordination, but no generally accepted econometric model of the kind required by Williamson exists, and—given the lack of consensus among scholars (reinforced by the poor results of all existing econometric exchange rate models)—I am afraid that it will take a long time to get agreement on such a common model. In the meantime, different econometric models will turn out different FEERs, thus creating additional confusion in the minds of policy makers.

However, let us assume for the sake of argument that the previous problems have been solved, namely that all agree on an econometric model that is able to translate the targets for external and internal balance into exchange rate targets with a very narrow confidence interval. My second point is that, even in this case, it would not be so easy to determine a FEER. One reason is that, if there are non-linearities, the solution may not be unique. This is not surprising. As is well known, even in the simplest flow approach to exchange-rate determination there may be multiple equilibria (Gandolfo 1986: Sect. 12.3). Another reason is that there are various possible combinations of the usual policy tools (monetary policy, fiscal policy, etc.) that can be used to achieve external and internal balance, and each of these combinations would give rise to a different FEER. In fact, in a full econometric model, the FEER is an endogenous variable that depends on everything else, not only on the targets for internal and external balance. But this observation still remains in the traditional context of given targets and instruments. If we move to the more modern approach of optimal control we get still more striking results. One is that, by using optimal control techniques, it is even possible to make the current exchange rate compatible with external and internal balance, provided that the policy tools are optimally managed. I say this not because I like being whimsical, but because I have been carrying out optimal control experiments with a continuous time econometric model of the Italian economy (Gandolfo, Padoan, and Petit 1986; Gandolfo and Petit 1987). These experiments have shown that, by optimally managing fiscal and monetary policy, it would have been possible to achieve both internal balance (higher growth and lower inflation) and external balance, *with the exchange rate following its historical path exactly*. On the other hand, the same internal and external targets could have been obtained by optimally managing the exchange rate in conjunction with fiscal and monetary policy. The result of this experiment has been an exchange rate varying through time. It follows that, in this case, to implement the target zone proposal, one should envisage a sort of "movable" zone. Of course with different objective functions and/or models, one might have obtained different results, but this is not relevant here. The point is that both in the traditional context and in the optimal control context *the FEER is not uniquely determined*.

John Williamson concludes his chapter by asking skeptics to "explain why my criteria are erroneous or incomplete, or why I have mislabelled some of the cells in the table." I am not a skeptic, but as a discussant I feel that his challenge has to be met. I believe that the criteria are incomplete, and I would add at least one: the need for international reserves. My impression is that the target zone proposal would require a higher amount of international reserves than, for example, the unmanaged float. I also believe that the zones could not withstand the capital flows that now move about in the international financial system. My opinion is that at least one of the cells is mislabelled: this is (7,3). If one looks at the fiscal policies in the industrialized countries one sees that they are divergent and that there are persistent difficulties in correcting fiscal imbalances. Because of this, the burden of adjustment under a system in which the exchange rate is targeted is likely to fall on monetary policy, which could be very costly in terms of internal balance. Furthermore, with misaligned fiscal policies and with monetary policies geared towards exchange-rate targeting, national governments may be tempted or forced to resort to protectionist trade policies.

To conclude: The target zone is an interesting proposal, but I am not so sure that it is definitely superior to its competitors and, in any case, I believe that further studies are needed before passing from theory to practice.

2

Over- and Undervalued Currencies: Theory, Measurement, and Policy Implications

Ulrich Camen and Hans Genberg

1. INTRODUCTION

Dissatisfaction with the performance of the world economy under floating rates has led to proposals for reform of the international monetary system that focus in one way or another on observed fluctuations in real exchange rates. Policy rules designed to limit these fluctuations often center on measures of over- and under-valuation (misalignment) of currencies. These measures vary in complexity from relatively simple purchasing power parity calculations to significantly more intricate ones involving multi-equation simulation models. Despite the frequent applications of the proposed methods in the literature,[1] there is generally very little discussion of the basic meaning and usefulness of the concept of misalignment itself. Our aim in this chapter is to fill this gap. After arguing that commonly used measures of misalignment are likely to be misleading guides for policy except in particular situations, we conclude that using real exchange rates as targets for policy is undesirable.

The chapter is organized as follows. Section 2 presents some important facts about real-exchange-rate movements in major countries during the period 1960–86. Taking a longer time horizon than is usual allows us to identify several features of real-exchange-rate behavior that are often overlooked. These features suggest that it may be quite difficult to find an appropriate standard of reference against which to measure misalignments. Section 3 takes up the problem of

Financial Support from the Fonds National Suisse de la Recherche Scientifique under grant no. 1.069-0.84 and from the Ford Foundation under grant no. 850-1013 is gratefully acknowledged.

defining such a standard. Two commonly used methods are evaluated and found deficient in important ways. In particular, we demonstrate that these standards provide useful targets for policy only in the special case of purely monetary disturbances. In the presence of real shocks they are likely to be misleading. In Section 4 we present theoretical models in which both real and monetary shocks influence real exchange rates. We show that they do so often in rather complex ways that make it difficult to infer the nature of the disturbance from observations on exchange rate and interest rate movements. Section 5 surveys some of the relevant empirical literature. We show that real shocks have been important sources of medium- and long-term real-exchange-rate movements. In the final section we return to the question of real-exchange-rate targeting. Drawing on the theoretical analysis we warn against using real exchange rates as targets of policy when real shocks are present. In view of the empirical evidence we conclude that this warning should be taken seriously.

2. STYLIZED FACTS

One underlying assumption of proposals in which the real exchange rate constitutes a target for policy is that the evolution of the long-run equilibrium exchange rate can be identified. To show the difficulties involved in doing so we start by describing the behavior of the real effective exchange rate in a historical perspective. In Figures 2.1 and 2.2 the rates for six representative industrial countries have been plotted, starting in 1960 and using the average values of both 1960 and 1980 as based periods.[2]

Two general observations can be made at the outset. Inspection of charts for a larger group of fourteen industrial countries reveals that the real effective exchange rate has been surprisingly stable over a 27-year period in roughly one-third of the cases. The rates of these countries stay within 15 percent of the 1960 base period. The high short-term volatility during the flexible compared to the fixed-exchange-rate period, a characteristic that is well known for bilateral nominal and real rates, is also found for real effective rates. Given the high correlation between nominal and real exchange rates these short-term changes can be attributed almost exclusively to variation in the nominal rates.[3]

Two main types of long-term movements of the real effective rates can be identified in the charts. For one group of countries the rate in the mid-1980s is roughly the same as the one at the beginning of the 1960s. For this group of countries, which includes the United States, Britain, and Germany, the real rate deviates strongly from its 1960 value only during the 1970s, with the British rate starting to diverge earlier than the rates of the two other countries. These countries illustrate very well the importance of choosing a base period. If, for instance, 1960 is chosen, it appears that the 1970–85 period contains the largest "misalignments," contrary to the impression one gets if, say, 1980 is adopted as a base.[4]

The long-term behavior of the real rate of a second group of countries is

Figure 2.1
Real Effective Exchange Rates: United States, West Germany, and Japan

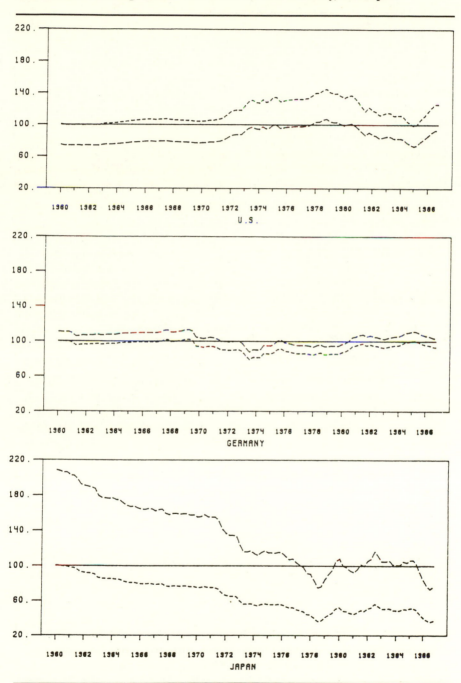

Figure 2.2
Real Effective Exchange Rates: Britain, Switzerland, and Denmark

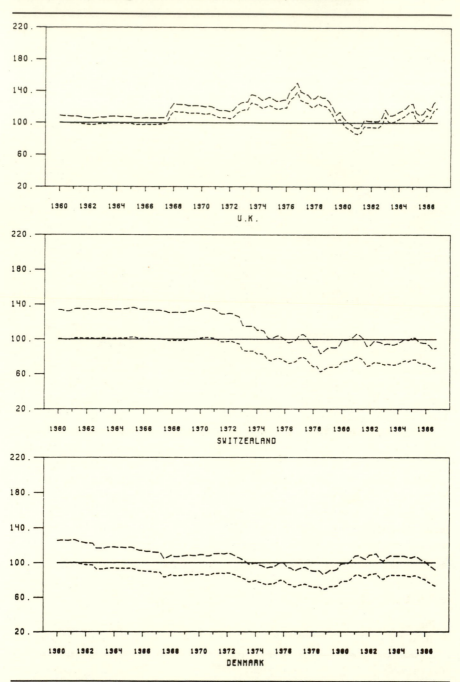

characterized by trend changes that in some cases are quite steady (Japan, Denmark) and in others appear to be stepwise (Canada, Switzerland). The most outstanding example is the case of Japan, whose real effective rate shows a strong trend appreciation during all of the 1960s and 1970s. A crucial question for the measurement of Japan's equilibrium real exchange rate is whether events in the 1980s have permanently broken this trend. If so, what are these events, and if not, what are the reasons for the flattening of the real rate path in Japan's chart, starting about 1979?

A further notable feature of the charts is that trend-like patterns are in general present from the start of our sample and can therefore not be related to the introduction of flexible exchange rates.

Given the varied experience represented in the six charts, it does not appear obvious what part of real-exchange-rate movements can be ascribed to "fundamentals" and what part to "misalignment." Different countries seem to require different treatments. Clearly we do not want to represent the "fundamental equilibrium" by a constant or a simple steady trend for all. But what should be used instead, and what are the policy implications of a given choice? This is the topic of the remainder of the paper.

3. OVERVALUED RELATIVE TO WHAT? IN SEARCH OF A STANDARD

Terms such as "overvalued," "undervalued," and "misaligned" imply the existence of a standard of reference.[5] What that standard is may depend on the purpose of the analysis. *In what follows we assume that these concepts will be used as a guide for policy.* To be specific, we analyze the desirability of using monetary policy to attempt to reduce currency misalignments. Throughout we focus on real rather than nominal exchange rates.

Two of the most common standards of reference for measurements of over- or undervaluations are the purchasing-power-parity value and what we call the "external-balance" value. In this section we show that, nonwithstanding their popularity, both of these standards are deficient in important respects. In particular, we demonstrate that they are useful as targets for monetary policy only in very special circumstances and that they may be uninformative or clearly misleading in others. We conclude that more comprehensive models of exchange-rate determination are needed both for understanding historical events and for formulating policy.

3.1 Purchasing Power Parity

Purchasing power parity calculations are perhaps the most readily applied method for getting numerical estimates of the degree of over- or undervaluation of a currency. Two practical problems, especially, have to be kept in mind when this method is used. One relates to the choice of price index to be used in the calculations. Much has already been said in the literature on this subject and there is little need to repeat this discussion here.[6] It suffices to notice that in practice not only the size but also the sign of deviations from purchasing power parity may depend on which of a number of plausible indexes is used.[7]

The second practical problem stems from the fact that almost all available price or cost indices are such that absolute purchasing power parity calculations are impossible. This means that the choice of a base period is of great importance. In the previous section we saw that substantially different impressions of the size of deviations from purchasing power parity can be conveyed by changing the base period.

Apart from being subject to these practical problems, the purchasing power parity method is also fraught with certain conceptual difficulties. At least since the well-known article by Balassa was published in 1964 it has been admitted that differences in growth rates between countries can give rise to so-called biases in purchasing power parity comparisons. These stem from the fact that relative price changes can occur in the face of technological progress. These price changes may differ between countries due to the existence of non-traded goods. Disturbances other than productivity change that impinge on this process of price determination are thus likely to create types of biases in purchasing power parity calculations similar to those documented by Balassa. Some of these will be discussed in Section 4 below.

3.2 The External Balance Method

The failure of purchasing power parity calculations to explain nominal-exchange-rate movements during the past decade[8] has shifted the emphasis toward the use of some form of external balance criterion for quantifying exchange-rate misalignments. Artus (1978) describes a version of this method in some detail, and Williamson (1985a) uses a related model to calculate target zones for real exchange rates in a recent study that has received much attention. In its most simple form the external balance method makes use of an equation such as 2.1, which describes the determinants of the trade balance. This equation is solved for the real exchange rate (e^T) that generates the target (not necessarily zero) trade balance (TB^T), given the domestic and foreign income levels as in (2.2).[9]

$$TB = tb(e, y, y^*) \tag{2.1}$$

$$e^T = e(TB^T, y, y^*) \tag{2.2}$$

The overvaluation of the home currency is then calculated as e/e^T.

While the procedure just described might seem attractive, it too is fraught with a number of problems relating both to technical issues such as the appropriate form of Equation 2.1 and to more fundamental ones calling into question the approach itself. Leaving technical issues aside, we start by elaborating on the fundamental problems by embedding Equation 2.1 in a standard textbook, open-economy, macroeconomic model. In so doing we shall show that there is in general nothing optimal or desirable associated with the real exchange rate e^T as defined in Equation 2.2.

To illustrate the weaknesses of the "external-balance" method it is sufficient to make use of a simple version of a standard open-economy macroeconomic model. We will use a slightly modified Mundell-Fleming model, which consists of:

a goods market equilibrium condition

$$y = a(y,r) + g + tb(y,y^*,e) \tag{2.3}$$

a money market equilibrium condition

$$M/E = L(y,i) \tag{2.4}$$

and an interest parity condition

$$r = r^* \tag{2.5}$$

In addition to the notation already introduced we define $a(. .)$ as domestic private sector absorption, g as government expenditures, $r(r^*)$ as the domestic (foreign) real interest rate, and M as the domestic nominal money supply. In the model we assume that the supply of domestic output is perfectly elastic, that (in view of the fixity of nominal prices) there is no difference between nominal and real interest rates, and that exchange-rate expectations are static.[10] Furthermore, asset accumulation as a result of fiscal or trade imbalances is not treated explicitly.

Equilibrium in the model is illustrated in Figure 2.3, which differs from standard representations only in that the real exchange rate rather than the real interest rate is measured on the vertical axis. The money market schedule, LM, is drawn for a given foreign real interest rate and a given stock of money. It has a negative slope because a devaluation (an increase in E and e) reduces real money balances, which requires a fall in output for equilibrium to be re-established. In the goods market, an increase in e creates an excess demand for domestic goods. An increase in output along the IS schedule is thus necessary to maintain equilibrium. Finally, trade is balanced along the TB schedule.

Imagine now that we have two targets of policy, internal balance and external balance. The former is for simplicity assumed to be attained if $y = y^f$, and the latter obtains if $tb = 0$. At E_0 both conditions are satisfied. Suppose this equilibrium is disturbed by an increase in spending on domestic goods due, for example, to a domestic fiscal expansion. The equilibrium will move to E_1, which

Figure 2.3
Fiscal Expansion and the Internal and External Equilibrium

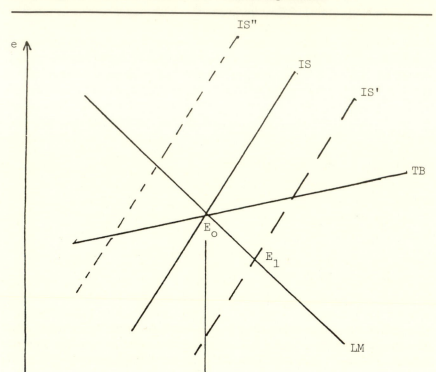

entails an increase in domestic output, a real appreciation of the domestic currency, and a current account deficit.

Is the exchange rate out of line at E_1? The external balance method for
measuring exchange-rate misalignment would respond yes and refer to the vertical distance between the tb-locus and E_1 as the degree of overvaluation of the
domestic currency. Would it follow that using monetary policy to "correct" this
overvaluation is desirable? Definitely not. Doing so would displace the equilibrium upward along the IS' schedule, reducing the external imbalance but
moving the economy further away from internal balance.

It is sometimes suggested that the external balance calculation should be
carried out using a "cyclically adjusted" output level. This may be taken to mean
that over- or undervaluation should be measured relative to the exchange rate
prevailing at E_0. A monetary policy aimed at stabilizing the exchange rate at this
value over a cycle generated by movements of the IS schedule between IS' and

IS'' would be exactly the wrong thing to do, as far as output stability is concerned.[11] Again, using the exchange rate at E_0 as a guide for monetary policy does not improve economic performance.

In recognition of the fact that two targets require two policy instruments it has been suggested that monetary policy should stabilize the real exchange rate at the level consistent with external balance, *assuming that fiscal policy is used to stabilize output at the full employment level.* If this assumption is correct, the implication for monetary policy is that it should *not* react to the "overvaluation" at E_1 because fiscal policy would bring the economy back to E_0. If the assumption is not correct we are back in the situation discussed in the previous paragraph, where a real-exchange-rate-oriented monetary policy would be counter-productive.

The conclusion of the above argument is that measures of exchange rate misalignment based on the external-balance calculations do not provide useful signals for the conduct of monetary policy in situations like those depicted in Figure 2.3, where goods market disturbances perturb the economy. This follows despite the fact that we have constructed the model so as to give monetary policy the power to permanently influence real variables.[12]

Suppose, in contrast to the above, that the economy was disturbed by a shock to the *LM* schedule due, say, to an increase in the demand for money. The resulting appreciation and trade balance surplus could be used to calculate a measure of overvaluation either at the current level of output or at a cyclically adjusted level. Following the previous analysis it is simple to show that monetary policy reacting to this measure would be stabilizing for both external and internal balance. This is an application of the well-known result[13] that the optimal policy in response to monetary disturbances in to fix the nominal exchange rate. The usefulness of measures of exchange rate misalignments for the conduct of policy thus depends critically on the sources of shocks to the economy and on the exchange rate consequences of these shocks. In the absence of direct knowledge about these shocks, policy makers must rely on information contained in observed variables such as interest rates and exchange rates. In the following section we show that it is difficult to draw inferences from data on *exchange rate and interest rate movements* about the nature of the shock that has disturbed the economy and hence about the appropriate policy response.

4. MODELS OF REAL EXCHANGE RATE DETERMINATION

It is useful to partition the discussion of real-exchange-rate determination according to the type of model that is used in the analysis. Broadly speaking one can distinguish between, on the one hand, purely real models, in which markets continuously clear and where modifications in output and expenditure patterns give rise to relative-price and real-exchange-rate changes, and on the other hand more macro-oriented models, in which monetary disturbances also have real effects due to some form of short-run rigidity in the system. Sections 4.1 and 4.2

discuss the main conclusions that emerge from each of these types of model. Our intention is not to provide an exhaustive analysis of the determinants of real exchange rates but rather to show that similar movements in real exchange rates (and interest rates) can occur in response to very different shocks, even in relatively simple models. Since the optimal policy response depends critically on the source of the disturbance, it follows that simple feedback rules that link monetary and fiscal policy to exchange rate or interest rate movements are unlikely to be appropriate. This conclusion is reinforced by the analysis in section 4.3, which treats briefly some consequences of so-called speculative bubbles and of irrational behavior.

4.1 Real Determinants of Real Exchange Rates

The real exchange rate measures the relative price of *goods,* as opposed to the nominal exchange rate, which measures the relative price of *monies.* In searching for an analytical framework within which one can discuss the determinants of the equilibrium real exchange rate it is thus necessary to turn to a framework in which relative prices are present in a non-trivial way.

In order to determine which relative prices are likely to be particularly important, we start by defining the real exchange as $e = EP^*/P$, that is as the ratio of the foreign to the domestic price level, both measured in terms of the domestic currency. If each index is composed of nontradables, exportables, and importables, it is relatively straightforward to show that

1. an increase in the price of non-tradables relative to tradables at home (abroad) will appreciate (depreciate) the domestic currency in real terms, and

2. an improvement in the domestic terms of trade will appreciate the domestic currency in real terms if the weight of domestic exportables is larger in the domestic price index than in the foreign price index.

Accordingly, any model purporting to explain movements in the real exchange rate must be capable of accounting for changes in the relative price of non-traded goods in the two countries and for changes in the terms of trade. Similarly, statements about over- or undervaluation of the real exchange rate must take account of movements in these same variables. In a recent series of papers, Frenkel and Razin[14] have developed a useful framework for analyzing the determinants of real interest rates and real exchange rates both in a small country and in a two-country setting. In this section we summarize some of the more pertinent results that emerge from the Frenkel-Razin analysis.

In the model used by Frenkel and Razin, expenditure and saving functions are derived on the basis of intertemporal maximization. The distribution of current spending among different types of goods depends on relative prices. Output is typically treated as exogenous, and relative prices (current period as well as intertemporal) are determined by market-clearing.

Consider now the effects on relative prices and the real exchange rate of the following shocks.

An Increase in Domestic Output

If the increase occurs in the present period only, an excess supply of current-period goods will result. This will depress the real rate of interest. In an internationally integrated capital market, the reduction in the rate of interest rate will be transmitted to the foreign country, where it will lead to an excess demand for non-traded goods. On this account then the domestic currency tends to depreciate in real terms. However, in the home country, relative prices are likely to change as well. If the increase in output is concentrated in the sector producing non-tradables, an excess supply of these will result and their relative price will fall. This will reinforce the real depreciation of the currency. If the increase in output occurs in the traded-goods industry instead, the relative price effect is likely to go in the opposite direction, partially or fully offsetting the previous real-exchange-rate effect. The effect on the real exchange rate via the terms of trade depends partly on the source of the increase in output and partly on conditions similar to those found in the literature on the transfer problem. The latter are relevant because differences in marginal propensities to spend on exportables and importables (at home as well as abroad) determine how the terms of trade react to expenditure increases.

So far we have seen that the exact source of the change in income as well as specific parameters in expenditure functions are important for both the quantitative and qualitative effects on the real exchange rate. It is also of interest to ask what happens if the current increase in output is interpreted as a sign that income will increase even more in the future. In this case *future* goods will be in excess supply and the rate of interest must increase. Foreign wealth will therefore decrease, creating an excess supply of their non-traded good. Modifications in the terms of trade again depend on transfer criteria, since domestic wealth increases and foreign wealth falls. The overall effect on the real exchange rate is uncertain.

An Increase in Government Spending

The analysis of this type of disturbance parallels in many ways that of an increase in income. The importance of the composition of government spending as between non-traded, export and import goods is obviously of great importance. The timing (current versus future) of the spending is also highly relevant.

A Tax Cut

A current tax cut financed by borrowing generates wealth effects unless Ricardian equivalence is present. The real rate of interest increases, which reduces foreign wealth. The effect of lower current taxes on disposable income implies an increase in domestic private-sector wealth. The consequences for relative prices again depends on "a multitude of 'transfer problem' criteria,"[15] and the effect on the real exchange rate cannot be determined without knowledge of both the parameters of spending functions in each country and the temporal distribution of the tax cuts.

A Transfer of Wealth to the Domestic Economy

The consequences of an exogenous wealth transfer can be analyzed with the techniques suggested above. Domestic spending will increase and foreign spending will fall. The relative price of non-traded goods will change accordingly, implying a real appreciation of the domestic currency. Terms of trace effects will depend on "transfer criteria."

It should be clear from this discussion that substantial and detailed information is in principle required to reach unambiguous conclusions regarding the effects of government policies and other exogenous disturbances on real exchange rates.

4.2 Sticky Prices, Expectations, and Monetary Effects

The simplest way to introduce the influence of monetary disturbances on the real exchange rate is to specify a model that incorporates some form of nominal price stickiness. An extreme form of such a model was analyzed in section 3.2 where it was assumed that the price of domestic output was completely fixed. In this framework we established that an increase in the demand for money would appreciate the domestic currency in real terms and reduce output. Introducing partially flexible prices and relaxing the restrictive assumption that expectations are static does not change the qualitative nature of these results in important ways, but introduces additional sources of exchange rate movements. Consider, for instance, a price adjustment rule of the type

$$P^d = \psi(y - y^f),$$

and expectations formation mechanisms defined by

$$\pi^e = P^d + (1 - \alpha)\hat{e}^e$$

and

$$\hat{e}^e = \theta(\bar{e} - e),$$

where a $\char94$ indicates a percentage rate of change, P^d stands for the price of domestic output, π for the domestic rate of inflation, and $\bar{e}$ for the expected future real exchange rate. Combining these assumptions with a conventional IS–LM model allows us to analyze the effects of exogenous shocks in familiar diagrams.[16] In Figure 2.4 the IS and LM loci have the same interpretation as before, whereas points along TB now imply current account balance. Each locus is drawn for a given value of $\bar{e}$ and their slopes are modified relative to Figure 2.3

Figure 2.4
Monetary Shocks and the Internal and External Equilibrium

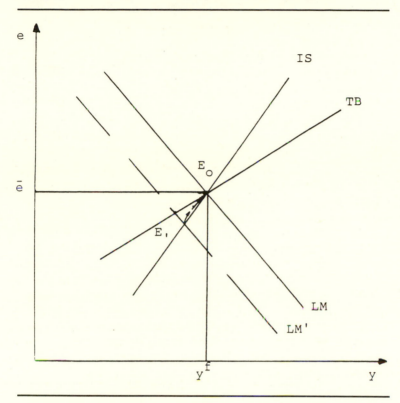

as a result of the interest-rate consequences of differences between y and y^f and between $\bar{e}$ and e. Furthermore, the *LM* locus will shift down over time when the price of domestic output increases, that is when the economy's equilibrium lies to the right of y^f.

Consider first the consequences of an exogenous increase in the demand for money. The temporary equilibrium point moves from E_0 to E_1. The familiar conclusions from the Dornbusch (1976) analysis emerge—an appreciation of the currency in both real and nominal terms, a decrease in output, and a current account deficit. The nominal interest rate may increase or decrease, since reductions in output and the real exchange rate may under- or overcompensate the increase in money demand.[17] Over time, as the price of domestic output falls, the economy returns to the initial equilibrium.[18]

A balanced-budget fiscal expansion shifts both the *IS* and the *TB* loci to the right (Figure 2.5). Since e must fall in the long run as a result of the switch in expenditures toward domestic goods,[19] the *LM* curve will shift downward. Temporary equilibrium involving an appreciation of the currency, an increase in

Figure 2.5
Balanced-Budget Expansion and the Internal and External Equilibrium

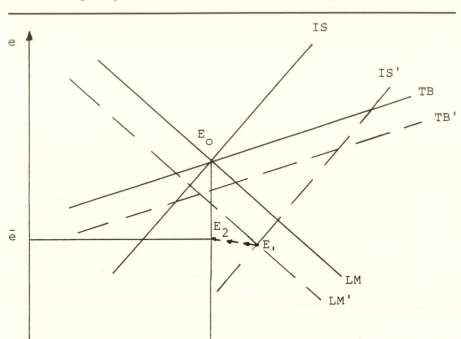

output, and a current account deficit will be established at E_1. Both the real and nominal rate of interest are likely to be higher at E_1 than at E_0. The consequences of increases in P^d and the current account deficit will lead to a long-run equilibrium at a point like E_2.

Suppose finally that the economy is perturbed by the expected *future* increase in government expenditures financed by a tax increase (Figure 2.6).[20] In the current period, only the effect of the reduction in e is present.[21] Both the real and the nominal rates of interest decline, increasing spending and money demand. Equilibrium moves from E_0 to E_1 in the short run.[22] When the expenditure increase actually takes place the economy will experience an expansionary phase (point E_2) before settling down at the long-run equilibrium at E_3.

The motive behind the analysis in Figures 2.4–2.6 is to illustrate that qualitatively the same exchange rate movement may be associated with different interest rate behavior and/or different output behavior in the short run, depending on the type of disturbance that is being considered (see Table 2.1). Hence, while it is possible to infer the exchange rate, interest rate, and output consequences once

Figure 2.6
Expected Future Fiscal Expansion and the Internal and External Equilibrium

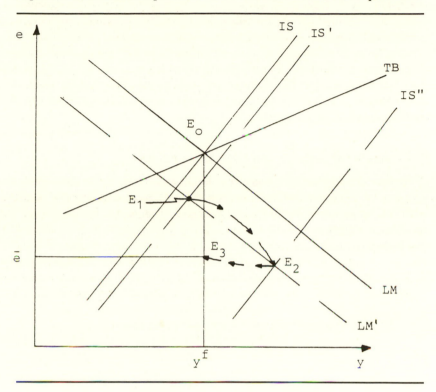

Table 2.1
Comparison of the Temporary Equilibrium (E_1) with the Initial Equilibrium (E_0)

Type of shock	e	r	i	y
Money demand (Figure 2.4)	down	up	up (down)	down
Current fiscal (Figure 2.5)	down	up (down)	up (down)	up
Future fiscal (Figure 2.6)	down	down	down	down

Note: i stands for the nominal interest rate. Parentheses indicate a less likely outcome.

the disturbance is known, the analysis suggests that the inverse may be difficult. Unless very detailed information exists, it may not be possible to infer the nature of the shock from the state of the economy. If, for instance, only e and i were observed frequently enough to serve as guides for policy, we see from the table that a money demand shock and a current fiscal shock would be indistinguishable. The implication of this for the usefulness of concepts such as under- and overvaluation as well as for using exchange rates as targets or indicators of policy will be discussed in section 6.

4.3 Irrational Behavior and Speculative Bubbles

We have seen that stabilization of the nominal exchange rate is desirable in the presence of monetary disturbances. Such stabilization may also be desirable when exchange rate movements are unrelated to economic fundamentals. The speculative-bubble hypothesis has attracted special attention in this context.[23] It can be formalized by starting with the open interest parity condition: $i = i^* + Es_{t+1} - s_t$, and expressing the expected change of the nominal exchange rate (s) as a weighted average of the deviation of the actual value from the long-run equilibrium value ($\bar{s} - s_t$), and the rate of change in the spot rate ($s_{t+1} - s_t$):

$$i - i^* = p_t (\bar{s} - s_t) + (1 - p_t) (s_{t+1} - s_t)$$

or

$$s_{t+1} - s_t = 1 / (1 - p_t) \{i - i^* + p_t (s_t - \bar{s})\}$$

The weights are the probability p_t that the bubble will burst in the coming month and $1 - p_t$ that the appreciation will continue for one month. The rate of change of the exchange rate will be higher the larger the deviation of the current from the long-term equilibrium value and the higher the probability of a crash. This type of speculative bubble is rational, as all market participants are aware that the current exchange rate deviates from the fundamental rate, but the bubble will be sustained by the belief that it grows faster, thus providing existing asset holders with a necessary expected return. Whether speculative bubbles of this type can explain recent movements in exchange rates is basically an empirical question, which will be discussed in the next section.

5. EMPIRICAL EVIDENCE

Given the importance of the sources of shocks for the formulation of successful short-run stabilization policies, it is essential to know whether movements of the real exchange rate are brought about by real disturbances or by speculative bubbles and monetary shocks. In the following we review briefly the empirical literature on exchange rate determination to give an answer to two questions: Are 'bubbles' important? and Can any real shocks be identified, or are monetary shocks all that matter?

Several recent studies have tested formally for the existence of speculative bubbles. The overall outcome appears to be that some short-term deviations of bilateral exchange rates from values implied by economic fundamentals may have been partly the result of speculative bubbles. Meese (1986), for instance, rejects the hypothesis of no rational bubbles for the dollar/Deutschmark and dollar/pound rate, using monthly data over the period 1973 to 1982 and employing a monetary model of exchange rates to determine the exchange rate consistent with fundamentals.[24] His results for the dollar/pound rate are not robust with respect to a sample split, and the test results for the dollar/yen rate were considered inconclusive because the empirical performance of the monetary approach exchange rate equation was highly unsatisfactory.

To assess these findings it is crucial to keep in mind that the performed tests are tests of the joint hypothesis of (1) the adequacy of the underlying exchange rate model, (2) no process switching, and (3) no bubbles. Process switching refers here to the anticipation by agents of changes in the underlying economic environment.[25] Meese's findings are therefore conditional on the assumed monetary exchange rate model and the stability of the specified autoregressive process for the relative money supplies and real incomes. Testing the robustness of his results with respect to the underlying assumptions leads Meese to qualify his findings as mixed evidence of asset market bubbles. Recent evaluation of bubble tests that have been applied to stock prices suggests that the above limitations are critical for the conclusion to be drawn from these tests. The studies show that the evidence that stock price fluctuations do not accord with market fundamentals could be attributed to a misspecification of the rate implied by fundamentals.[26] This evidence, together with the unsatisfactory empirical performance of models of exchange-rate determination in the past, indicates that the evidence on bubbles in bilateral exchange rates must be interpreted with great caution.

For our purposes the relevance of the bubble tests is even more questionable. For even if bubbles exist in the very short run, it appears highly improbable that they can explain the observed medium- and long-term swings of dollar rates during the flexible-exchange-rate period, and as we shall see, there is some evidence that models based on "fundamentals" can.

What evidence does exist with respect to real versus nominal determinants of real exchange rates? One set of studies investigates the sources of real exchange rate variability by using cross-section studies. Edwards (1986) finds for a sample of developing countries that while nominal exchange rates are the major source of short-term real-exchange-rate variability, real disturbances, especially the terms of trade, are important determinants of long-term variability. A study by De Grauwe and Rosiers (1984) confirms the importance of the variability in a country's money growth for explaining real-exchange-rate variation (about 40 percent) but at the same time shows that a major portion of the variability is unexplained by nominal factor.

In a recent paper (Sachs 1985), Jeffrey Sachs adopts the strategy based on "fundamentals" and argues that the appreciation of the dollar relative to the DM since 1977 can be accounted for by movements in the real-interest-rate differential and the differential growth in output relative to Germany. The dependence of the real exchange on the real-interest-rate differential is derived from two conditions describing equilibrium in asset markets: the uncovered interest parity condition and the Fisher relationship. These two relationships imply that the *real*-interest-rate differential is equal to the expected depreciation of the *real* exchange rate. If it is assumed, as Sachs does, that the long-run real exchange rate is fixed, then the only way in which agents will rationally expect the real rate to depreciate from its current value is if the currency always appreciates in real terms when the real-interest-rate differential increases. The dependence of the real rate on the growth rate differential can be explained with reference to the effect of biased technological change on relative prices, as in section 4.1.

The empirical evidence Sachs presents for the real \$/DM rate during the period 1977:1–1984:4 is quite favorable to his model; about 90 percent of the variance during this period can be accounted for by the two factors discussed in the previous paragraph. Sachs is thus able to explain the appreciation of the dollar since 1977 with "fundamental" variables. There is no need to resort to overvaluation arguments.[27]

In view of the thorough empirical work carried out by Meese and Rogoff (1983a, 1983b, 1985), in which they show that the performance of empirical exchange rate models is quite poor, the findings of Sachs are surprising. One possible explanation for the discrepancy between the two sets of results might be that the real-exchange-rate–real-interest-rate-link documented by Sachs is specific to the 1977–84 period and the \$/DM rate. However, Feldstein (1986) confirms Sachs' findings for the entire flexible exchange rate period.[28] In addition, he identifies a strong impact of expected future U.S. budget deficits. Another result of interest is that the change in the growth of the U.S. monetary base has a significant coefficient.

Taken together, this empirical evidence suggests that both real and nominal factors were important in explaining the pattern of the real exchange rates over the flexible exchange rate period.

6. CONCLUDING REMARKS: REAL EXCHANGE RATES AS TARGETS OR INDICATORS

On the basis of the theoretical and empirical results we have derived we are now in the position to draw some conclusions for exchange rate policy. In section 3 we showed that the policy implications of a given exchange rate movement depend crucially on the nature of the disturbance responsible for that movement. In particular, targeting (fixing) the real exchange rate to its purchasing power parity or "external balance" value was shown to increase output variability in the presence of real disturbances. Only in the case of monetary disturbances or in the presence of speculative bubbles would it be optimal to stabilize the exchange rate.[29] These conclusions continue to be valid, even in the extended framework of section 4. Compare, for instance, the implications of the disturbances analyzed in Figures 2.4 and 2.5. As before, using monetary policy to maintain the exchange rate at $\bar{e}$ in the case of the money demand disturbance (Figure 2.4) is clearly still desirable. The economy would never diverge from E_0. Analogously, using monetary policy to maintain the initial real exchange rate, the long-run equilibrium rate $\bar{e}$, or any other rate in between is still counterproductive, as far as output stability is concerned in the case of the fiscal shock (Figure 2.5).[30] By applying both monetary and fiscal policy in the appropriate doses it would perhaps be possible to stabilize the economy at full employment and $\bar{e}$. But this presumes knowledge of the location of $\bar{e}$, which implies knowledge of the nature of the initial disturbance. It thus follows that identification of the sources of exchange rate movements is crucial for the conduct of discretionary stabilization policy or for the design of feedback rules for monetary or fiscal policy that depend on $\bar{e}$. The analysis in section 4 was designed partly to show that this identification is likely to be very difficult, on the basis of readily available data on the state of the economy. For instance, it was shown that the same exchange rate and interest rate movements may occur in response to substantially different types of shocks.

In section 4 we also demonstrated how different types of fiscal and other real shocks imply distinct long-run stationary real exchange rates, that is distinct values of $\bar{e}$. Suppose that currency misalignment is defined relative to this rate. It follows that this measure of misalignment can only be constructed conditionally on particular values of exogenous variables. But which values of the exogenous variables should be chosen? Should one use the current stance of fiscal policy, or maybe a fiscal policy that would maintain "internal balance," given the current values of other exogenous variables? How should anticipated policy changes abroad be treated? In general there is nothing optimal about any of these choices, and, as already shown, they do not carry any particular implications for monetary policy.

One might argue that a proper measure of the degree of misalignment is the difference between the current equilibrium rate and the rate that would prevail if monetary and fiscal policy were used appropriately to move the economy along the optimal adjustment path toward full employment and current account balance. This is an empty definition of misalignment if policies will not be used optimally. Alternatively, if policies are meant to be set optimally, but the implementation has not yet taken place, then it is an unnecessary and basically unhelpful definition, since it is really *policies* that are "misaligned." Speaking of misalignment of the *exchange rate* instead diverts attention away from the real problem.

We have tried to demonstrate that the real exchange rate is frequently an inappropriate target for policy and that the notion of misalignment is unhelpful at best. Our analysis also implies that the exchange rate is likely to be a poor indicator both of the state of the economy and of the stance of policy. As an illustration of the latter,[31] consider the link between the dollar and the policy mix. It used to be argued that the high and rising dollar in the early 1980s was a sign of excessively expansionary fiscal policy in the United States. Does this mean that the currently low value of the dollar indicates a "correct" or even too restrictive policy? Of course not. The large budget deficit in the United States tells the appropriate story about the stance of U.S. fiscal policy; the value of the dollar does not. Similarly, a high or low or rising or falling dollar does not give an unambiguous indication of the stance of monetary policy. We conclude that it is unsuitable to design or evaluate policy on the basis of real exchange rate movements. Using either ultimate target variables or direct instruments of policy for this purpose is more appropriate.

APPENDIX

The model used in section 4.2 is an extended Mundell-Fleming model similar to those used in Branson and Buiter (1983) and Sachs and Wyplosz (1984). The following equations define the model:

$$y = a(y^c, r, eb^*) + g + tb[a(.\ .\ .\ .\ .), e] \tag{2.6}$$

$$y^d = y - t + r^* eb^* \tag{2.7}$$

$$M/P = L(y, i) \tag{2.8}$$

$$P = P^{d\alpha}(E \cdot P^*)^{1-\alpha} = P^d (EP^*/P^d)^{1-\alpha} = P^d e^{1-\alpha} \tag{2.9}$$

$$r = r^* + \alpha \hat{e}^e \tag{2.10}$$

$$i = r^* + \hat{e}^e + \hat{P}^{d^e} \tag{2.11}$$

$$\hat{P}^d = \psi (y - y^f) \tag{2.12}$$

$$\hat{e}^e = \Theta (\bar{e} - e) \tag{2.13}$$

$$e\hat{b}^* = tb[.\ .\ .\ .\ .\ .] + r^* eb^* \tag{2.14}$$

where $a(a^*)$ is domestic (foreign) private sector absorption; b^* is domestic holdings of foreign bonds; E is the nominal exchange rate (units of domestic currency per unit of foreign currency); e is the real exchange rate ≢ the inverse of the terms of trade ≢ EP^*/P^d; $\bar{e}$ is the steady-state equilibrium real exchange rate; g is real government spending; $i(i^*)$ is the domestic (foreign) nominal interest rate; M is the nominal money supply; P^d is the (domestic currency) price of the domestic good; P^* is the (foreign currency) price of the foreign good; P is the domestic consumer price index; $r(r^*)$ is the domestic (foreign) real interest rate; t is real tax revenue; tb is the trade balance in real terms; y is real output; y^d is real disposable income; and y^f is full-employment output.

Equation 2.6 states that the demand for domestic output equals the sum of private sector absorption, real government spending, and the trade balance. Absorption is a positive function of disposable income and wealth (proxied by the real value of holdings of foreign bonds), and a negative function of the real rate of interest. Government spending falls exclusively on the domestic good, whereas the trade balance depends on domestic and foreign absorption and on the real exchange rate, defined as the inverse of the terms of trace. Equation 2.7 defines disposable income as domestic real output minus tax payments plus interest earnings on holdings of foreign bonds.

Money market equilibrium is defined in Equation 2.8. Note that the nominal stock of money is deflated by the domestic consumer price index, which implies that the exchange rate enters directly. The demand for real money balances depends on real output and the nominal interest rate in standard fashion.

The consumer price index is defined in Equation 2.9 as a weighted average of the prices of the domestic and the foreign good. The weights represent the consumption shares, and as a consequence $1 - \alpha$ should be related to the marginal propensity to import.

The expressions for the domestic real and nominal interest rates found in Equations 2.10 and 2.11 are derived from the uncovered interest parity condition and the Fisher relationship as follows. The uncovered interest parity condition states that $i = i^* + \hat{E}^e$, where the superscript e denotes an expected value and a $\hat{}$ a percentage rate of change. Subtracting and adding $\hat{P}^{*e}$ from the right side yields $i = r^* + \hat{E}^e + \hat{P}^{*e}$, which, using the definition of the real exchange rate, can be transformed into $i = r^* + \hat{e}^e + \hat{P}^{de}$. Since $r = i - \hat{P}^e$, the last expression implies (using Equation 2.9) $r = r^* + \alpha\hat{e}^e$.

The price of the domestic good is assumed to adjust to the difference between current output (which is equal to the demand) and full-employment output as in Equation 2.12. Equation 2.13 states that the expected rate of change of the real exchange rate is proportional to the difference between the steady-state equilibrium rate and the current rate.

Equation 2.14, finally, shows that the rate of accumulation of foreign bonds is equal to the current account balance, that is to the sum of the trade balance and the interest earnings from abroad.

Rather than supplying complete solutions for the entire dynamic adjustment path of the model in response to shocks to all the exogenous variables, we shall provide steady-state and impact effects of a few illustrative cases.

As a result of the forward-looking nature of exchange rate expectations, the steady-state solution for the real exchange rate is required to calculate the impact responses of the endogenous variables. Setting $y = y^f$, $e = \bar{e}$, and $b^* = 0$, Equations 2.6 and 2.14 can be solved for the steady-state values of e and b^*.[32] The two equations can be written in linearized form as follows:

$$\begin{pmatrix} tb_e\,(a_w + cr_0^*)\,(1-m) \\ tb_e\, - ma_w + (1-mc)r_0^* \end{pmatrix} \begin{pmatrix} \bar{e} \\ eb^* \end{pmatrix} = \begin{pmatrix} 1-c(1-m) \\ mc \end{pmatrix} y^f$$

$$+ \begin{pmatrix} -\,[1-c(1-m)] \\ -mc \end{pmatrix} g$$

$$+ \begin{pmatrix} -(a_r + ce_0b_0^*)\,(1-m) \\ ma_r - (1-mc)e_0b_0^* \end{pmatrix} r^*$$

$$+ \begin{pmatrix} -tb_{a*} \\ -tb_{a*} \end{pmatrix} a^*$$

where

$$tb_e = \frac{\partial tb}{\partial e}, \; a_w = \frac{\partial a}{\partial(eb^*)}, \; c = \frac{\partial a}{\partial y^d}, \; m = \frac{\partial tb}{\partial a}, \; a_r = \frac{\partial a}{\partial r}, \; tb_{a*} = \frac{\partial tb}{\partial a^*}$$

and where a $-$ indicates a steady-state value and a subscript 0 indicates an initial value.

$$\bar{\Delta} = \begin{vmatrix} tb_e \; (a_w + cr_0^*) \; (1-m) \\ \\ tb_e - ma_w + (1-mc)r_0^* \end{vmatrix} = tb_e \; [a_w - (1-c)r_0^*] < 0$$

The last inequality sign follows if $a_w > (1-c)r_0^*$, a condition that is related to the stability of the system (see Sachs and Wyplosz, 1984, for a similar expression), and which we assume to be fulfilled. Using the above equation system it is easily established that

$$\frac{d\bar{e}}{dM} = 0$$

$$\frac{d\bar{e}}{dy^f} = -\frac{1}{\bar{\Delta}} [1-c(1-m)][ma_w - (1-mc)r_0^*] > 0$$

$$\frac{d\bar{e}}{dg} = -\frac{d\bar{e}}{dy^f} < 0$$

and

$$\frac{d\bar{e}}{da^*} = -\frac{th_a^*}{tb_e} < 0$$

provided $ma_w - (1-mc)r_0^* > 0$, which we assume to be the case.

Using the solution for $\bar{e}$ obtained above, we can now obtain impact responses of the model to changes in the exogenous variables. To calculate these impact responses we treat P^d and b^* as fixed. The relevant linearized equation system for the temporary equilibrium values of e and y takes the form

$$\begin{pmatrix} 1 - c(1 - m) & -(1 - m) \; [\frac{tb_e}{1-m} + a_w b_0^* - a_r \alpha\theta + cr_0^* b_0^*] \\ L_y + L_i\psi & 1-\alpha-L_i\theta \end{pmatrix} \begin{pmatrix} y \\ e \end{pmatrix} =$$

$$\begin{pmatrix} 0 \\ 1 \end{pmatrix} M + \begin{pmatrix} 0 \\ -1 \end{pmatrix} P^d + \begin{pmatrix} tb_{a^*} \\ 0 \end{pmatrix} a^* + \begin{pmatrix} 1 - \gamma - c(1 - m) \\ 0 \end{pmatrix} g$$

$$+ \begin{pmatrix} (1 - m)(a_r + cb_0^*) \\ -L_i \end{pmatrix} r^* + \begin{pmatrix} (1 - m)a_r \alpha\theta \\ -L_i\theta \end{pmatrix} \bar{e} + \begin{pmatrix} (1 - m)(a_w + cr_0^*) \\ 0 \end{pmatrix} b^*$$

$$+ \begin{pmatrix} 0 \\ -L_i\psi \end{pmatrix} y^f$$

$$\Delta = [1 - c(1 - m)][1 - \alpha - L_i\theta] + (1 - m)[\frac{tbe}{1-m} + a_w b_0^*$$
$$- a_r \alpha\theta + cr_0^* b_0^*][L_y + L_i\psi] > 0$$

provided $L_y + L_i\psi > 0$.

The effects of a balanced-budget increase in government spending can now be written

$$\frac{dy}{dg} = \frac{dy}{dg}\bigg|_{d\bar{e} = 0} + \frac{dy}{d\bar{e}} \cdot \frac{d\bar{e}}{dg} = \frac{[1 - c(1 - m)][1 - \alpha - L_i\theta]}{\Delta} + \frac{dy}{d\bar{e}}\frac{d\bar{e}}{dg}$$

$$\frac{de}{dg} = \frac{de}{dg}\bigg|_{d\bar{e} = 0} + \frac{de}{d\bar{e}} \cdot \frac{d\bar{e}}{dg} = \frac{-[1 - c(1 - m)][L_y + L_i\psi]}{\Delta} + \frac{de}{d\bar{e}}\frac{d\bar{e}}{dg}$$

$$\frac{di}{dg} = \theta\left(\frac{d\bar{e}}{dg} - \frac{de}{dg}\right) + \psi\frac{dy}{dg}$$

$$\frac{dr}{dg} = \alpha\left(\frac{d\bar{e}}{dg} - \frac{de}{dg}\right)$$

$$\frac{dtb}{dg} = -m\frac{da}{dg} + tb_e\frac{de}{dg} = -m\ [c\left(\frac{dy}{dg} - 1 + r_0^*b_0^*\frac{de}{dg}\right) + a_r\frac{dr}{dg}$$

$$+ a_wb_0^*\frac{de}{dg}] + tb_e\frac{de}{dg}$$

where $d\bar{e}/dg$ has already been defined and where

$$\frac{dy}{d\bar{e}} = \frac{1}{\Delta}\begin{vmatrix} (1 - m)a_r\alpha\theta - (1 - m)\ [\frac{tb_e}{1-m} + a_wb_0^* - a_r\alpha\theta + cr_0b_0^*] \\ -L_i\theta & 1 - \alpha - L_i\theta \end{vmatrix}$$

$$\frac{de}{d\bar{e}} = \frac{1}{\Delta}\Big([1 - c(1 - m)](-L_i\theta) - (1 - m)a_r\alpha\theta\ (L_y + L_i\psi)\Big) > 0$$

Although the signs of the multipliers are not unambiguous for all parameter values, it can be established that when the exchange rate response of the trade balance (tb_e) is sufficiently large then

$$\frac{dy}{dg} > 0, \frac{de}{dg} < 0, \frac{di}{dg} > 0, \frac{dr}{dg} > 0, \text{ and } \frac{dtb}{dg} < 0$$

The consequences of the other shocks considered in the main text can be calculated in an analogous manner.

NOTES

1. At one stage, estimating the overvaluation of the dollar became somewhat of a growth industry. See Armington (1985), Krugman (1985), Levich (1985), Marris and Martin (1985), Marris (1985), and Williamson (1985a).

2. The real effective exchange rates have been calculated on the basis of bilateral nominal exchange rates for fourteen industrial countries, using consumer price indices, bilateral trade weights, and the geometric average procedure.

3. Mussa (1986).

4. The "overvaluation" of the dollar in the early 1980s also looks very different, depending on which base period is used.

5. On various meanings of over/undervaluation, see Frankel (1985).

6. See, for instance, Officer (1976) for a thorough review.

7. See Morgan Garanty, *World Financial Markets*, May 1978.

8. See, for instance, Genberg (1978) and Frenkel (1981). Note that the failure of *very short-term movements* of nominal exchange rates to correspond to purchasing power parity calculations does not necessarily disqualify the later as standards for determining the size of over- or undervaluations. Other considerations, such as the biases noted in the previous section, would have to be invoked to justify such a conclusion.

9. Equation 2.1 can be thought of as a compact form of the following: $TB = X(e,y^*) - e\ IM(e,y)$, where TB is the trade balance measured in terms of the domestic good, $e = EP^*/P$ is the real exchange rate, P is the domestic-currency price of the domestic (export) good, X is domestic exports, E is the nominal exchange rate, P^* is the foreign-currency price of the foreign good (domestic import good), IM is domestic imports, and y and y^* are domestic and foreign income, respecively.

10. These assumptions allow us to illustrate our main arguments in the most simple fashion. Introducing more realistic features such as (partially) flexible prices and expectations that are not static (see section 4.2) would strengthen our case but make it perhaps less transparent. In a complete discussion of the performance and desirability of alternative exchange rate rules, these additional features would of course have to be taken into account.

11. This conclusion is of course analogous to that derived by Poole (1970) in a different context.

12. In a framework where monetary policy has only *temporary* real effects it has been shown that a policy of reacting to deviations from purchasing power parity may destabilize the inflation rate. See Genberg (1981) and Adams and Gros (1986).

13. See for instance Henderson (1984).

14. See the Bibliography for a sample of these papers.

15. Frenkel and Razin (1985: 619).

16. See the Appendix for a formal presentation of the model used in this section.

17. The model may in other words generate either "overshooting" or "undershooting" of the nominal exchange rate.

18. The path involves more than a move along a stationery *IS* curve as a result of current-account-induced wealth effects on spending and money demand.

19. Government spending is assumed to be more heavily concentrated on domestic goods than private sector spending.

20. In order to avoid the undesirable implication that the implementation of the policy would entail a jump in the exchange rate that could be foreseen, we assume that the *date* of the implementation is unknown.

21. This abstracts from possible effects of changes in human wealth (discounted value of disposable income) on current absorption.

22. It is assumed here that the *LM* curve shifts down by more than the *IS* curve. This will in fact occur if the trade balance is sufficiently exchange rate elastic.

23. Speculative bubbles in the context of rational expectation models were discussed by Blanchard (1979) and applied to exchange rate movements by Dornbusch (1982).

24. Woo (1984) finds evidence for bubbles in the German, French, and Japanese bilateral exchange rate with the United States, using a portfolio-balance model. Evans (1986) cannot reject the existence of bubbles in the dollar/pound rate. His test does not allow discrimination between rational bubbles of the type described in the previous section and excess volatility due to nonrational expectations.

25. Obstfeld (1985). Flood and Garber (1983) introduced the term "process switching."

26. Diba and Grossman (1975), Flood et. al. (1985).

27. In a slight extension of his empirical test, Sachs also shows that fiscal policy differences between the two countries can account for the movements in the real interest rate differential. The expansionary fiscal policy pursued in the United States is thus seen as a major reason for the strong dollar. A similar conclusion is reached in Branson (1985).

28. Similar regressions for the $/yen and DM/yen rates by the authors yield comparable results.

29. In these cases the *nominal* rate should be fixed.

30. The cumulated price increase during the adjustment process from E_1 to E_2 would also be larger with this policy.

31. That the exchange rate is not an unambiguous indicator of the state of the economy was already illustrated in Table 2.1 in section 4.

32. We assume throughout that government expenditures are entirely tax financed, so that $t = g$.

3

Exchange Rate Management and International Coordination

Emil-Maria Claassen

This chapter deals with three basic questions:

1. Why should there be exchange rate management? The answer is far from evident—as usual among economists—and an agreement can only be found for dampening the short-run volatility of the exchange rate.

2. How should one intervene in the foreign exchange market in order to attain the desired exchange rate? Fortunately, in this field the answer is more clear-cut. Interventions to be effective should be of the nonsterilized type. However, over the long run, such interventions have a predominant impact only on the nominal exchange rate. Proper international coordination is also advisable, since it avoids an increase in world inflation, such as that of the 1970s.

3. How could one manage the exchange rate by a proper mix of domestic policies? This question concerns the management not of the nominal exchange rate but of the real exchange rate. The policy mix concerns mainly monetary and fiscal policy. The answer is disastrous for (real) exchange rate management, although fiscal policy coordination would have avoided the dramatic real appreciation and depreciation of the dollar during the 1980s.

The following three sections try to answer successively these three basic questions in a more sophisticated way according to our professional rules of the game.

1. WHY EXCHANGE RATE MANAGEMENT?

Since the adoption of floating exchange rates, changes in the nominal exchange rate have been large. One percent in a day, 5 percent in a month, and 20 percent in a year are not unusual. Table 3.1 presents the major movements in the dollar/mark and dollar/yen exchange rates over several months or years (day-to-day or month-to-month volatility is not shown).

These movements have been mainly real. The large fluctuations in nominal exchange rates have not been offset by differences in national inflation rates since these have been much smaller. Figure 3.1 shows the evolution of the nominal and real effective exchange rate of the dollar with respect to the currencies of the Group of Ten over the period 1979 to 1985.

Do these exchange rate movements represent serious market failures in the

Table 3.1
Variability in the Nominal Exchange Value of the U.S. Dollar, 1970–86*

Percent appreciation (+) or depreciation (−) of U.S. dollar*

Period	Spot exchange rate with German mark	Spot exchange rate with Japanese yen
June 1970 to March 1973	−22.6	−27.0
March 1973 to July 1973	−17.0	+1.0
July 1973 to January 1974	−20.5	+12.6
January 1974 to March 1975	−17.6	−3.4
March 1975 to September 1977	+0.2	−7.3
September 1977 to October 1978	−20.9	−31.2
October 1978 to May 1979	+3.8	+19.0
May 1979 to July 1980	−8.4	+1.2
July 1980 to August 1981	−43.2	+5.5
August 1981 to November 1981	−10.9	−4.4
November 1981 to November 1982	+14.6	+18.3
November 1982 to January 1983	−6.5	−11.8
January 1983 to January 1984	+17.7	+0.5
January 1984 to March 1984	−7.6	−3.7
March 1984 to February 1985	+27.1	+15.6
February 1985 to July 1986	−34.8	−39.1
June 1970 to September 1977	−36.0	−25.7
September 1977 to July 1980	−24.8	−17.1
July 1980 to February 1985	+89.0	+17.8
February 1985 to July 1986	−34.8	−39.1
June 1970 to July 1986	−40.8	−55.8

*Underlying spot exchange rates are monthly averages of daily rates.

Source: Ronald I. McKinnon, "Money Supply versus Exchange-Rate Targeting: An Asymmetry between the United States and Other Industrial Economies," in H. Giersch, ed., *Macro and Micro Policies for More Growth and Employment* (Tübingen: Mohr, 1988), 245–68.

Figure 3.1
Nominal and Real Effective Dollar Exchange Rates, 1979:1–1985:4*

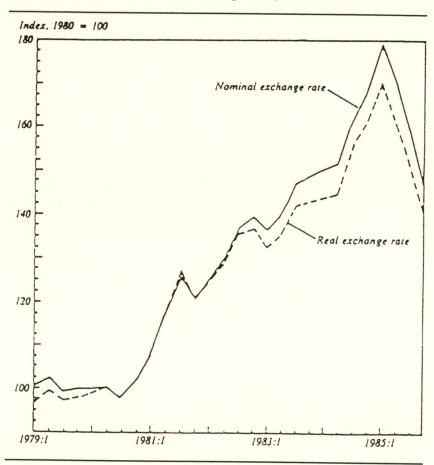

*Quarterly data. The nominal exchange rate is based on the Federal Reserve series for the weighted average nominal exchange value of the U.S. dollar against the currencies of the Group of Ten industrial countries. The real rate is adjusted for changes in the consumer price index. A rise in either index is an appreciation of the dollar against foreign currencies.

Source: Branson (1986: 177). Reprinted with permission from the *Brookings Papers on Economic Activity* (Washington, D.C.: 1986).

foreign exchange market, or do they reflect a healthy flexible exchange rate regime? When there are market failures, then a case for exchange rate management can be made. However, even if the foreign exchange market is efficient, should one nevertheless intervene in order to reduce the excess variability of the exchange rate and, if so, do the monetary authorities know the appropriate exchange rate?

1.1 Market Failure

The postulated inefficiency or "irrationality" of the foreign exchange market has a long history in economic literature. The assertion by Ragnar Nurkse (1944) that destabilizing speculation was dominant during the period of floating rates in the 1920s and the counter-argument of generally stabilizing speculation put forward by Milton Friedman (1953) are well known. In the most recent literature, this debate has re-emerged in terms of "rational bubbles," "sunspot equilibria," and "self-fulfilling runs," all representing cases of destabilizing speculation by rational market participants (see e.g., Blanchard 1979; Flood and Garber 1984; Obstfeld 1986; Evans 1986).

The inefficiency is sometimes ascribed to risk aversion, which would not be justified by the underlying fundamentals, thus pushing currencies into "overvaluations" (and, by this, other currencies into "undervaluations"). Or there are bandwagon effects—speculation feeding upon speculation, again without any regard to the basic determinants. They can even become self-fulfilling by analogy to the vicious-and-virtuous circle argument. In the presence of these destabilizing speculations, it is often argued that government should step in and manage the exchange rate.

The possibility that there may be an absence of stabilizing speculation is recognized by Milton Friedman (1953), and in such circumstances he proposed an intervention policy of "leaning against the wind." The Central Bank should become a speculator replacing insufficient stabilizing market speculations and, moreover, realize a profit from such interventions. However, Friedman (1953: 175–76) also argued it was unlikely "that government officials [risking funds that they do not themselves own] are better judges of the likely movements in the foreign exchange markets than private individuals [risking their own funds]."

Exchange rate management can only be recommended when the monetary authorities have superior information than that available to the market. An alternative if not the preferable strategy by central banks would be to release the relevant information to market participants and to abstain from intervention. Empirical studies (e.g., Levich 1978) have shown that foreign exchange markets are efficient (in the sense that prices always reflect fully the available information such that unusual ex ante speculative profits cannot be realized).

1.2 Excess Variability

The observable excess variability of the exchange rate can be conceived to consist of two parts: *volatility* (i.e., "short-run variability from hour to hour, day to day, week to week or month to month" around a trend) and persistent *misalignments* (i.e., "a persistent departure of the exchange rate from its long-run equilibrium level"; Williamson 1985a: 9–10). For Williamson, volatility is a "troublesome nuisance rather than a major cause of concern" (p. 45). However, exchange rate management in practice has been concerned mainly with volatility, and reform proposals with misalignments.

In the recent exchange rate literature, volatility is explained by the equilibrium forces of the financial asset markets. The exchange rate, viewed as the relative price of two currencies, is always an equilibrium price (from the point of view of financial markets), and according to this viewpoint there is no basis for exchange rate management. However, although the exchange rate is well behaved from the point of view of financial markets, it can diverge from the "equilibrium" exchange rate, conceived as a relative price of goods, as much between domestic and foreign traded goods (terms of trade) as between tradables and non-tradables. The main reason for this discrepancy lies in the slow adjustment of goods prices and quantities to any disturbance (Dornbusch 1976). In this respect, exchange rate management could be considered to be a substitute for a quicker adjustment process in the real sector of the economy. It then has the task of accelerating the exchange rate movement toward the equilibrium rate of the real sector. In so doing it would avoid the misallocation of resources that result from a temporary change in the terms of trade (with respect to the production sector of tradables) and in the relative price of tradables and non-tradables.

A completely different issue for exchange rate management concerns the question of whether, over the long run, there remain "persistent misalignments" in our present system. If this hypothesis is valid, then an additional interpretation of exchange rate management would emerge in terms of monetary reform, since this may prove the most efficient way to tackle such problems.

1.3 Which Long-Run "Equilibrium" Exchange Rate?

After nearly 15 years of turbulence in the foreign exchange markets, economists still cannot agree on what is the fundamental long-run "equilibrium" or desired exchange rate at which management should aim. There are two competing schools of thought—that of balanced trade and that of purchasing power parity. In the most recent debate, the main protagonist of one school is John Williamson (1986) and of the other Ronald McKinnon (1986a).

According to the principle of balanced trade, the exchange rate should roughly equilibrate imports and exports by allowing for the need to make the debt-service requirements and to take into account the "underlying capital flow over the cycle" (Williamson 1986: 166). Branson (1986: 185) mentions even as a possible long-run equilibrium rate the one that sets the full-employment current account balance at zero. The focus on the current account is reminiscent of the elasticity approach to the balance of payments of the 1930s to 1950s, in which one had to worry about the trade deficits because international (private) capital movements were moribund. The approach neglects—in a world of capital mobility—the possibility of long-lasting net-creditor countries and net-debtor countries and, by this, the advantages of an international division of savers and investors. Furthermore, as a matter of course, any real shock to the economy implies a revision of the exchange rate target, since real shocks influence the current account.

The purchasing power parity approach to exchange rate targeting is only concerned with nominal exchange rates. This approach reminds one of the debate of the 1920s in particular with respect to the division of goods into tradables and non-tradables (Oppenheimer 1974). Official exchange rate targets should be set to correspond to national price levels of tradable goods so that the real purchasing power of currencies is roughly identical in terms of tradable goods. A terms-of-trade effect on the exchange rate is ruled out, and the only real exchange rate that is allowed to vary is the relative price between tradables and non-tradables.

The reform proposals put forward by Williamson (1985) and McKinnon (1986a) have in common the desire to manage the exchange around the fundamental long-run equilibrium rate, the first author according to the current account balance criterion and the second according to the purchasing power parity criterion. The aim of these proposals is to establish a set of international "rules of the game" for domestic policy makers (Sachs 1986a). By imposing these rules, the autonomy of domestic policies is limited, since the main reason for the misalignments is seen to the pursuit of divergent domestic policies, which create the excess variability of the exchange rate.

2. HOW TO INTERVENE IN THE FOREIGN EXCHANGE MARKET?

At the very outset, it should be emphasized that intervention policies in the foreign exchange market, like any other monetary policy, have, in principle, no long-lasting effect on the real exchange rate. Monetary policy as a nominal phenomenon can only have nominal effects in the long run, effects on the price level provided that one excludes long-run money illusion and a long-run impact on the real interest rate. Consequently, there is in principle a *long-run* neutrality of money on the real exchange rate.

In the *short run,* monetary policy in the sense of exchange rate management can be used for two different purposes:

a. It can be utilized for employment reasons in terms of an expansionary monetary policy, since the "overshooting" phenomenon can take place implying a short-run real depreciation of the home currency. The real depreciation generally represents an employment bonus to the extent that exports rise and imports fall. To the extent that the expansionary monetary policy has been pursued mainly for the employment effect resulting from a temporary real depreciation, it can be called a policy of exchange rate management of the "beggar-thy-neighbour" policy kind. In the following, we exclude this target of exchange rate management for monetary policy.

b. The other purpose of exchange rate management is the aim to influence nominal exchange rates in order to reduce the excess variability (in the sense of volatility) as was discussed in section 1. By assuming that the authorities have chosen a nominal exchange rate target, the present section discusses a rather technical aspect concerning the question of how the target could be realized with the most appropriate mix of monetary-policy instruments; other macropolicies will be discussed in section 3.1. (1) The centre of the debate concerns the traditional distinction between sterilized and nonsterilized interventions on the one hand and the underlying assumption about the degree of substitutability of domestic and foreign financial assets on the other hand. (2) Furthermore, the effectiveness of intervention policies will be increased by a proper international coordination scheme of nonsterilized interventions. (3) Finally, to the extent that such an international cooperation pattern does not exist, world inflation is likely to increase as observed in the 1970s.

2.1 Sterilized versus Nonsterilized Intervention Policy

The effects of sterilized and nonsterilized interventions have been analyzed by Branson (1979), Marston (1980), Genberg (1981), Mussa (1981), Obstfeld (1982, 1983), and Tryon (1983). The analyses of these effects also constitute the main object of the Jurgensen Report (1983), presented by the working group on exchange market intervention established at the Versailles summit meeting.

When a central bank intervenes in the foreign exchange market, from an analytical point of view it purchases or sells (interest-bearing) bonds denominated in foreign currency in exchange for domestic currency. This type of monetary policy has two immediate effects: the stock of bonds denominated in foreign currency held by the public (at home and abroad) is changed and simultaneously the domestic monetary base is changed. This intervention policy is called "nonsterilized." If at the same time the central bank also sells or purchases bonds denominated in domestic currency ("domestic credit") in exchange for domestic currency such that the monetary base is unaltered, the intervention policy is termed "sterilized." The exchange rate effects of the two types of intervention policy differ from each other depending upon whether one assumes perfect or imperfect substitutability between domestic and foreign bonds.

To the extent that one works with the hypothesis of perfect substitutability, the country concerned will not be able to change its real interest rate beyond the real interest rate parity, since the above hypothesis implies perfectly integrated capital markets in the world economy. A sterilized intervention policy will only have an impact on daily or weekly exchange rates; over a longer period it is completely ineffective. Obstfeld, having studied the sterilized intervention policy of the Bundesbank, comes to the conclusion (1983: 184–85): "The model's verdict was that the Bundesbank has little if any power to influence the exchange rate over that time span [a month] without altering current or expected future money-market conditions [i.e., without conducting unsterilized interventions]." On the other hand, nonsterilized intervention is exactly equivalent to an open market operation and produces the same macroeconomic effects as conventional monetary policy. Thus, exchange rate management is possible with a nonsterilized intervention policy (or any other monetary policy instrument). However, only over the short run will it be able to have an impact on the real exchange rate due to the phenomenon of overshooting. Over the longer run, once the internal price has adjusted to the new outstanding money stock, a nonsterilized intervention policy creates roughly an equivalent change in the nominal exchange rate.

Under the hypothesis of imperfect substitutability between domestic and foreign bonds, the results for nonsterilized intervention remain the same even though the short-run impact on the exchange rate will be higher, since the domestic real interest rate is not linked any more strictly to the foreign rate via real interest rate parity. Over the short run, sterilized intervention will also be effective. Imperfect substitutability implies that the expected returns on assets denominated in different currencies will differ by a "risk premium" such that the real interest rate parity does not hold anymore. The risk premium in turn depends, for a given risk aversion, on the relative supplies (or outstanding stocks) of domestic and foreign bonds. Since the monetary authority changes the composition between the two stocks when it conducts sterilized foreign exchange market operations (or, in more conventional terms, the composition of the source of the monetary base—domestic credit and international reserves—is changed), it will have an impact on the exchange rate.

2.2 Coordination of Exchange Rate Management

As de Grauwe (1983) and Claassen (1983) have shown, international coordination of intervention policies makes a lot of difference for the efficiency of exchange rate management. In the following, we shall remain in the (simpler) framework of perfect substitutability. Consequently, only nonsterilized operations will have a (short-run) impact on the real exchange rate. Since intervention means that the domestic country gains reserves and another country loses reserves (or vice versa), it makes a big difference for the efficacy of exchange rate management whether the foreign authorities sterilize or do not sterilize their reserve losses.

Choosing a two-country framework, one could look at two countries outside the United States, or at two countries where the first one represents the United States and the other one the rest of the world (ROW). We shall follow the second option, since the present dollar standard imposes on the United States an "unconscious" behavior of sterilization. However, similar results can be derived from a two-country model outside the United States (e.g., for two countries within the European Monetary System), where one country—most probably the surplus country, that is the country that tries to avoid an appreciation of its currency ("leaning against the wind")—systematically pursues a sterilized intervention policy.

As McKinnon (1982: 330) has shown, the sterilization policy of the United States is not consciously pursued but instead is "passive" to the extent that the

Federal Reserve System does not know it is pursuing a sterilization policy, since it is induced by the ROW-country's willingness to hold international reserves in the form of U.S. Treasury bonds. The U.S. sterilization policy "is *passive* because the Federal Reserve is not consciously sterilizing with offsetting changes in its own domestic asset position. Rather, the American money supply is insulated from changes in official reserves by the willingness of foreign central banks to hold nonmonetary U.S. government debt." Thus, for instance, if the ROW-country avoids an appreciation, it eventually uses, with the aid of the Federal Reserve System as a broker, its reserve inflows to purchase U.S. Treasury bonds or bills in the U.S. market.

The disadvantages of this "asymmetrical type of cooperation" are twofold. On one hand, a relatively large amount of reserves is needed for intervention. On the other hand, the world quantity of money changes, since the intervening country's money supply varies. The case of "symmetrical cooperation" (both countries do not sterilize) is the optimal one, or the "most fruitful" one, because the intervention policy for influencing the exchange rate is efficient, the need for international reserves is the lowest, the world quantity of money remains unchanged, and the adjustment burden is shared equally between the United States and the ROW-country.

2.3 Asymmetrical Cooperation and the World Inflation of the 1970s

In a pure flexible exchange rate system, there is no relation whatsoever between international reserves and the money supplies of various countries, because the former simply remain constant (expressed in U.S. dollars). In a managed system of floating exchange rates, there is, again, no link at all when sterilized intervention policies are pursued, whereas there is a strong link when nonsterilized intervention policies are pursued. If, furthermore, the United States follows a policy of sterilization, the impact of nonsterilized intervention policies of other countries on the *world* quantity of money will be greatest.

By looking at yearly world data on growth rates (for the ten major industrial countries, the growth rates for the world money supply and for the world price level are weighted averages of national growth rates using gross national product weights of 1970), McKinnon (1982: 321–24) finds strong evidence of a link between international reserves, the world quantity of money, and the world price level for two periods, 1971–72 and 1977–78 (when the dollar was under attack), as the figures reproduced in Table 3.2 indicate. There was only partial non-sterilization in the countries outside the United States and a sterilization of the U.S. quantity of money. The weight of the U.S. quantity of money within the world quantity of money is about 50 percent. The resulting world price inflation had a two-year lag.

In a more recent paper (1986) McKinnon shows why the asymmetrical cooperation of exchange rate management (partly nonsterilized interventions by ROW

Table 3.2
Growth Rates of U.S. Money Supply, of International Reserves, of World Quantity of Money, and of World Price Level (percent)

Year	U.S. Money Supply (M_1)	International Reserves (dollars)	World Money Supply (M_1)	World Price Level
1970	4.3	74.8	8.19	4.4
1971	6.5	142.0	11.77	3.1
1972	9.1	14.7	12.73	4.1
1973	5.7	8.9	7.65	12.9
1974	3.0	–0.8	6.51	21.9
1975	5.5	0.2	9.22	7.5
1976	5.9	6.2	7.36	6.6
1977	8.2	47.6	10.27	6.6
1978	8.2	33.5	10.98	5.6
1979	8.0	–19.9	7.60	11.1
1980	5.3	0.8	4.88	13.5

Source: McKinnon (1982).

Figure 3.2
U.S. Effective Exchange Rate and the Rest of the World's Money Supply

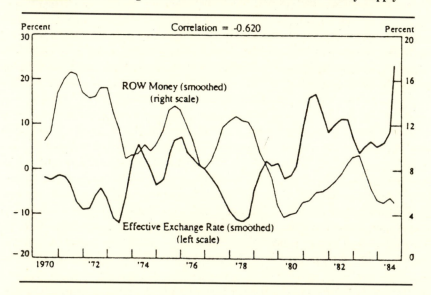

Source: McKinnon (1986: 218). Reprinted courtesy of Ronald McKinnon.

and always sterilization by the Federal Reserve) has tended to synchronize the international business cycle as far as monetary shocks are concerned. In Figure 3.2 a strong negative correlation is shown between quarterly rates of change in the dollar exchange rate and money growth rates in ROW. Both variables are used (or smoothed) with a five-quarter moving average. When the dollar is rising (i.e., appreciating), ROW's central banks intervene ("leaning against the wind" by selling reserves and buying their own currencies) for reasons of exchange rate management, and their money growth rates tend to be reduced collectively. Conversely, when the dollar is falling (i.e., depreciating), partly nonsterilized intervention operations by ROW (creating money against the purchase of reserves) increase their money supply growth rates. To the extent that the appreciation of the dollar was caused by tight U.S. monetary policy (and similarly that the depreciation of the dollar was induced by loose U.S. monetary policy)—a hypothesis that is not always evident for the 1980s—the total world stock of money must fluctuate cyclically, and the basic reason is that the "Federal Reserve has not typically responded to these fluctuations in the dollar exchange rate in an offsetting fashion" (McKinnon 1986: 216).

3. HOW TO MANAGE THE REAL EXCHANGE RATE IN THE PRESENCE OF REAL SHOCK

The most remarkable case of divergence from purchasing power parity over the recent period of floating rates is the real appreciation of the U.S. dollar since the end of 1980 to 1985 (see Fig. 3.1). This period has witnessed a major real shock: the "formidable" U.S. debt-financed budget deficit since 1981, which has been accompanied by fiscal contraction in Europe and Japan. The "excessive" real appreciation of the dollar cannot be considered as a "rational bubble," but rather it reflects a change in the fundamentals as far as the divergent fiscal policies (coupled with minor divergences concerning tightness of monetary policies) are concerned.

Implicitly, the excess variability dealt with in the preceding sections was created by monetary or financial disturbances (money supply shocks or portfolio shifts), and the proper response was monetary policy to manage the exchange rate. Nominal shocks hit the nominal fundamentals of the exchange rate, real shocks affect the real fundamentals and thus the real exchange rate. By definition, these real shocks emerge in the real sector (i.e., in the goods market), and their origin can be traced to the supply or demand side. Among the real cost push effects, there have been the worldwide oil price increases and the increase in taxation of labor income (social security contributions and personal income tax) constituting real supply shocks, which have characterized the 1970s (de Grauwe and Fratianni 1985). Real demand shocks are those of an increase (or decrease) in autonomous consumption (i.e., fall in savings), investment, or bond-financed budget deficits. The case of fiscal expansion in the United States and of (relative) fiscal contraction in Europe and Japan is the major real shock of the 1980s.

1. Since it was not a "common" but rather a "divergent" real shock (because of divergent fiscal policies) to the world economy, there had to be a change in the real exchange rate between the United States and the ROW in a world of high capital mobility.

2. The response of the ROW could have been a real exchange rate management via a proper monetary–fiscal policy mix, but the contrary occurred, probably for reasons of real interest rate management.

3. In this particular policy configuration no case can be made for a traditional international coordination of exchange rate management in terms of (nonsterilized) intervention policies.

3.1 Real Shocks in a World of Capital Mobility

In the recent closed economy literature, there is still an ongoing debate as to whether public debt constitutes net wealth for the global economy. As one can expect, some economists (e.g., Barro 1974) deny the net wealth aspect and some others argue for it (e.g., Buiter 1985). One of the essential conditions according to which public debt would not represent net wealth concerns the possibility that taxpayers fully discount their future tax liabilities (which arise to service the debt). According to this hypothesis, a bond-financed budget deficit would imply a reaction by private agents to increase their amount of savings, which in the limit could correspond exactly to the volume of the budget deficit. In such a case, a bond-financed budget deficit is equivalent to a tax-financed budget "deficit" (the so-called Ricardo equivalence theorem), and its impact on the real macroeconomic variables would be zero (except for the long-run implications of a higher part of government expenditures in GDP). There would consequently not be any other real effect in an open economy, so that the real shock in the form of a bond-financed budget deficit would be completely absorbed by the domestic economy. In the following, we shall assume that public debt is not neutral; the book by Frenkel and Razin (1987) represents an interesting contribution since they assume only a certain degree of public debt neutrality.

Flexible exchange rates do not insulate national economies from a real shock emerging in one of these economies—and in particular in a large economy like the United States—to the extent that there is some degree of capital mobility. In the traditional sense, a high degree of capital mobility stands for a high degree of substitutability of domestic and foreign financial assets. According to the terminology of the more recent literature, capital mobility refers to the possibility of capital controls. We shall use the term "capital mobility" in the sense of both interpretations.

When there is complete capital immobility, the domestic economy works like a closed economy. In this case, flexible exchange rates would insulate the concerned economy absolutely from the rest of the world. Since the balance of payments coincides with the trade balance, any bond-financed budget deficit would be fully financed by domestic savings via a rise in the domestic interest rate. This type of economy was probably in the mind of those economists who in the 1950s advocated a regime of floating exchange rates, since the stabilization policy of an individual country would be autonomous, that is, independent of foreign economies (Purvis 1985: 725). At the present time, this model of an economy represents the "ideal" type of an open economy for the proponents of capital restrictions (like Liviatan 1980; Tobin 1982; and Dornbusch 1986) in order to minimize or nullify the impact of capital flows on the volatility of exchange rates.

In a world of capital mobility, the budget deficit will be financed jointly by domestic and foreign savings. According to the hypothesis of perfect capital mobility for a small open economy (which, by definition, has no impact on the real world interest rate), the budget deficit would be totally financed by external savings (i.e., by capital inflows). To the financial transfer must correspond a real transfer in terms of goods. The real transfer is made possible through a real appreciation of the domestic currency, which includes (under normal elasticity conditions and by ignoring short-run J-curve effects) less exports and more imports. Consequently, the budget deficit creates a total crowding-out effect, not with respect to domestic absorption (which remains unchanged) but with respect to net exports. This crowding-out is realized by the change in the real exchange rate—a traditional result of the "old-fashioned" Mundell-Fleming model. Through the real exchange rate effect, domestic goods are available for government expenditures via less export and via a switch from import substitutes to imported goods.

If the budget deficit takes place in a big country—say the United States—the adjustment process will differ, since one has to work with a two-country model: the United States and the ROW. We still remain under the hypothesis of perfect capital mobility. The rise in the U.S.-bond-financed budget deficit increases the real world market interest rate. Consequently, there is some crowding-out of private expenditures in the United States and some other crowding-out of private expenditures in the ROW, the first creating excess savings in the United States and the second one excess savings in the ROW. It follows that the budget deficit is financed partly by domestic savings and partly by foreign savings via capital inflows. The corresponding transfer of goods from the ROW to the United States is realized by the real appreciation of the U.S. dollar involving a current account deficit in the United States and a corresponding current account surplus in the ROW. From the point of view of a two-country model, the former crowding-out effect of "net exports" (described for a small country) is actually a crowding-out effect of domestic *and* foreign private absorption.

The case of imperfect capital mobility (in the sense of imperfect substitutability between domestic and foreign financial assets) would produce a higher real U.S. interest rate and a lower real appreciation of the dollar. The reason is that under imperfect capital mobility, the internal real interest rate can rise by much more than the external one (or, more precisely, much more than the real interest rate parity condition would predict; this additional divergence is called a "risk premium"). Consequently, more domestic excess savings are available, less foreign excess savings are necessary, and it follows that capital inflows are lower.

From the above description of the adjustment mechanism under various assumptions about the degree of capital mobility, the following general result can be put forward. Bond-financed budget deficits of the domestic economy constitute a real shock to the domestic *and* foreign country; the same reasoning can be developed for an autonomous increase in domestic consumption or investment. These real shocks influence the real world market interest rate and provoke a switch of savings in the world economy from the ROW to the United States via capital movements. To the net capital movements must correspond net trade flows, which are brought about by a change in the real exchange rate. In this sense, the system of flexible exchange rates does not allow macroeconomic independence except for the case of capital immobility.

Since bond-financed budget deficits lead to a real appreciation, continuously increasing budget deficits involve a continuous ongoing real appreciation over time. Consequently the continuous increase in the U.S. budget deficit from 1981 to 1985 could explain the *trend* of the U.S. real exchange rate (Fig. 3.1) (Branson 1986; Frenkel 1986; Dornbusch 1986). Other factors could have played an additional role: tight monetary policy in 1980–81 and relatively loose monetary policy in 1985; the expectation effects with regard to an appreciation as a consequence of the Kemp-Roth tax bill in 1981 and with respect to the depreciation as a result of the Gramm-Rudman-Hollings bill of 1985, according to which the U.S. budget deficit will be gradually reduced over the following years.

3.2 Exchange Rate Management versus Interest Rate Management

How could the rest of the world have reacted to the real shock brought about by U.S. fiscal policy? In particular, would an appropriate exchange rate management have avoided the tremendous fluctuations in the real exchange rate of the U.S. currency over the 1980s? Proper real exchange rate management could only be conducted by influencing the real fundamentals of the exchange rate, and the proper policy tool would be fiscal policy or a monetary–fiscal policy mix. In the following we shall concentrate on possible fiscal policy reactions (Corden 1986).

Figure 3.3 illustrates the fiscal policy reactions of the ROW, which we shall call Europe (standing for all other OECD members). The European fiscal policy parameter is the size of Europe's budget deficit (*BD*). The real exchange rate of European currencies is represented by *e*, where an increase in *e* signifies a real depreciation of European currencies, which is equal to a corresponding real appreciation of the U.S. dollar. The trade-off line *T* describes the results of our theoretical arguments (exposed in section 3.1) but is now applied to Europe. An increase of Europe's bond-financed budget deficit implies a real appreciation of Europe's currencies (the slope is mainly determined by the degree of capital mobility and by the elasticity of the trade balance with respect to the real

Figure 3.3
Budget Deficits and the Real Exchange Rate: Real Exchange Rate Stabilization versus Real Interest Rate Stabilization

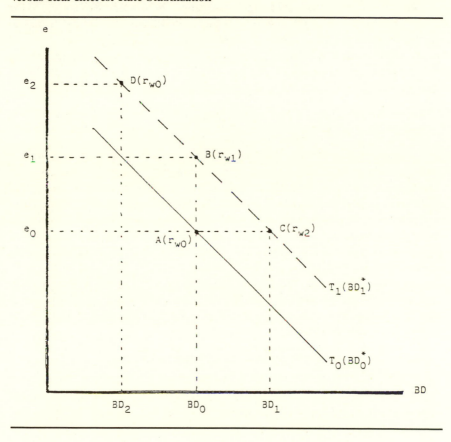

exchange rate). The T_0-line is constructed for a given U.S. budget deficit (BD_0^*). The initial situation may be characterized by point A. An expansionary fiscal policy of the U.S. (BD_1^*) shifts the T_0-line to the position T_1. There can be three fundamentally different fiscal policy reactions by Europe:

No Fiscal Policy Reaction (point B)

This case underlies implicitly our two-country model of section 3.1. On one hand, there is a real appreciation of the U.S. dollar, which corresponds to a real depreciation of Europe's currencies (e_1). On the other hand, there is an increase in the real world market interest rate from r_{w0} to r_{w1}. The real shock inside the U.S. economy has been transmitted to Europe in the form of a real depreciation of Europe's currencies and an increase in the real interest rate.

*Expansionary Fiscal Policy Reaction for Reasons of Real Exchange
Rate Stabilization (point C)*

The real exchange rate would remain unchanged between both areas (e_0) to the extent that Europe expands in line with the United States by raising its budget deficit from BD_0 to BD_1. However, there would be a still sharper rise in the real world interest rate (i.e., from r_{w1} to r_{w2}). In both parts of the world the budget deficits are financed totally by internal savings via the additional increase in the real interest rate. Consequently, the real exchange rate remains unchanged.

*Restrictive Fiscal Policy Reaction for Reasons of Real Interest Rate
Stabilization (point D)*

To the extent that the Europeans are annoyed about the rise in the real interest rate (considering the real depreciation of their currencies as stimulating for employment), they are only able to reduce the real interest rate by a contractive fiscal policy. Provided that they want to reestablish the initial real interest rate r_{w0}, they have to reduce their budget deficit by an amount that compensates for the increase in the U.S. budget deficit, so that the real interest rate in the world capital market remains constant. The increased savings as a consequence of lower European budget deficits serve for the complete financing of the U.S. budget deficit (when assuming perfect capital mobility). The corresponding trade transfer of goods from Europe to the United States can only be realized by a still stronger real appreciation of the dollar, that is, by a still stronger real depreciation of European currencies.

It is now interesting to observe what actually happened in Europe in the 1980s on the fiscal side. The trend was more in the direction of a restrictive fiscal policy (especially for Britain, Japan, and West Germany). Consequently, the relevant evolution of the real exchange rate was that between points B and D on the T_1-line. Thus, Europe's fiscal policy has intensified the size of the change in the real exchange rate. Whether this policy has been conducted consciously for reasons of real interest rate stabilization or for reasons of public debt consolidation remains an open question. It is probable that both reasons have played a role, despite the tremendous repercussion on the United States/Europe real exchange rate.

3.3 The Uneasy Case for Exchange Rate Coordination in the Early 1980s

The title of this section is borrowed from Sachs' "The Uneasy Case for Greater Exchange Rate Coordination" (1986a). When fundamentals change, as in the case of the new fiscal policy mix between the United States and the ROW, then the real equilibrium exchange rate also changes. In the case of real shocks, there cannot be found any reasonable ground to propose exchange rate management and, by this, any exchange rate coordination (Frenkel 1986; Branson 1986;

Dornbusch 1986). On this point, the three eminent experts in the field, William Branson, Rudiger Dornbusch, and Jacob Frenkel, are in full mutual agreement:

[A] shift in fiscal policy, much as occurred beginning in 1982, will generate an equilibrium adjustment in the real exchange rate as part of the financing process. This movement is probably being reversed now, as the Gramm-Rudman legislation brings real interest rates and the exchange rate down. A monetary policy that attempted to frustrate this movement probably would be a mistake now, as it would have been in 1982. (Branson 1986; 186–87)

The lesson is that large international divergences in monetary or fiscal policy will be reflected in exchange rates. To avoid these fluctuations, bad policies must be avoided. Accommodating a poor fiscal policy by exchange-rate-oriented monetary policy simply adds yet another folly. (Dornbusch 1986: 222)

If indeed the root cause for the current difficulties lies in the fiscal positions of the United States, Europe, and Japan, then the solution for the problems does *not* call for a monetary reform, for tariffs and protectionism, for taxes on capital flows (or for other measures which throw sand in the wheels), nor does it call for intervention rules. Rather, it calls for a restoration of fiscal order in which the United States adopts a more contractionary fiscal stance while Europe and Japan adopt a more expansionary stance. I believe that the central difficulties with the current regime do not rest with the exchange-rate system or with the exchange-rate policies; rather, they rest with the overall mix of the uncoordinated macroeconomic policies. (Frenkel 1986: 62–63)

Consequently, if one wants *more real exchange rate stability,* the only way to do it is to coordinate fiscal policy among countries. This means that fiscal policy autonomy is sacrificed to an exchange rate target. In the real world, such a plea for international fiscal policy coordination must remain a vain hope, since it would imply fiscal conversion—all countries pursue, at the same rhythm, either expansion together or contraction together.

Furthermore, as we have shown in section 3.2, this fiscal convergence implies a sacrifice of real interest rate stability. Behind the background of changing fiscal policies over time combined with fiscal convergence, more real exchange rate stability implies *more real interest instability.* Thus, worldwide fiscal expansion raises real interest rates and worldwide fiscal contraction lowers them.

Proponents of target zones such as John Williamson (1985a) go even further in believing that the implementation of target zones for exchange rates constitute "a first step in educating governments to pursue good policies" (Dornbusch 1986: 222). It should be remembered that there is an endless debate going on in Europe concerning the "merits" of the European Monetary System. The existence of the EMS could indicate that coordination works. However, critics of this mini-Bretton-Woods system with an adjustable peg consider it in fact as nothing more than a "German Monetary Area" with "occasional crises, realignments, and capital controls" (Dornbusch 1986: 218).

Instead of more real exchange rate stability, one could also defend the opposite view of *real exchange rate flexibility* to the extent that changes in the real exchange rate are an outcome of justifiable real shocks in the world economy. Max Corden (1986) has put forward this point. Real shocks are justifiable when they respond to the adjustment of actual stocks to desired stocks. A fall in the savings ratio represents the case where the actual wealth ratio exceeds the desired one. An increase in private investment is the adjustment of the actual capital stock to the desired stock. A large decline in savings or a large rise in investment has similar effects on the real interest rate and the real exchange rate as large budget deficits—the former rises and the latter falls. Thus, the real exchange rate instability has to be compared with the gains from stock adjustment:

When Japanese savings are being transferred to the United States in order to finance tax cuts or private investment in the United States the process might be regarded as optimal. Hence the much maligned current account "imbalances" may be optimal. There are gains from trade in financial assets against goods, as there are in goods–goods trade. The Japanese want to export more goods and import more bonds in return, and the Americans want to trade in the opposite direction (Corden 1986: 429)

CONCLUDING REMARKS

The conclusions about the degree of exchange rate management and of international coordination are as follows:

1. Financial markets are efficient. From the point of view of the financial sector, the current exchange rate is always the correct equilibrium rate. However, this correct rate can be the wrong one from the point of view of the real sector. Excess fluctuations of the terms of trade and of the relative price between tradables and nontradables could be dampened by exchange rate management. A crucial assumption for exchange rate management concerns the perfect knowledge, by the monetary authorities, of the fundamental equilibrium real exchange rate.
2. Concerning the choice of the proper monetary policy mix for effective exchange rate management, non-sterilized intervention policies are doubtlessly superior to sterilized ones. The reason is that one of the monetary fundamentals—the outstanding stock of money—is altered. However, such a policy will not have a long-lasting impact on the real exchange rate to the extent that the internal price level adjusts. International symmetrical coordination of exchange rate management (and here of non-sterilized intervention policies) is seen to be the most efficient—in particular between the United States and the "rest of the world." Such a coordination would produce the greatest impact on the exchange rate (for a given amount of reserves used by the intervention operation) and would avoid world inflation pressures.
3. A case against exchange rate management must be made in the presence of real shocks. The shock of divergent fiscal policies to the world economy over the

1980s illustrates this. In a world of capital mobility, a bond-financed budget deficit will be financed, to a large extent, by foreign savings. In order to ensure the real transfer in terms of more available traded goods, the real exchange rate has to appreciate. This real appreciation is nothing more than a reflection of the change in the real fundamentals of the exchange rate. Exchange rate management of the non-sterilized intervention type and, a fortiori, international coordination of such intervention policies, would be a nuisance to the international monetary system (and over the long run it could only change the nominal exchange rate). Consequently, if any international coordination should be implanted in order to avoid the real shock, it could only be on the level of fiscal convergence—a hopeless hypothesis in the present circumstances (as is the plea for a symmetrical cooperation of non-sterilized intervention policies between the United States and the ROW).

COMMENT BY

Douglas D. Purvis

Emil-Maria Claassen's chapter provides a useful survey of a number of the important issues pertaining to the international coordination of economic policies. I find myself in agreement with much—indeed most—of what he has written, and hence I will address most of my remarks to issues that he did not take up. However, before turning to remarks that relate directly to his chapter, I will make a number of remarks on the more general theme of the role of real phenomena in understanding exchange rates and in formulating exchange rate policies.

GENERAL REMARKS

The Role of Real Disturbances

The importance of real phenomena to the discussion is perhaps most clearly seen by comparing Claassen's conclusions with those reached in the other two chapters in this session. Claassen is in almost complete agreement with Camen and Genberg, and disagrees sharply with John Williamson. Claassen stresses the role of real factors in influencing exchange rate developments, and Camen and Genberg stress further the difficulty for the analyst and policy maker alike in disentangling the effects of those real phenomena from purely monetary influences. Williamson, on the other hand, gives relatively short shrift to the importance of real phenomena and is extremely sanguine about the problems involved in identifying and compensating for real disturbances. Hence, despite using a rather common theoretical framework, Williamson reaches conclusions diametrically opposed to those reached by Claassen and by Camen and Genberg.

PPP Benchmarks

A related issue is the relevance of purchasing power parity (PPP) measures as a benchmark for evaluating exchange rate developments and for assessing whether a particular currency might be over- or undervalued. My own, perhaps revisionist, view of the PPP doctrine is that it simply represents the operation of the neutrality of money in an open economy. That is, it is a comparative statics proposition that says that relative prices, and hence the real exchange rate, will be unaltered (in the long run) by monetary disturbances. PPP is not simply an arbitrage proposition, and hence it should not be confused with the Law of One Price.[1] Most importantly, the PPP doctrine does not imply that relative prices, including real exchange rates, should not be expected to change.

Thus only in circumstances where monetary factors can be shown to clearly dominate exchange rate developments can PPP estimates be used as a benchmark to judge the over- and undervaluations of currencies. One such situation is hyperinflation; another is when very long-run comparisons are made in a world where real shocks are transitory and thus net out over time. The last decade, which witnessed wild swings in the relative prices of oil, food, and other commodities, exploding public sector deficits, and huge changes in real interest rates, does not seem to me to be an appropriate situation for using PPP benchmarks. Despite the short shrift Williamson gives to real disturbances, the general approach he puts forward for calculating equilibrium real exchange rates has the advantage of, in principal, allowing for real factors in a way that PPP benchmarks do not.

Overshooting and Misalignment

A useful and commonly used model for evaluating exchange rate misalignment, and one consistent with the view of PPP set out above, is the Dornbusch overshooting model (elaborated to incorporate income effects on money demand and the liquidity effects of exchange rate movements; see, e.g., Devereux and Purvis 1986). In that model, nominal disturbances give rise to zero long-run effects on the real exchange rate, but nonetheless cause a temporary misalignment. Real shocks give rise to both a long-run change in the real exchange rate and to a temporary misalignment, and the temporary misalignment can be either positive or negative.[2] This underlines the problems involved in disentangling the two types of effects stressed by Camen and Genberg.

Nominal and Real Exchange Rate Adjustment

A final general comment I would like to make concerns the interaction between nominal exchange rate changes and adjusting to real phenomena. The classic case in favor of flexible exchange rates put forward by Milton Friedman sought to exploit the correlation between real and nominal exchange rate changes, now so often cited as one of the problems of the operation of the current "system" of flexible exchange rates. The view, also stressed by Mundell in his "Optimal Currency Area" paper, is that in the presence of domestic nominal rigidities, real changes can often be most effectively achieved by a currency realignment. The argument is analogous to the case for adopting Daylight Savings Time each spring.

It now seems clear that there is a fallacy of composition involved in extending the analysis from a once-for-all realignment to a system of freely fluctuating, market-determined exchange rates. The latter involves the creation of asset markets, and hence allows for the possibility of a number of manifestations of speculative behavior—in particular the (perhaps efficient, but also in some sense excessive) sensitivity of asset prices (in this case exchange rates) to information flows (see Camen and Genberg, Chapter 2, this volume).

These phenomena give rise to volatile nominal exchange rate behavior and, given nominal rigidities, therefore to real exchange rate volatility. Thus rather than becoming a vehicle by which real changes can be effected and adjusted to, nominal exchange rate changes become a source of real disturbances with real consequences for the economy.

John Williamson stresses these speculative disturbances. While I disagree with his policy proposal, I think that he has identified and addressed an extremely important issue. The essential problem is to maximize the role of exchange rate changes in facilitating required real adjustments, while minimizing the potential for "unwarranted" exchange rate changes to set off otherwise unnecessary real adjustments in the economy.

SPECIFIC COMMENTS

Let me now turn to Emil-Maria Claassen's chapter. Section 1 provides a useful survey of the events giving rise to the current interest in exchange rate management. He documents the by now well-known correlation between real and nominal exchange rates, and draws the useful distinction between short-run volatility of exchange rates and the (often persistant) misalignment of currencies. This leads to a comparative discussion of the "exchange rate management" proposals put forward by John Williamson (see above) and Ronald McKinnon.

Here Claassen states, correctly in my view, that one important reason for currency misalignments is the pursuit of divergent domestic policies in various countries. This relates to Camen and Genberg position (Chapter 2)—they stress the importance of "fundamentals" (including policy) in explaining exchange rate developments, and conclude that the evidence in favor of "bubbles" is rather weak. But in the presence of exploding public sector deficits, one can also question the "sustainability" of current policies. In this situation the distinction between fundamentals and bubbles is harder to identify, since one must ask how rational markets will respond in the face of potentially unsustainable policies.[3]

In section 2 Claassen reviews the literature on foreign exchange market intervention. Here we get a clear, if somewhat pedestrian, discussion of the role of asset substitutability in differentiating between sterilized and unsterilized intervention, and a useful extension that further discusses the McKinnon hypothesis and associated policy proposals. The only real issue I take with this discussion is the rather sanguine view it puts forward with regard to activist intervention of the "leaning against the wind" variety. Just as the distinction between real and nominal shocks is important, so is the distinction between transitory and permanent shocks. With transitory shocks only, a "leaning against the wind" policy is ideal—it smooths fluctuations and helps promote "orderly market conditions." With permanent shocks, however, leaning against the wind can prove counterproductive.

For example, suppose a permanent disturbance occurs that calls for a 10 percent depreciation of the domestic currency, but that the central bank intervenes to "lean against the wind," so that the currency only depreciates in the first instance by 4 percent. To the extent that market participants correctly perceive that eventually the currency will depreciate by the full 10 percent, then the central bank's policy creates a speculative opportunity *and* provides liquidity to the speculators. The important lesson is that exchange market intervention is capable of feeding speculation as well as mitigating it.

I turn now to the most substantive part of the Claassen chapter, part 3, which deals with real exchange rate policies in the presence of real shocks. The major shortcoming that I identified is its lack of strategic considerations. A key issue when analyzing international policy coordination is that any policy action, or any policy regime, sets up incentives for policy reactions in the rest of the world. Thus in order to understand the consequences of alternative domestic policies, whether cooperative or not, it is necessary to take into account changes in both the domestic policy and those in the rest of the world.

For example, consider Claassen's analysis of the effects of fiscal restraint in the early 1980s in Japan and Europe (JEurope for short). His interpretation is that JEurope reacted to U.S. fiscal expansion with fiscal restraint, "essentially for reasons of real interest rate management." That view takes the U.S. fiscal position as given, and in particular does not allow for any U.S. fiscal reaction to the JEuropean policies.

An alternative view, perhaps heretical in some quarters but not inconsistent with the facts, is that Keynesian-style fiscal expansion was being used to fuel the U.S. recovery in this period. The key point is that from the perspective of U.S. aggregate demand, JEuropean and U.S. fiscal expansion are substitutes; to the extent that JEuropean fiscal restraint occurs, there is incentive created for increased U.S. fiscal deficits. Hence the JEuropean fiscal response may well serve to exacerbate the problem (the U.S. fiscal deficit) that it was responding to.

A more productive JEuropean response might have been to undertake fiscal expansion. This would have reduced the perceived need for U.S. deficits from the point of view of U.S. demand management. As a result the real interest consequences of the policy would not have been as drastic as Claassen's analysis—with its *given* U.S. fiscal stance—would suggest. Further, while the aggregate fiscal deficits of Western industrialized countries may have been increased somewhat, the distribution of those deficits would have been more balanced. The JEuropean fiscal expansion would have also stabilized real exchange rates, and given a significant reduction in the U.S. deficit, it would not have destabilized world real interest rates.

Thus one interpretation is that even if real exchange rate stabilization were desirable, in this case it would have been more efficaciously achieved by JEuropean fiscal expansion rather than monetary contraction.[4] The more general point for the theme of this conference is that the question of whether to stabilize real exchange rates is not the only relevant one; how to do it is also important.

The potential for U.S. policy reaction is also relevant to Paul De Grauwe's chapter in this book. One strong incentive for intra-JEuropean cooperation is to create an economic bloc strong enough to induce desired U.S. policy responses. Thus I feel he underestimates the incentives for JEuropean cooperation and that, similar to Claassen, his analysis of the consequences of JEuropean fiscal restraint is misleading in that it treats U.S. policies as given.[5]

The above are, however, only minor qualifications to the analysis. In particular, they do not upset Claassen's general conclusion that "a case must be made against [real] exchange rate management in the presence of real shocks."

CONCLUDING REMARKS ON REAL EXCHANGE RATE TARGETING

In light of the above considerations, my view is that

• if one is confident of being able to identify the equilibrium real exchange rate;

- if one is confident that multilateral cooperation is capable of prescribing an appropriate set of policies to achieve that equilibrium real rate;

- if changes in the equilibrium real rate can be quickly identified and agreed upon;

- if policies can be changed quickly and take their effect with a lag short enough to ensure that they remain appropriate given the changes in the equilibrium real exchange rate; and

- if adopting this regime does not cause speculative behavior that changes the operation of the system so as to render the agreed-upon policies inappropriate and perhaps exacerbate other policy problems;

then it is appropriate to adopt targets for real exchange rates. Otherwise, it is not.

I do not believe we can be sure of *any* of these required steps, much less *all* of them. Thus while I think John Williamson's policy prescription has provided a useful forum for constructive debate and for bringing focus to several key issues, as a piece of policy advice it is sheer technocratic folly.

Williamson's estimates of "FEERs" for a large number of countries represents a bold and imaginative exercise. The approach has considerable appeal, and by and large the estimates represent thoughtful and careful work. For the country with which I am most familiar, Canada, I felt quite comfortable with the judgments he made in developing targets for the capital account, but I was struck with how much judgment was called for, and how wide the range of elasticity estimates available was with which to go from a capital account target to a FEER estimate. While the estimate he came up with seemed sensible, I can only imagine what harm could be done by a room full of creative bureaucrats and politicians using this approach to rationalize policies motivated by considerations less pure than Williamson's.

NOTES

1. Williamson identifies PPP with LOOP in some of his writings. The distinction between them, and the conditions under which PPP can be violated while LOOP is maintained, are discussed in detail in Bruce and Purvis (1985).

2. That is, nominal shocks always give rise to real exchange rate overshooting, but real shocks can cause either over- or under-shooting. Further, the "long-run" real effects can be reversed in the "very long run" once the cumulative stock effects of the deficits are taken into account. See, for example, Claassen and Krauss (1986).

3. For example, the recent performance of the U.S. dollar is often cited as an example where fundamentals fail to provide an adequate explanation, and thus "bubbles" must be resorted to. But, as noted in the earlier footnote, a reasonable model of parameter values suggests that a fiscal deficit will first lead to a real appreciation of the home currency as demand is transferred toward the home good, but will later lead to a real depreciation as the transfer of wealth abroad leads to a shift of demand toward the foreign good. Superficially, this story fits the U.S. case. Adding expectations complicates the dynamics, as rational agents bring forward in time expected future exchange rate changes. Adding consideration that the current projected fiscal stance is not in some sense sustainable makes hypothesis testing even more difficult.

4. That is, somewhat surprisingly, the optimal response to the widely disparaged U.S. monetary/fiscal mix may well have been to imitate it.

An important related point, developed in detail in Asikoglu (1986), is that the real structures of economies influence the incentives created by their policy choices. If JEurope can be characterized as "real wage rigid," then JEuropean monetary policy is neutral both in terms of its "domestic" effects and in terms of the incentives it creates for U.S. policies. However, JEuropean fiscal expansion remains substitutable with U.S. fiscal expansion in terms of U.S. aggregate demand.

5. Intra-European cooperation is analyzed in detail by Asikoglu (1986).

4

The Role of the SDRs in the International Monetary System

Jürgen Schröder

The special drawing right (SDR) is an international reserve asset created by the International Monetary Fund (IMF) in order to supplement existing reserves. Although the aim was to make the SDR the principal international reserve asset, at present—seventeen years after the first SDR allocation—there are only about 20 billion SDRs, less than 5 percent of all non-gold international reserves. Newly created SDRs are allocated to the members in proportion to their quotas in the Fund. Figures 4.1 and 4.2 show that the distribution of SDR holdings is quiet uneven and that this unevenness has increased in recent years. The SDR holdings as a percentage of non-gold reserves, as well as relative to cumulative SDR allocations, are much larger for industrial countries than for capital-importing developing countries and countries with debt-servicing problems. This means that, on average, the latter two groups are net users of SDRs, that is, they take SDR-related credit, whereas the former group is the net holder of SDRs, that is, they give SDR-related credit.

Against the background of this disequilibrium in the market for official SDRs, this chapter will investigate whether the SDRs should, in future, play a more important role and, if so, in which respect the characteristics of the SDRs have to be changed to ensure that they are more evenly distributed. This is a necessary condition for getting the required majority of votes in favour of an increase in SDR allocation. To answer these questions it is necessary to recall the arguments that were put forward in the 1960s in favor of creating SDRs. Further, it is necessary to discuss the changes in the international monetary system in the 1970s and 1980s and what these changes implied for the role of SDRs in the international monetary system.[1]

Figure 4.1
SDR Holdings as a Percentage of Non-Gold Reserves for Selected Country Groups

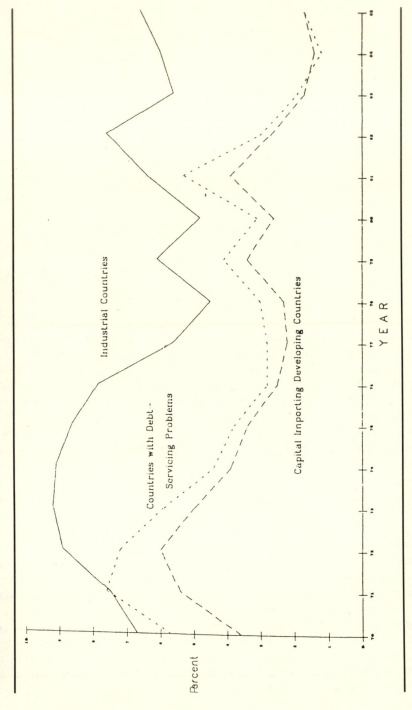

Source: International Monetary Fund, *International Financial Statistics.*

Figure 4.2
SDR Holdings as a Percentage of Cumulative SDR Allocations for Selected Country Groups

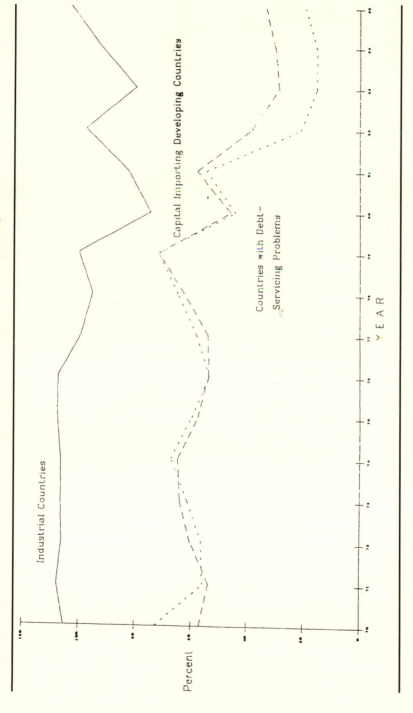

Source: International Monetary Fund, *International Financial Statistics*.

A CRITICAL REVIEW OF THE ORIGINAL ARGUMENTS
FOR CREATING SDRS

There were three reasons that led to the creation of the SDRs. All three were related to the U.S. dollar, the main international reserve asset, and they are therefore all connected with one another.

The following two arguments became well known under the name 'Triffin Dilemma' because Triffin was the first to consider these problems.[2] First, it was believed that without a new international reserve asset, a shortage in international reserves would emerge. This was so because, to provide the rest of the world with the necessary international liquidity, the United States would have to produce a continuously growing balance of payments deficit but would not be able to do this without endangering the stability of the international monetary system.

The second argument, which is very closely related to the first, dealt with the U.S. commitment to convert officially held U.S. dollars into gold at a fixed price if foreign central banks wanted this. It was argued that the creation of SDRs would reduce the use of the U.S. dollar as an international reserve and thereby increase the confidence in the gold convertibility of the officially held dollar reserves, which would add to the stability of the Bretton Woods System.

A third argument dealt with the asymmetries inherent in the gold-dollar reserve system. It was said that the United States as a reserve currency country had an advantage compared to non-reserve-currency countries, because it could easily finance its balance of payments deficits by issuing claims denominated in its own currency. Moreover, because it had been observed empirically that in growing economies there was a tendency for central banks to try and hold constant the ratio between imports of goods per period and the stock of international reserves, the United States could enjoy in each period an absorption in excess of domestic production to the amount of the increase in the dollar reserves of the central banks of all non-reserve-currency countries. The introduction of an international reserve asset would reduce this asymmetry and thereby reduce the advantage accruing to a reserve currency country. The discussion went even further in this respect. It was argued that the substitution of the dollar by the SDR would not only remove this undue advantage but would also reverse the asymmetry in favor of developing countries. By allocating the SDRs to the developing countries, this system could provide a useful link between foreign aid and the creation of international liquidity.[3]

These arguments for SDR allocations are implicitly based on assumptions that are questionable. The danger of a shortage in international liquidity rests on the assumption that central banks want to keep a certain ratio between international reserves and imports. The main purpose for holding international reserves is to use them in the future for financing a balance of payments deficit. The alternative to financing is to adjust the economy, usually via depreciation, so as to get rid of the external disequilibrium.[4] The main argument for financing the deficit instead of adjusting the economy is that the adjustment costs are usually very high and should be spread over time via a temporary financing of the deficit.[5] The adjustment costs consist of a decrease in absorption relative to production in order to free resources so that export- and import-competing products can be produced.[6] The larger the foreign exchange reserves and the less costly it is to acquire and to use them, the larger the temptation to postpone the necessary adjustment. However, a postponement of the adjustment usually increases the adjustment costs. This can lead to instability in the whole economic system because eventually the adjustment has to take place. From this point of view the introduction of SDRs adds to economic instability because, unlike earned reserves, their allocation costs nothing, and unlike borrowed reserves they cost less to use. Therefore, the more SDRs are allocated, the greater the temptation for balance of payments deficit countries to postpone necessary adjustments.

The argument that a reserve currency country has the advantage of receiving international seigniorage is only one side of the coin. The price for this privilege is that a reserve-currency country carries a much larger responsibility for world economic stability than a non-reserve-currency country. To avoid world inflation and to keep its currency attractive as an international reserve medium, the reserve-currency country has to carry out a policy that ensures stability at home and gives the rest of the world just the desired amount of international liquidity. The Bretton Woods system failed because the United States did not meet this responsibility.

On the other hand non-reserve-currency countries also have advantages when a national currency instead of the SDRs serve as international reserves. Earned international reserves can be invested in the capital market of the reserve-currency country. The received interest income offsets the real transfer due to the seigniorage.

THE CHANGE IN WORLD MONETARY CONDITIONS IN THE 1970S AND 1980S AND THE ROLE OF THE SDRS

Basically there were four major changes in the international monetary system after the SDRs were introduced. All four changes made an international reserve asset like the SDR less necessary than was believed in the 1960s.

First, in 1971, two years after the decision was made to allocate the first SDRs, the United States suspended its commitment to convert officially held dollar reserves into gold. Therefore the argument that an international reserve asset had to be created in order to reduce the burden on the U.S. dollar and thereby to strengthen the gold convertibility of officially held dollars became obsolete. The suspension of gold convertibility had, of course, an impact on the characteristics of the SDRs. The SDRs were no longer based on a given weight of gold but, instead, on a basket of national currencies. Further, the interest rate on the SDRs was continuously raised from 1.5 percent, which was close to the zero interest rate of gold, to rates closer to yields that were earned on other typical foreign exchange reserves.

Second, with the final breakdown of the Bretton Woods system in 1973 most major industrial countries moved to flexible exchange rates. Although this important step by no means implied clean floating, external disequilibria were now removed by exchange rate changes to a much larger extent and much faster than had been the case during the fixed exchange rate period prior to 1973. Therefore, from this point of view, the need for foreign exchange reserves and therefore for an international reserve asset like the SDR was reduced.

Third, the liberalization in international capital movements that was made possible mainly by the transition to flexible exchange rates, the deregulations in national and international financial markets, and the enormous technical progress in these markets made them much wider and deeper. These developments implied that the supply of international reserves for each country became almost unlimited, so that any demand by central banks can now easily be satisfied. Therefore, as long as the international capital markets continue to function, there is no danger of a shortage in international liquidity and therefore no convincing economic reason for creating SDRs. Of course, the less creditworthy a country is the tighter the conditions it faces in borrowing in these private markets, especially in terms of interest rates. However, this is an economic law in national and international credit markets that each household and each firm has to face. There is no reason for an exception to be made when the borrowers are governments or central banks. The argument that SDR credits are necessary for the neediest countries (i.e., for those who have serious balance of payments problems and have therefore either no access to the international capital market or only on conditions that are much worse than using their allocated SDRs) is not convincing when a loose monetary and/or fiscal policy caused the external disequilibrium. The less expensive it is to finance the deficit, the fewer economic incentives there are for countries to bring their houses into good economic order.

Fourth, the movement to a multi-currency reserve system changed the asymmetry in the international monetary system. As other national currencies like the DM and the yen serve more and more as international reserves, Germany and Japan also have the advantage of the international seigniorage. However, like the United States, they also carry more responsibility for the functioning of the international monetary system than non-reserve-currency countries. The movement toward a multi-reserve-currency system increases the potential supply of international reserves and thereby diminishes the asymmetry between the United States and the rest of the world. For both of these reasons there is less need for SDRs than was believed in the 1960s.

THE CURRENT SITUATION IN THE MARKET FOR OFFICIAL SDRS

At present the market for official SDRs is characterized by a severe disequilibrium. The demand for SDR credit, that is, the wish to use their allocated SDRs, by balance of payments deficit countries is much larger than the supply of

SDR credit, that is, the wish to hold more SDRs than their SDR allocation, by balance of payments surplus countries. The reason for this disequilibrium can easily be explained. For balance of payments deficit countries, it is cheaper to use SDRs than to borrow on the international capital market in order to finance the deficit. The interest rate they have to pay when using their allocated SDRs is a combined market interest rate, which is a weighted average of interest rates on selected *short-run* instruments in the money markets of the five countries whose currencies are in the SDR basket. These short-term money market instruments are as follows: a market yield on three-month U.S. Treasury bills, a three-month interbank deposit rate in West Germany, a three-month interbank money rate against private papers in France, a rate on two-month (private) bills in Japan, and a market yield on three-month British Treasury bills.[7] The weight of these individual interest rates in the SDR interest rate corresponds to the weights of the five currencies in the SDR basket. Due to their low creditworthiness, balance of payments deficit countries would not be able to get short-term credit in the five money markets at such favorable conditions. Further, until 1981 there was a reconstitution requirement: in a five-year period each country had to hold on average 30 percent of its allocated SDRs. In 1981 this reconstruction requirement was dropped. Since then balance of payments deficit countries can use their allocated SDRs for an unlimited time to finance external imbalances. This means these countries receive long-term loans and pay short-term interest rates when using their allocated SDRs.[8] Not only do balance of payments deficit countries receive a substantial subsidy when using their SDRs, they are also extremely liquid assets for these countries. If they do not find a balance of payments surplus country that will buy their SDRs voluntarily, then they inform the IMF of their balance of payments need. The Fund then designates a particular balance of payments surplus country or a country that has sufficient foreign exchange reserves as buyer of the SDRs from the deficit country.

On the other hand, for balance of payments surplus countries the holding of SDRs beyond their allocated SDRs is less attractive than holding other reserve assets. Because of their limited use the surplus countries are stuck with the official SDRs, once they are designated to buy them, until they themselves run into balance of payments problems. This means that those countries who conduct a sound economic and monetary policy, and therefore have to buy and hold the SDRs, are forced to invest in long-term illiquid foreign exchange assets for which they receive interest equal to that of short-term liquid assets. Economic reality tells us, however, that the interest rate differential is usually the other way around. The interest rates on assets that are relatively less liquid and that have a relatively long maturity are higher than the interest rates on short-term liquid assets, so as to induce investors to hold the former. Often the argument is put forward that the exchange value of the official SDR is generally much more stable than that of any single currency in the SDR basket. This is correct. However, central banks can obtain the same stability of their foreign exchange reserves portfolio if they tailor their private SDR basket according to their own needs. They have the advantage of being much more flexible if they mix their own private SDR cocktail rather than hold official SDRs.

The IMF rules basically provide two ways in which potential surplus countries can protect themselves from holding too many unwanted SDRs. First, there is the acceptance limit, which says that the Fund cannot force a country to accept SDRs from other members or from the Fund itself if its SDR holdings are already 300 percent of its SDR allocation. This rule gives each potential balance of payments surplus country protection within the given amount of total SDR allocations. However, when new SDRs are allocated, the absolute amount of the acceptance limit increases in proportion to new allocations for each country. Since a majority of 85 percent of the Fund's voting power is necessary for a new allocation of SDRs, potential surplus countries have an indirect second way of protecting themselves against being designated to hold too many unwanted SDRs. Given the uneven distribution of the existing 20.4 billion SDRs, it is not surprising that potential balance of payment surplus countries and reserve currency countries use this second possibility to avoid being forced to pile up too many unwanted SDRs.

FUTURE ROLE OF THE SDRS

The future role and possible usefulness of the SDRs cannot be judged without saying something about the future international monetary order in general. There is one long-term and two short-term scenarios. For those who are convinced that a clean flexible exchange rate system is the best way to solve international monetary and economic problems, there is no future for the SDRs. In such a system, the exchange rate takes care of the external equilibrium. Any intervention in the foreign exchange market by central banks must be rejected. Therefore, foreign exchange reserves and thus SDRs are not necessary. It is generally agreed that a necessary condition for a clean float to work is a sound economic and monetary policy in the countries concerned. Otherwise huge volatilities in the real exchange rates, with all their negative consequences, might occur.

For those who doubt that a clean float will be the best solution for a stable international monetary system, a sound monetary and economic policy of the countries concerned is a necessary but not a sufficient condition for stable real exchange rates. They argue that the case for flexible exchange rates was put forward in the 1950s and 1960s, when the exchange rate or the balance of payments situation was mainly determined by current account transactions, because there were restrictions on international capital movements and generally underdeveloped international capital markets. As pointed out above this changed completely in the 1970s and 1980s, so that international capital transactions play a dominant role in determining the real exchange rate and the balance of payments situation, at least in the short and medium run. The liberalization and the huge technical progress in financial markets led not only to a substantial increase in international capital mobility but also to an enormous increase in the speed at which this capital can react to practically any actual and expected economic and, especially, political "news." As goods markets react much more slowly to external disturbances than financial markets, a substantial deviation of the nominal exchange rate from purchasing power parity (i.e., a substantial volatility of the real exchange rate) can be the result. In order to avoid this volatility temporary foreign exchange market intervention could become necessary and therefore SDRs as international reserves could be useful. Even if one is in favor of intervention for this reason, this is no argument for carrying out the intervention with interest-rate-subsidized SDR credits. In an environment in which all countries keep their economic houses in order, each central bank should be able to borrow the necessary foreign exchange in the well-developed international capital markets.

The last, long-term scenario may seem far fetched; however, it is worth discussing. It can be argued that in future, national currencies will become less and less suitable as international reserves, especially as international transactions money, and, for the same reason, national governments and central banks will become less and less able to conduct economic and monetary policies oriented toward internal goals. If this is correct, then the SDR could have an important role in a future international monetary system. The arguments for this possible long-term scenario are as follows. It is well known that a national money cannot become an international reserve medium by law. There has to be a general consensus that a certain national currency has the qualities necessary to fill this role. Most important, the currency has to be stable compared with other currencies and must be expected to remain stable in the future. A necessary and important condition for stability is a stable monetary and economic policy in a stable political environment. This internal stability is necessary but not sufficient. A country whose currency fulfills the role of an international reserve medium also has to be immune to world market instabilities. This is more the case the less open the economy is (i.e., the smaller the export and import shares of GNP are). On the other hand, the foreign economic relations and the non-tradable sector must be large enough to satisfy other countries' wish to use the money and capital market of this country without causing negative impacts on key economic variables. To fulfill these two economic conditions simultaneously, the country must have a large share of world GNP and, at the same time, small export and import shares of domestic GNP. Although such a country is not very open, exports and imports are relatively large compared with world exports and imports, because it is a large country. The United States was and is the country that fulfills these conditions best, although this advantage is diminishing. In 1960 U.S. GNP was 40 percent of world GNP, and exports as well as imports over GNP were roughly 4 percent. About 20 years later, its share of world GNP was down to about 30 percent, whereas export and import shares had increased to about 10 percent. This means that the objective conditions for the U.S. dollar to be used as international money have deteriorated because the United States and the dollar have become more vulnerable to economic disturbances caused in world markets.

It might be that these world economic developments have been one reason (among others—for instance, the loose monetary and economic policy in the Johnson and Carter eras) that the Deutschmark and the yen were partly substituted for the U.S. dollar as international reserve currency. However, from the point of view of these objective conditions, both these currencies are much less suitable than the dollar as international reserve currencies. Although monetary and economic policies have been relatively stable in these countries, the GNP of each of them in 1980 was roughly only 10 percent of world GNP. The exports and imports over GNP were roughly 30 percent in Germany and 15 percent in Japan. In the period of 1960 to 1980, these ratios increased by almost 100 percent in Germany and by 50 percent in Japan. This means that both countries, especially Germany, are, compared with the United States, not only relatively small but also extremely open. Therefore, these countries and their currencies are much more vulnerable to disturbances in the world market than the United States and the dollar. That these relatively vulnerable national currencies have taken over the functions of international money could imply a substantial potential increase in the instability of the international monetary system.

Furthermore, in order to get the advantages of a further increase in international division of labor and of further positive growth rates of real GNP, especially in less developed countries, not only will export and import over GNP in all countries permanently increase, but the relative economic size of the large industrial countries will also permanently diminish. This implies that with a continuous international integration process in the goods markets as well as in the capital markets, not only will single countries and their currencies become more and more vulnerable to disturbances on the world market, but they will also be less and less able to conduct successful independent monetary and economic policies without endangering free international goods and capital movements.

Assuming such a long-term international economic development, there are good economic arguments for a future world central bank and one world money.[9] Keeping in mind that this scenario is far fetched one could argue that here could possibly lie the future comparative advantage of the SDR as an international reserve asset, backed by the international community. If this is correct, then the monetary characteristics and the usability of the SDRs should gradually be enhanced, and an increase in SDR allocation should be favored in order to make a larger use of them possible.[10]

INCENTIVES VERSUS REGULATIONS IN THE MARKET FOR OFFICIAL SDRS

If SDR allocation is to be increased, a prerequisite is equilibrium in this market—that is, the difference between the wish to use SDRs for financing balance of payments deficits and the wish of the surplus countries to hold SDRs as foreign exchange reserves must be reduced. This gap could be removed by introducing regulations or by using market incentives. From the point of view of efficiency, incentives are superior to regulations. Recently a proposal was made to reintroduce a reconstitution requirement in order to get the necessary majority of voting power for a new SDR allocation.[11] One argument in favor of this regulatory measure is that in private credit markets it is impossible to get a credit at fixed conditions without time limits. Therefore, to make SDR credit more comparable to credit in private international capital markets, reintroduction of reconstitution could be recommended. However, this measure does not solve but only disguises the disequilibrium in the market for official SDRs. If this measure is combined with an increase in SDR allocation, potential balance of payments surplus countries could be forced to hold even more unwanted SDRs than before. This would hardly be a solution to the current problem.

What has to be done is to increase the incentives for holding SDRs and to decrease the incentives for using them. With given risk and liquidity of the SDRs, this two-sided effect can best be obtained by increasing the interest rate on SDR allocations and SDR holdings. This measure would bring the costs of the SDR credit more in line with the costs of reserves borrowed in private international financial markets. The result would be that potential deficit countries would be less eager to use their allocated SDRs for financing balance of payments deficits and therefore would become more conscious of the need for external equilibrium. On the other hand, an increase in the SDR interest rate would make the SDRs more attractive as international reserve assets, so that balance of payments surplus countries would become more willing to hold them. There is, however, the danger that too great an increase in the SDR interest rate could work in the opposite direction, that the preference for holding SDRs beyond the allocated amount would become greater than the preference for using them to finance balance of payments deficits. This would, contrary to the intention, reduce the use of the official SDRs. However, if the SDR interest rate is not too far above the interest rate that would prevail if there were a free market for official SDRs, then there will always be deficit countries who prefer to use SDR credit. The ideal interest rate would be the free market interest rate for official SDRs. However, as long as there is no free market, an interest rate a little above the free market interest rate is better than one below it, for getting the necessary majority to increase SDR allocations.

SUMMARY

In the first part of this chapter the arguments, put forward in the 1960s in favor of SDR allocations, were critically reviewed. Next, the important changes in the international monetary system in the 1970s and 1980s were described and it has been shown that these made the allocation of SDRs less necessary than originally expected. After having discussed the existing disequilibrium in the market for official SDRs, the latter's chances for becoming the main international reserve asset in the future were examined. It has been argued that, in the short run, there is no need for an international reserve asset like the SDRs, regardless of whether there are flexible or some kind of fixed exchange rates. However, it is possible that in the long run, when all the countries are very open economically, an asset backed by the international community could be useful. Although this is rather speculative, it is the only argument for an increase in SDR allocation. However, this increase can, and should in reality, only be made if the existing disequilibrium in the market for official SDRs is removed. An increase in the interest rate on official SDRs seems to be the proper policy for reaching equilibrium in the SDR market, because it reduces the incentive for balance of payments deficit countries to finance their deficits with SDR credit and it increases the incentives for balance of payments surplus countries to hold SDRs as international reserves.

NOTES

1. For this see also IMF (1987).

2. Triffin (1963).

3. For a most recent proposal in this direction see Sengupta (1986).

4. An extensive discussion of "Adjusting versus Financing" is found in Seidel (1984).

5. For an extensive development of this point see especially Kenen (1986).

6. A decrease in real investment is generally also possible. However, that would worsen the country's long-run economic and balance of payments situation.

7. See IMF (1985: 45).

8. This is probably the explanation for the unevenness in 1981 of SDR holdings, as a percentage of cumulated SDRs increased substantially between industrial countries on the one hand and capital-importing developing countries as well as countries with debt-servicing problems on the other, as can be seen from Figure 4.1.

9. For the functioning of and the problems arising from a world central bank, see especially Fischer (1983).

10. For an increase in the usability of the SDRs see Kenen (1983).

11. See Williamson (1984: 38–41).

COMMENT BY

Pascal Salin

Jürgen Schröder presents a very comprehensive and subtle chapter on the roles of SDRs, as they have been considered at their creation, as they evolved, and as they could be in the future. We broadly agree with Jürgen Schröder on many issues, but we may be more sceptical on the usefulness and the future of SDRs. In the present comment, we do not intend to guess at the future of SDRs, but to analyze further their possible roles. Our discussion would apply to ECUs as well.

DEFINITION OF SDRS

SDRs are claims on the IMF. As any modern currency they are claims on a specific organization and their liquidity depends on their specific characteristics and on the capacity of the issuer to guarantee their convertibility into other currencies or some commodity.

Let us make a comparison between SDRs and, for instance, dollars issued by different banks. A claim on the Chase Manhattan Bank, denominated in dollars, is considered as perfectly substitutable for a claim in dollars on the Chemical Bank, because there exists a system to guarantee perfect convertibility at a fixed price between both assets (the Fed, in that case).

There was, at the beginning, perfect substitutability between one SDR and one dollar. SDRs could have been named IMF-$ instead of SDRs, as well as dollars held at the Chase Manhattan Bank could be named Chase dollars. In the case of SDRs, however, the convertibility guarantee was not given by the Fed, but by the IMF itself. In that sense, the IMF was—and still is—very similar to any Euro-dollar bank that creates its own system of guarantee. The only differences are the following:

- The IMF is a public international bank and not a private bank (which means that it cannot fail, but also that it bears less responsibility than a private bank).
- There are explicit rules for issuing SDRs, whereas Euro-dollars are issued according to discretionary rules. However, the periodical decisions to "allocate" SDRs proceed from a discretionary process.

When it was decided that SDRs would be defined in terms of a basket of currencies, their nature was not really modified. The new definition implied differences in the average change in purchasing power and in the degree of risk, but the change was not the same for SDR holders who were generally using dollars and for others. Differences in return and risk between two possible definitions of SDRs (dollars or a basket of currencies) can be dealt with by different rates of return on SDR balances.

REASONS FOR CREATING SDRs

There were and are three usual and different justifications for creating SDRs, which are recalled by Jürgen Schröder:

1. The first justification rests on the existence of an assumed *general* shortage of international liquidity. (As Jürgen Schröder reminds us, SDRs were intended to "supplement" existing reserves.) This is a fallacy, since people desire real balances and not nominal balances. Therefore, the best way to create (real) cash balances—those that are really needed—is to destroy (nominal) cash balances. It means that there is no such thing as an "unsatisfied need for liquidity" and, even more, that there is never any reason to create money.

The widespread belief in the necessity to meet the supposed general need for (international) liquidity is also based on another misconception, namely the usual misunderstanding of the working of a fixed rate system (or any system of predetermined exchange rate, as a system of dirty floating). In such cases, national money creation has to be adjusted on reserves and not the reverse. The idea that there could be a "need for international liquidity" is completely wrong. It just happens too often that national money creation in a great number of countries is too rapid in comparison with existing "international reserves," but it does not mean that international reserves are too low.

Schröder reminds us of the initial arguments in favor of SDRs, mainly defended by Robert Triffin, namely the risk of a "shortage of international liquidity" or the unability of the United States to maintain the convertibility of dollars into gold. These arguments, in our opinion, stem from a fundamental misunderstanding of economic theory and monetary principles.

Schröder is rightly critical of this argument, according to which there could be a general shortage of liquidity. However, he ought to point out more strongly that, in a system of fixed rates, the role of reserves is not "to keep a certain ratio between international reserves and imports," nor "to finance a balance of payments deficit." In fact, reserves ought to be *the* instrument for monetary regulation in a system of fixed rates where, by definition, monetary policy has to be adjusted to the exchange rate target. The decrease of reserves thus plays the role of a signal, if ever monetary creation has been too expansionary. In that sense it is not quite correct to say that "the alternative to financing is to adjust the economy, usually via depreciation." For one thing, there is no need for "financing," and for the other, the solution to a "disequilibrium" problem is not depreciation but monetary restraint.

Schröder argues that financing the deficit might be justified because the adjustment costs might be too high, so that it could be valuable to slow the process of adjustment. In any event, financing implies a complete reversal of the working of the system; instead of adjusting monetary creation to the level of reserves, central banks adjust the amount of reserves to the quantity of money (with the possible consequence of a balance of payments deficit). Thus, there is a risk that instead of smoothing the process of adjustment, financing leads to a perpetuation of disequilibria. In fact, Schröder is perfectly aware of this risk, as he writes that "the introduction of SDRs adds to economic instability because . . . their allocation costs nothing . . . and the more SDRs are allocated, the greater the temptation for balance of payments deficit countries to postpone necessary adjustments."

2. It is sometimes considered that, rather than a general need for international liquidity, there is a specific need of some countries, either because they have "balance of payments problems" or because they have "development needs" (which would justify the "link" proposal). Let us start with the first aspect. Such a justification is fallacious since

- Balance of payments problems never exist (only inconsistent policies exist).
- There is no reason to give credit at preferential conditions to the authorities of countries where money management is the worst.

In fact, the authorities of these countries issue too much money and they say they have not enough international liquidity (they pretend, for instance, to guarantee perfect substitutability between their currency and the dollar, but they do not adjust their monetary policy to this target).

As regards the link proposal, I certainly agree with Schröder that it implies trying to reach two goals with only one tool. More precisely, this argument rests on a confusion between money creation and credit. Even if money is usually created against credits in the modern world, the goals of monetary policy have nothing in common with the transfers made through credit.

3. A last reason for creating SDRs was to deprive the United States of some of its "power" to create dollars or, more generally, to avoid the asymmetrical character of the international monetary system. However, when a producer is efficient in producing any good, one cannot say that he has too much power and that other producers might be

entitled to do counterfeiting. The only acceptable solution is to outcompete him by proposing a better good.

As Schröder reminds us, one argument for creating SDRs was to suppress the asymmetries of the gold-exchange standard. However, this asymmetry was desired in the sense that there was a private demand for dollars, and central banks—which were free to decide otherwise—had decided to intervene in dollars. If may be that the problem would appear quite different if, instead of speaking of dollar creation by the United States, one would speak of dollar creation by U.S. banks. The problem is not one of an uneven monetary power or uneven distribution of the seigniorage gain, but one of specialization. It just happened that U.S. banks were specialized in the production of the relatively most demanded currency, the dollar.

There is no more reason to redistribute the profit from this specific activity than there would be to redistribute the profit from any other activity, under the pretext that any specific country is particularly specialized in this activity!

THE REAL ROLE OF SDRs

Banks, in the modern world, are institutions that play two main roles: they issue money and they are financial intermediaries. In which respect does the IMF, as issuer of SDRs, play one or the other role?

The IMF as a Source of Money Creation

It is difficult to assess whether the world quantity of money would be lower if SDRs did not exist. SDRs are created against non-marketable claims on monetary authorities. The beneficiary of such a distribution of claims has the right to obtain national currencies against its stock of SDRs, within the framework of the specific rules concerning the management of SDRs. If, for instance, the monetary authorities of a country are allowed to exchange SDRs against dollars, is the total creation of dollars in the world increased? In principle, monetary authorities have the option of "sterilizing" such external influences, by deciding a more restrictive monetary policy to compensate for this source of money creation. Whether they use this possibility or not is an open question.

Whatever the answer is, it remains true that the first justification for SDR creation (the need for liquidity) is not valid, since, as we already stressed, there is never any reason for creating money and even less for creating official reserves. The SDR system induces the adjustment of reserves to national money creation, instead of the reverse. This role is negative since it implies a behavior of monetary authorities just opposite to the logic of money regulation in a fixed rate system.

Moreover, this system can be considered "unfair," since it means transferring resources, via the inflation tax, from "virtuous countries" to "vicious countries," that is, those with bad monetary management. In that respect the proposal made by Schröder— the payment of a "market interest rate" on SDRs—makes the system fairer, at least if the interest is paid by the country that uses (spends) its SDRs.

Schröder rightly points out that the working of the international monetary system has changed since the time when SDRs were first created, since the end of the convertibility of dollars into gold and the shift to more flexible exchange rates made reserves less useful. As the role of SDRs as international reserve assets in a fixed rate system was already debatable, it is even more so in the new environment. More and more, SDRs are credits, attributed to countries under the pretext of balance of payments problems.

The IMF as a Financial Intermediary

The countries that *use* their SDRs (i.e., which exchange them against national currencies) get more resources, which means that there is a real transfer from the countries that keep their SDRs to those that spend them.

It is usually said that these transfers are intended to finance "balance of payments deficits." We have already said why such a justification cannot be accepted. In fact, national monetary authorities that have been unable to enforce a monetary policy compatible with their exchange rate target (fixed rate or dirty floating) are looking for a way to continue their policy of excessive spending or, at least, to smooth the return to more coherent policies.

One cannot see any justification for giving credit at preferential conditions to the authorities that have been the worst managers in the world, at the expense of other ones that have behaved better. On this point I strongly agree with Schröder. Moreover, the fact that the IMF thus participates in a safety network induces irresponsible behavior from the authorities that borrow or from the banks that lend.

In fact, SDRs are not a currency, but a means to transfer credit to some countries; those credits have two characteristics: a low interest rate and a denomination in terms of a basket of currencies instead of a national currency. Therefore, SDRs do not contribute to a clarification of the process by which money is created in the world, nor to an improvement of adjustment processes.

Schröder underlines that there has been a transfer of SDRs from the group of capital-importing countries and countries with debt problems to the group of industrial countries, and he cares about the solutions for a "more even distribution." In fact, there are two different phases to be distinguished: in a first round, SDRs are allocated (i.e., distributed), and this very process of money creation is questionable since, normally, money has to be bought against present commodities or future commodities (financial assets). The free distribution of money balances implies either a non-optimal quantity of money or a mere replacement of some reserve assets by SDRs (i.e., a different distribution of seigniorage). In a second round, SDRs are transferred from country to country through a process of (more or less unvoluntary) "redistribution."

In a completely voluntary system, where monetary authorities would freely decide how many reserve assets of any sort to buy, the very notion of an "uneven" distribution would be meaningless. In the actual system of allocation and designation, there is no valid criterion to evaluate what is an "even" distribution.

THE FUTURE OF SDRs

The proposals made by Schröder—namely to increase the incentives for holding SDRs and to decrease the incentives for using them, for instance by reintroducing a reconstitution requirement or by paying a market interest rate—would be possible solutions to present problems. However, another question would arise: What would be the role of the IMF in such a case? In fact, any bank could play the same role, namely to extend credit to a country that is supposed to have "balance of payments problems." Therefore, there is no specific reason to have one more bank (the IMF) to play this role, and, particularly, a public bank, that is, a bank that may behave in a less responsible way than a private bank. Schröder believes that the "ideal interest rate would be the free market interest rate for official SDRs." However there is no reason for a political body (as is the Board of the IMF) to agree on such a "rational" proposal, since the countries represented on the Board have to negotiate an interest rate on non-personal forced savings and transferred via inflation tax.

The fact, stressed by Schröder, according to which "the market for official SDRs is characterized by a severe disequilibrium," means that SDRs are not particularly desired assets and that central banks, if let free to decide, would not be particularly willing to hold SDRs under present conditions. However, as SDRs are not perfectly transferable between monetary authorities, the conditionality imposed by the IMF to accept any transfer of SDRs is a lever to get policy reforms, which a private bank might obtain less easily.

In that sense it can be said—at least if the policy prescriptions of the IMF are efficient, which is debatable—that the IMF plays a third role, beyond those of a financial intermediary and a money issuer, that of an expert in macroeconomic policy. The less expensive this expertise is, the more it is demanded. In that sense, the IMF may have more chances to play a role as an expert if its credit conditions are attractive and the interest rate paid on the use of SDRs is low.

I certainly do not believe that this expertise in favor of badly managed countries could be considered as a sort of "public good" that could justify preferential credit conditions and a low interest rate on SDRs. It may rather be considered as a specific sort of foreign aid, which consists in bringing consulting services to a country that is supposed to be lacking them (although the bad management of the country may be due to the working of the "political market" more than to the lack of expertise, which, in any event, could be bought anywhere in the world at a relatively low cost). If this view is valid, and if one desires to give foreign aid in priority to badly managed countries rather than to other ones—even if some of the latter are poorer—it would be better not to charge a market interest rate on SDRs and IMF credit or to charge a low rate. If not, there is no specific justification either for SDRs or, even more, for the IMF.

Schröder also suggests that SDRs could be used as a means of intervention in a situation where the mobility of capital could cause a great instability of real exchange rates. However, it is difficult for monetary authorities to evaluate what ought to be equilibrium real exchange rates at any time. Moreover, SDRs do not constitute an independent currency. They are nothing but a basket of national currencies, and it is even more difficult to assess the effects on real exchange rates of a multiple-currency intervention.

Finally, I strongly disagree with the proposal made by Jürgen Schröder according to which SDRs, in spite of their inadequate characteristics in the short run, could have a very important role to play in the long run as a world money issued by a world central bank. It is difficult to understand by which miracle monetary management, which seems to be so difficult in modern times in any national framework, could lead to world stability if dependent on a world central bank subject to diverging political pressures. There is, in fact, no option other than giving individuals the greatest number of options between existing currencies or currencies to be created to meet the needs of the market.

CONCLUSION

As bureaucracies tend to survive, so will SDRs. But there is no clear justification for their existence. In fact, reserve assets have only one role, which is to be a tool for regulation. We do not believe that monetary regulation by a world bank via a fiat money is either possible or desirable. For the time being, SDRs do not play a role for monetary regulation. They are nothing but a constraint on currency diversification of their reserves by central banks and they are used for financing badly managed countries.

However, the IMF benefits from a monopoly position by issuing this so-called currency, the holding of which is imposed to some central banks. Economic theory has underlined for a long time that monopolies are bad, but it has not sufficiently stressed that only public monopolies can survive without any effort. SDRs will survive, whatever their role (and the same is true for ECUs, the use of which benefits from some specific privileges).

As economists we know the role of the market and we believe sometimes that we play our role as experts whenever we propose to introduce a market symbol in a non-market system (for instance, to pay a market interest rate on SDRs). However, is it not better to make a plea for the disappearance of non-market systems?

5

Exchange Rate Regimes for LDCs

Bela Balassa

The purpose of this chapter is to evaluate the usefulness of alternative exchange rate systems for developing countries. The discussion will proceed on the assumption that the present international monetary system (or non-system) will continue to operate, so that developing countries will have to be prepared for substantial fluctuations in exchange rates—in nominal as well as in real terms—between the currencies of the major developed countries. Subsequently, the implications of removing this assumption will be briefly indicated.

Section 1 will review the proximate objectives the exchange rate regimes of developing countries may appropriately serve. These objectives include eschewing foreign exchange restrictions, maintaining realistic exchange rates, limiting uncertainty for business decision making, and reducing fluctuations in macroeconomic relationships.

Section 2 will evaluate alternative exchange rate regimes from the point of view of the stated objectives, on the assumption that the rate of inflation in the country concerned equals the trade-weighted average of inflation rates in its trading partners. Freely floating exchange rates, dual exchange rates, pegging to a particular currency, pegging to the SDR, and pegging to a trade-weighted basket will be considered in this section.

Section 3 will admit the possibility of differences in inflation rates in the country concerned and in its trading partners, on the average. It will further consider the question if the conclusions are affected in the event of the transformation of the international monetary system. The principal alternative is the target zone system, which has attracted much attention recently.

1. PROXIMATE OBJECTIVES OF EXCHANGE RATE REGIMES IN DEVELOPING COUNTRIES

Eschewing exchange restrictions may be considered to be one of the objectives of exchange rate regimes in developing countries.[1] Such restrictions introduce arbitrariness in the process of decision making and involve a cost to the national economy. This cost relates to the misallocation of resources as well as to rent seeking.

The efficient allocation of resources requires the free availability of foreign exchange to all users, with the market allocating foreign exchange among competing claimants. Under exchange restrictions, rationing by an administrative authority replaces rationing by the market. Rather than competition on the market, we have competition for the favors of the decision makers, so as to obtain the rents inherent in the scarcity of foreign exchange.

Non-market allocation of foreign exchange is inefficient, since the information dispersed among agents in the market is not available to an administrative authority, even if it wished to reproduce market processes. In practice, the authority will rely on rules of thumb and will respond to pressures on the part of users, when the outcome is influenced by the relative bargaining power of the participants, generally favoring large over small firms. Also, the process will often involve bribery so as to partake in the rent accruing to the recipients of foreign exchange.

Rent seeking, too, involves economic costs. There is a cost involved in spending time and energy on obtaining foreign exchange from the administrative authority, rather than producing foreign exchange through exports and import substitution. Furthermore, to the extent that foreign exchange allocation is based on existing capacity (trading outlets in the case of consumer goods and production capacity in the case of inputs), competition for rents will involve the duplications of capacity (Krueger 1974).

Exchange rate regimes should also aim at *maintaining realistic exchange rates,* defined as rates that ensure the attainment of balance of payments targets. An appropriate overall target for developing countries is the continuing inflow of foreign capital.

This target is predicated on the assumption that the marginal productivity of capital is higher in developing countries than the rate of interest they pay on foreign loans. One reason for this is that developing countries have a lower ratio of capital to labor than developed countries; another is that they can apply existing technology that has originated in the developed countries.

The amount that may be borrowed is limited, however, by considerations of creditworthiness, which call for avoiding increases in the ratio of foreign debt to exports beyond certain limits. Once these limits are exceeded, there will be a need to reduce the debt or, at least, to reduce its ratio to exports. This, in turn, will necessitate financing interest payments, in full or in part, from export proceeds. Realism in exchange rates will then require an allowance for the foreign exchange needs of interest payments on the foreign debt.

Over- and undervaluation of the currency should thus be defined with respect to the concept of realistic exchange rates. At the same time, overvalued exchange rates distort the allocation of resources by discriminating against traded goods in favor of non-traded goods. They discourage exports and encourage imports, thereby giving rise to a balance of payments deficit over and above acceptable levels of foreign borrowing. As a result, pressures are generated to subsidize exports and to protect imports, which tend to create discrimination among trading activities, with attendant economic costs.

Undervalued exchange rates, too, have an economic cost. To utilize the expression introduced by Corden (1981), they involve "exchange rate protection" in discriminating against non-traded goods in favor of traded goods. As a result, a surplus is generated in the balance of payments that involves the misallocation of resources in investing in foreign financial assets, even though higher returns can be obtained in domestic investments. Furthermore, the upgrading of the country's export structure is hindered by reason of the fact that exports, in which the country is losing comparative advantage, continue to be profitable at undervalued exchange rates.

The unfavorable economic effects of overvaluation are well documented in the development literature. They have been shown to have had an adverse impact on exports and, thereby, on economic growth in a wide variety of situations, ranging from the middle-income countries in Latin America (Balassa, Bueno, Kuczynski, and Simonsen 1986) to the poor countries of sub-Saharan Africa (Balassa 1984).

There is less experience with undervalued exchange rates in developing countries. Nevertheless, such a situation has arisen recently in the four East Asian NICs (Hong Kong, Korea, Singapore, and Taiwan), which have largely followed the U.S. dollar in depreciating their currencies with respect to other trading partners in recent years. The result has been an increasing accumulation of reserves, transforming the four East Asian NICs (in particular, Korea and Taiwan) from borrowers to lenders in international financial markets, which conflicts with their well-conceived interests (Balassa and Williamson 1987).

There is further need to *limit uncertainty for business decision making*. The pursuit of this objective will require avoiding fluctuations in exchange values around what is considered a realistic level. Such fluctuations discourage exports due to the exchange rate risk. At the same time, continued fluctuations may mean that exporters expect a reversal of the situation in cases when a realistic exchange rate has been established.

In the face of exchange rate uncertainty, firms may also forego export-oriented investments and the establishment of trading facilities abroad. Furthermore, the losses suffered at the time of unfavorable exchange rates may not be fully reversible, as market positions are lost and foreign buyers may permanently shift to other suppliers.

Mexico provides an example of large fluctuations in currency values since 1982. And Venezuela may be cited as a case where exporters did not expect the continuation of favorable exchange rates, and the facts have proved them right. In December 1986 earnings derived from nontraditional exports were shifted from the free trade exchange market, where the rate was about 24 bolivars to the U.S. dollar, to the newly established official rate of 14.5 bolivars to the dollar, with only partial compensation provided through increased fiscal credit to exporters. In turn, stability in currency values had favorable effects in the East Asian NICs prior to 1985.

Finally, it is desirable to *reduce fluctuations in macroeconomic relationships*. Such fluctuations, associated with large variations in exchange rates, interfere with the conduct of economic policy in developing countries and require holdings of large foreign exchange reserves, which have a cost to the national economy.

2. ALTERNATIVE EXCHANGE RATE REGIMES FOR DEVELOPING COUNTRIES

In this section, alternative exchange rate regimes will be evaluated on the assumption that the rate of inflation in the country concerned equals the trade-weighted average of inflation rates in its trading partners. It will further be assumed that disparate changes occur in rates of inflation among individual trading partners.

Among possible alternatives, several authors had summarily dismissed *freely floating exchange rates* for developing countries by reference to the existence of limited capital markets, restrictions on capital flows, thin foreign exchange markets, and the lack of sufficient reserves to finance external shocks in these countries.[2] In fact, until recently, there were practically no freely floating exchange rates in developing countries. This has changed, however, in the last several years.

Apart from Lebanon, which has maintained a freely floating exchange rate under adverse political conditions, Uruguay was the first developing country to adopt freely floating exchange rates, in the wake of its disastrous experience in attempting to use the exchange rate as an anti-inflationary device (see section 3 below). It has been followed by Bolivia, the Dominican Republic, Gambia, Ghana, Guinea, Nigeria, the Philippines, Sierra Leone, Zaire, Zambia, among which Ghana and Nigeria also have a preferential rate for debt service payments and government transactions.

Why, then, the sudden popularity of floating exchange rates? Wickham (1985) questioned the validity of the proposition put forward in the literature that freely floating exchange rates were not suitable for developing countries. He also provided evidence from empirical studies that the choice of currency regimes does not depend on the level of economic development.

But additional factors need to be introduced to explain the change in attitudes on the part of a number of developing governments. First, in countries where the rate is greatly overvalued, it is difficult to determine the appropriate (realistic) exchange rate. Second, governments, which are reluctant to undertake devaluations, can shift responsibility to the market for the depreciation of the currency. Third, business can plan with the understanding that the exchange rate will not become overvalued again.

Freely floating exchange rates also offer advantages over *dual exchange rates,* which usually involve a lower rate for commercial, and a higher rate for financial, transactions. While dual exchange rates have generally been adopted with a view of avoiding devaluations and/or reserve losses, they have led to the depreciation of the financial exchange rate. Differences between the two rates, in turn, involve discrimination among foreign exchange transactions, effectively taxing exports and the purchase of foreign financial assets and subsidizing imports and the sale of foreign financial assets.

The maintenance of dual exchange rates also necessitates strict foreign exchange controls. Despite these controls, the under-invoicing of exports and over-invoicing of imports are widely practiced so as to exploit the profit opportunities offered by the exchange rate differential. These actions represent a capital outflow, and hence have an adverse effect on the balance of payments.

It was observed that in Belgium and France, which made use of dual exchange rates, a rate differential in excess of 5 to 10 percent gave rise to widespread evasion. This conclusion applies, *a fortiori,* to developing countries, where the system of administration is weaker. At the same time, rate differentials in these countries have exceeded 100 to 200 percent in some cases. Such had been the case, for example, in Ecuador until August 1986, when the exchange rates applicable to private transactions were unified and the new exchange rate stabilized at about the midpoint between the two rates.

The use of freely floating rates also reduces reserve requirements under normal conditions. And while such reserves are needed in the event of external shocks, the financing of these shocks from foreign exchange reserves under a unified exchange rate regime avoids the temporary disturbance that real effects have on the balance of payments and on the national economy. This will, however, be the case under dual exchange rates, where the ensuing depreciation of the financial exchange rate creates demand for non-traded goods by increasing the domestic currency value of foreign assets, thereby leading to the deterioration of the balance of payments (Kiguel and Lizondo 1986).

Alternative exchange rate arrangements include pegging to a single currency, to the SDR, or to some other currency basket. In January 1987, 31 developing countries pegged their currencies to the U.S. dollar, 14 to the French franc, 5 to other currencies, 10 to the SDR, and 24 to other currency baskets. As shown in Table 5.1, these numbers represent a decline over time in the number of currencies pegged to the U.S. dollar and, to a lesser extent, to the SDR, as well as an increase in pegging to a currency basket based on trade weights.[3]

Pegging to a single currency offers advantages in part because the currency in question is also employed as an intervention currency and in part because business firms use it as a vehicle currency in which to invoice, to cover forward transactions in other currencies, to borrow, and to lend (Williamson 1987). It has also been shown that Latin American countries whose currencies were pegged to the U.S. dollar experienced substantially less inflation than other countries of the region, and the same result has been obtained in countries of the franc zone (CFA) as against other African countries (Connolly 1985). Furthermore, Patrick Guillaumont (1986) explains the greater openness of the CFA countries, in terms of their participation in international trade, by the stability of exchange rates and the convertibility of their currencies.

Fluctuations in the value of a currency to which a particular exchange rate is pegged will matter little as long as it accounts for the bulk of foreign exchange transactions for the country concerned. This has been the case for the CFA countries, even if one excludes other member countries of the EMS. It has been

Table 5.1
Exchange Rate Arrangements for Developing Countries (number of countries, as of January 31)

	1979	1981	1983	1985	1987
Pegged to a single currency					
US dollar	39	38	37	34	31
French franc	14	14	13	14	14
other currencies	7	4	5	4	5
total	60	56	55	52	50
Pegged to a basket					
SDR	12	15	15	11	10
trade weighted	15	18	18	25	24
total	27	33	33	36	34
Adjustment based on					
Set of indicators	4	3	4	5	5
Single currency			10	7	5
Other managed floating	2	23	14	15	17
Independently floating			3	6	12
total	24	26	31	33	39
Grand Total	111	115	119	122	123

Source: International Monetary Fund, *International Financial Statistics*, various issues.

less so for countries that link their currencies to the U.S. dollar. Thus, in 1976, France had a 39 percent share in the trade of the CFA countries, on the average, with these shares varying from 30 to 49 percent, whereas the corresponding average for trade with the United States was 24 percent for countries whose currencies were pegged to the U.S. dollar, with these shares ranging from 1 to 85 percent (Brodsky and Sampson 1984). Also, the dollar has shown larger fluctuations in effective terms than the French franc, even though several parity changes occurred within the EMS.

As a result, the currencies linked to the U.S. dollar have experienced considerable fluctuations over time with respect to other currencies, with an appreciation being followed by a depreciation in trade-weighted (effective) terms. A case in point is Hong Kong, whose effective exchange rate appreciated by 14 percent between October 1983, when its currency was linked to the U.S. dollar, and September 1985, the date of the Plaza Agreement, and depreciated by 29 percent between September 1985 and April 1987 (Balassa and Williamson 1987).[4]

Linking to a fluctuating single currency also gives rise to macroeconomic shocks. There are further adverse microeconomic effects as fluctuations in exchange rates create uncertainty for business decisions, and over- or undervaluation with respect to other currencies affects the country's competitiveness.

It has been shown that, compared with pegging to a single currency, *pegging to the 16-currency basket SDR* would have generally led to less instability in the effective exchange rates of the developing countries. The exceptions are pegging the currencies of some Caribbean countries to the U.S. dollar and pegging CFA currencies to the French franc (Helleiner 1981; Brodsky and Sampson 1984).

The SDR has since been transformed into a basket of only five currencies, thereby reducing its compensatory properties as far as exchange rate fluctuations are concerned, according to the law of large numbers. Nevertheless, the five-currency peg performed better in relation to the effective exchange rate than the 16-currency peg in the case of Jordan in the 1975–83 period. For the same country, linking to the U.S. dollar was shown to be superior to the SDR link in the first part of the period, while the opposite conclusion applied in the second part as well as for the period as a whole (Takagi 1984).

But, even though the SDR peg better approximates the *trade-weighted average of exchange rates* than the single currency peg, it still remains an imperfect approximation to the former. Thus, a more appropriate solution is to use a trade-weighted peg, including merchandise trade as well as service transactions in the calculations. The choice of this alternative makes it possible to minimize the macroeconomic effects of external shocks, reducing uncertainty for traders, and to limit the extent of over- and undervaluation of the currency.

At the same time, there are no technical obstacles to the use of a single intervention currency while employing a trade-weighted average to determine currency values (Takagi 1986). Also, exporters (importers) may utilize several vehicle currencies, depending on where they export to (import from), and may engage in forward market transactions in these currencies.[5]

Nevertheless, as first noted by Sylviane Guillaumont (1984), there may be a conflict between the requirements of macroeconomic and microeconomic stability. Thus, the trade-weighted average of the standard deviation of bilateral exchange rates may be greater if the rate is set so as to eliminate fluctuations in the trade-weighted (effective) exchange rate than if it is set in terms of the currency that accounts for the bulk of a country's trade.[6]

This hypothesis has been confirmed by calculations made by Paraire (1986) for the 1970–83 period in the case of all but one of the currencies of the Franc

Table 5.2

Trade-Weighted Averages of Standard Deviations of Exchange Rates in Bilateral Relationships, 1970–86

	Nominal Exchange Rates		Real Exchange Rates	
	Actual Rate	Trade-Weighted Rate	Actual Rate	Trade-Weighted Rate
Benin	5.535	5.579	n.a.	n.a.
Burkina Faso	2.996	3.850	8.75	8.26
Cameroon	3.524	3.900	4.75	5.06
Central Africa	3.046	3.926	4.22	3.85
Congo	4.198	4.822	6.07	5.81
Cote d' Ivoïre	4.583	5.008	7.38	6.86
Gabon	6.145	8.642	8.39	7.97
Mali	2.005	2.730	n.a.	n.a.
Niger	3.917	6.091	8.41	8.16
Senegal	3.219	4.378	7.50	6.81
Chad	3.728	4.437	n.a.	n.a.
Togo	4.644	4.774	7.14	7.04
Egypt	23.661	6.650	24.88	7.12
El Salvador	28.699	7.705	8.01	7.19
Ethiopia	8.623	7.187	10.11	9.87
Guatemala	7.423	8.709	7.54	8.06
Haiti	3.720	4.967	6.76	6.56
Honduras	4.948	6.246	5.19	5.37
Iraq	12.367	9.871	n.a.	n.a.
Liberia	8.613	6.078	7.63	6.75
Nicaragua	55.249	8.426	n.a.	n.a.
Oman	11.674	6.528	n.a.	n.a.
Panama	6.100	7.610	5.88	6.98
Paraguay	18.743	22.487	15.96	22.25
Peru	53.016	9.922	14.41	19.36
Syria	10.906	6.829	n.a.	n.a.
Trinidad & Tobago	13.106	3.706	7.27	5.68
Venezuela	15.606	5.411	13.66	4.85
Vietnam	349.725	6.172	n.a.	n.a.
Yemen, Arab Republic	11.291	6.182	n.a.	n.a.
Yemen, P.D.	7.734	6.324	n.a.	n.a.

Source: World Bank data base.

zone, the exception being Togo. It has been confirmed without exception if the real (inflation-adjusted) exchange rate is utilized.

The present author has reperformed the calculations for the countries of the franc zone for the 1970–86 period. His results are the same as those of Paraire using nominal exchange rates, but are inverted in all cases except one using real exchange rates (Table 5.2). At the same time, from the point of view of evaluating exchange rate systems, real rather than nominal exchange rates are relevant.

Further calculations have been made for the currencies of countries linked to the U.S. dollar, whose population exceeds 1 million. Sylviane Guillaumont's hypothesis is confirmed in five out of nineteen cases using nominal exchange rates and five out of twelve cases using real exchange rates.

Thus, while macroeconomic instability is minimized through the adoption of trade-weighted exchange rates, the objective of microeconomic efficiency may be better served if the country's currency is linked to that of its principal trading partner. The results are not conclusive, however.

3. EXCHANGE RATES REGIMES FOR DEVELOPING COUNTRIES UNDER ALTERNATIVE ASSUMPTIONS

If developing countries link money creation to the balance of payments, their inflation rates will approximate inflation rates in the country (countries) to whose currency their exchange rate is pegged. Such has been the case, in fact, in the Caribbean and the CFA countries referred to earlier.

In the absence of a link between money creation and the balance of payments, inflation rates may differ among the countries concerned. It has been claimed, however, that maintaining the peg will eliminate differences in inflation rates. The basis of this proposition is the so-called law of one price. As Sjaastad expressed it:

For an economy in which all goods are traded internationally, it is widely held that the internal rate of inflation is determined by the external inflation and changes in the exchange rate. This proposition is merely an extension of the "law of one price." To the extent that this law holds at every moment in time, the price level is completely determined, as is its rate of change. In such an economy, exchange rate policy is obviously sufficient to determine the rate of inflation, and there can be little question concerning the efficacy of that policy as a stabilization tool. (Sjaastad 1984: 85)

Sjaastad admits that "the presence of 'home' or nontraded goods complicates the analysis, as the exchange rate can affect the price of these goods only indirectly—through substitution effects, through expectations, or through both" (1984). But, he adds:

The general idea is that—under normal assumptions concerning preferences and production possibilities, and given the state of overall demand relative to production—there is but one price of home goods, relative to that of traded goods, which will clear the home goods market. Letting the nominal internal price of traded goods be determined by external prices and the exchange rate, this determines the *equilibrium* nominal price for home goods, and hence the equilibrium price level. (Sjaastad 1983: 85)

To examine the validity of this proposition, one needs to consider the process of adjustment in regard to standardized and differential products in the traded goods sector as well as in regard to non-traded goods. The answer is simple in regard to standardized commodities. For importables the domestic price will equal the international price plus transportation costs and the tariff, while for exportables the domestic price will be the international price less transportation costs. The law of one price will hold in this case, the adjustment period will be short, and—once adjustment is made—the rate of increase of domestic prices cannot differ from that of international prices.

Such will not be the case for differentiated traded goods that dominate the manufacturing sector, including practically all consumer goods and investment goods as well as a substantial proportion of intermediate products. For these commodities, the relationship between domestic and international prices will depend on the elasticity of substitution between the domestic and the foreign varieties of the product, in home markets for importables and in foreign markets for exportables. Correspondingly, prices and their rates of increase may diverge for a protracted period.

This conclusion applies *a fortiori* to non-traded goods. There is no micro-economic mechanism that would equalize the prices of these goods or their rates of change. In turn, macroeconomic mechanisms act but slowly through changes in overall demand conditions.

The exchange rate was used as an anti-inflationary device in the Southern Cone of Latin America (Argentina, Chile, and Uruguay) during the early 1980s. The following discussion concerns the experience of Chile, where the exchange rate was maintained fixed in terms of the U.S. dollar between June 1979 and March 1982.

The divergence in the rate of increase of domestic and foreign prices declined only slowly in Chile, and the divergence in the rate of increase of the domestic prices of non-traded and trade goods failed to decline (Balassa 1985). This is hardly surprising, given low product substitution elasticities in production and consumption in the short run and even in the medium run, particularly between traded and non-traded goods.

In the presence of sluggish adjustment in prices, then, using the exchange rate as an instrument to reduce the rate of inflation imposes a real cost on the economy. And the appreciation of the exchange rate in real terms is not undone at the time when domestic and foreign prices converge, so that the overvaluation of the exchange rate is perpetuated.

At the same time, the loss in export market positions may involve an element of irreversibility, as consumers shift to other suppliers. Also, as domestic producers are unable to compete with imports, the customary historical process of traders becoming producers may be reversed.

These considerations point to the inappropriateness of using the exchange rate as an anti-inflationary device. Rather, the exchange rate should be adjusted in line with the domestic–foreign inflation differential. This means maintaining the real effective exchange rate, rather than the nominal effective exchange rate, constant over time, barring permanent shifts in the underlying conditions.

Temporary shifts in the balance of payments, in turn, should be accommodated through changes in foreign exchange reserves and/or in the external debt. It would further be desirable to make increased use of the IMF Compensatory Financing Facility, designed to compensate for fluctuations in export receipts, and to establish an interest equalization scheme, to compensate for fluctuations in interest rates (Balassa, Bueno, Kuczynski, and Simonsen 1986).

The question remains if the above conclusions need to be modified in the event that variations in the values of the currencies of the major developed countries are reduced through, for example, the establishment of a target zone. The economic cost of pegging to a single currency will be lower in this case, but the use of a trade-weighted basket will continue to offer advantages.

For one thing, differing rates of inflation in different industrial countries will lead to changes in the target zones of their currencies. For another thing, account needs to be taken of fluctuations in currency values among developing countries that are trading partners or competitors for the country in question.

CONCLUSIONS

This chapter has suggested that alternative exchange rate regimes be evaluated by reference to the objectives of eschewing foreign exchange restrictions, maintaining realistic exchange rates, limiting uncertainty for business decision making, and reducing fluctuations in macroeconomic relationships. In view of these objectives, freely floating exchange rates appear superior to other alternatives.

If the adoption of a freely floating exchange rate were excluded, linking to a basket of currencies would be superior to linking to a single currency, unless the latter is the currency in which the bulk of a country's trade is carried out. In the second eventuality, the requirements of macroeconomic and microeconomic stability may come into conflict.

Reductions in U.S. trade shares and fluctuations in the value of the dollar may explain the decline over time in the number of currencies pegged to the U.S. dollar. These considerations apply, *a fortiori*, to the British pound, to which a number of currencies were pegged in the early postwar period, four currencies as late as 1979, and none in 1987. The desirability of avoiding fluctuations of currency values in effective terms also points to the superiority of trade-weighted exchange rates over pegging to the SDR, which is manifested in the shift from the latter to the former.[7] At the same time, there has been an increase over time in the number of freely floating rates.

NOTES

1. The word "proximate" in the title of the section indicates that these objectives are designed to serve ultimate economic goals such as growth and employment. For an excellent discussion of the requirements of internal and external balance, see Black (1976).

2. For a review of the literature, the reader is referred to Williamson (1985a).

3. Dual exchange rates are not shown separately in the statistics. However, Table 5.1 includes currencies that are neither freely floating nor pegged.

4. At the same time, pegging to the U.S. dollar has often been in name but not in reality. Thus, among the 31 currencies listed in Table 5.1 as dollar-pegged on January 31, 1987, only nine maintained their value in terms of dollars between 1973 and 1986 (the group includes the People's Democratic Republic of Yemen, which has less than 2 percent of its trade with the United States but has nevertheless chosen to maintain a constant relationship with the U.S. dollar).

5. A trade-weighted basket is customarily defined in terms of the composition of a country's exports and imports. An alternative procedure involves setting currency values on the basis of changes in the currencies of the country's competitors. While in the first case one considers substitution against the products of trading partners, in the second case substitution against the products of competitors is considered. The choice between the two alternatives should depend on the relative importance of these substitution relationships for the country concerned. One may also choose an intermediate solution by taking, for example, some average of the two weighting schemes.

6. A similar argument is made by Williamson (1987).

7. At any rate, the reported figures overstate the number of currencies that are *de facto* pegged to the U.S. dollar or the SDR. Thus, there are currencies "whose value for all intents and purposes was defined independently of the currency to which it ostensibly pegged" (Brodsky and Sampson 1984: 141). In 1979 there were 17 such currencies out of 39 ostensibly pegged to the U.S. dollar and 10 out of 12 currencies ostensibly pegged to the SDR, leaving Guinea and Jordan as the only "true" SDR peggers (Brodsky and Sampson 1984: 139–41).

COMMENT BY

Marcello de Cecco

What exchange rate regime should developing countries choose? Bela Balassa addresses this intricate subject first of all by defining the objectives that should be pursued by developing countries (or indeed, by *any* country) when engaging in the exercise of evaluating the merits and demerits of alternative exchange rate regimes. These objectives he lists as being the following: eschewing foreign exchange restrictions; maintaining realistic exchange rates; limiting uncertainty for business decision making; and reducing fluctuations in macroeconomic relationship. The objectives listed are rather unusual with respect to traditional literature on economic development, according to which these objectives should be considered as constraints imposed on the primary objective developing countries should pursue, which is the maximization of the growth rate of income per head for their citizens or, alternatively, of maximum growth rate of real GNP.

One could object that, by successfully pursuing Balassa's objectives and thus choosing the exchange rate regime compatible with them, countries will achieve maximum growth of real GNP. But I am not sure the latter will follow from the former.

What Balassa says about the objective of eschewing foreign exchange restrictions is, in my opinion, open to doubt. He dismisses exchange controls as if they were theoretically proven as inferior to a free foreign exchange market. He declares himself certain that, if foreign exchange and capital controls were removed, and realistic exchange rates established for developing countries, capital would freely flow there because, as he states, "developing countries have a lower ratio of capital to labour than developed countries and can apply existing technology that has been generated in the developed countries."

This is definitely one of the *loci classici* of debate among development economists. Without going into that debate, let us only note that it had not been officially declared closed in favor of the view Balassa expresses in his paper. The issue remains, to say the least, still very much undecided, with excellent arguments being made for and against Balassa's view.

To consider it a settled matter, however, is not necessary for the whole of Balassa's remaining arguments. In his concluding remarks, he states the superiority, for developing countries, of pegging to a basket over pegging to a single currency (with the correct qualifications he makes). This can still be accepted if his arguments on exchange restrictions and capital flows are dropped. Most of his considerations, however, cannot be made, if one is less of an elasticity optimist than he is with respect to developing countries' trade.

If one takes the line that elasticity pessimism is more in order, when developing countries' trade is considered, most of the adjustment mechanisms he analyzes will not work the way they are supposed to. It is definitely the case that elasticity optimism or pessimism should not be *fixed* intellectual positions. They should be adjusted according to forecasts about trends in world trade. One was justified, for instance, in being an elasticity optimist in the 1960s and 1970s, but pessimism should be more in order when forecasting elasticities in the 1980s and 1990s. What developing countries will be able to export very much depends on the willingness of developed countries to accept their imports. The space that was there to accommodate Japan and the NICs in the 1960s and 1970s was given by the running down of the relative monopoly of world trade Britain and the United States had after the Second World War. Now that their monopoly is gone, and purchasing power is not shifted to import-hungry countries like those of OPEC, there is just no reason to be an elasticity optimist any longer.

What exchange rate regime developing countries ought to choose for the remaining thirteen years of this century should be discussed against this much gloomier international trade prospect. It is my view that they ought to choose to align themselves to the exchange rate regimes of countries, or groups of countries, which give a guarantee of absorbing at least their raw material exports and half a guarantee of accepting their manufactured goods exports.

The countries that offer these guarantees are the European countries and Japan. Between them they absorb about 50 percent of total world imports and provide an even more impressive share of world exports. And, what is more important, foreign trade is essential to their economic well-being. Keeping in mind that the superiority of pegging to a basket is ascertained by Balassa over that of pegging to one single currency, it is perhaps worth suggesting that a number of developing countries may find it a good idea to peg to the ECU, an option Balassa does not explore in Chapter 5.

Because of the importance of EMS countries as trading partners, most European countries that are not members of the EMS are pegging to it anyway. This increases the share of trade developing countries have with official and *unofficial* EMS members over their total trade.

It has been proved by Masera that the reward-variability index of the ECU is not as good as that of the SDR for countries that are not members of the EMS. But it definitely is for EMS members. This means that since the countries officially or unofficially involved in the EMS are many, and all of them large traders, a developing country would, by pegging to the ECU, ensure stability for its exports proceeds but also for its import capacity, as it can shop with the ECU all around Europe without exchange rate fear. A good idea might also be to renegotiate the debt owed, mostly in dollars, to EMS countries, to transform it into ECU-denominated debt. It would make its management less a speculative and more an economic activity for developing countries' monetary authorities.

PART II

THE EUROPEAN MONETARY SYSTEM

6

PPP and the Peso Problem: Exchange Rates in the EMS

Susan M. Collins

How has the EMS exchange arrangement influenced the actual and anticipated behavior of member countries' exchange rates? This question encompasses a broad set of issues that are at the heart of analyses of the system's performance and prospects, and are of interest to policy makers as well as researchers. The issues are fundamentally empirical, and an understanding of how the exchange rate system has actually functioned should prove invaluable in selecting tractable but appropriate frameworks for theoretical and econometric analysis.

The purpose of this chapter is to discuss existing empirical work and to present new evidence about two aspects of exchange rate adjustments in the EMS. The first issue, purchasing power parity (PPP), is discussed in section 2. The section points out that realignments have played a critical role in real exchange rate shifts between EMS members, and turns to an analysis of the size of these adjustments. One widely held view is that a key objective of EMS exchange rate management has been to "discipline" high inflation members. This view has the implication that adjustments should only partially offset cumulated inflation differentials. A second view stresses international competitiveness. It implies that adjustments should more than offset past inflation differentials. The section first develops the two models, and then turns to the evidence to ask whether one or the other is supported in the data.

The second issue, discussed in section 3, is whether market expectations of realignments have implied recurrent "peso problems" for the EMS. The term refers directly to the persistent forward premium on the Mexican peso in the months preceding the 1976 maxi-devaluation, and more generally to the potential problems resulting from expectations of any change in regime or in the rules of the game. As discussed in the rest of the chapter, large realignments can be thought of as changes in the exchange regime. There is substantial evidence that market participants form expectations about the timing (and magnitude) of exchange rate jumps associated with realignments. In addition to influencing nominal variables (such as interest rates and forward exchange rates) these "peso problem" expectations may have real effects.

A brief description of the EMS exchange arrangement is given in section 1. Section 4 contains concluding remarks.

1. THE EMS EXCHANGE ARRANGEMENT

The members of the European Monetary System (EMS) engage in a unique and interesting exchange arrangement that combines aspects of fixed and flexible exchange regimes. The system is like a fixed regime in two respects. First, members maintain their currencies within narrow bands ($\pm$ 2.25 percent) of fixed central parities.[1]

Second, there have been a number of realignments of these central parities. Both because the timing and the magnitude of the adjustments are determined by monetary authorities and because the adjustments have frequently been large relative to the width of the bands necessitating exchange rate jumps, these realignments resemble devaluations or revaluations of fixed exchange rates. At the same time, the system does allow for some exchange rate flexibility.

Table 6.1 gives the dates and magnitudes of the eleven realignments that have occurred to date. Some (e.g., March 1981 and July 1985) involved an adjustment of one currency against the others, while others adjusted the bilateral exchange rates between all members.

2. PPP: REAL EXCHANGE RATES
AND COMPETITIVENESS

Because of the relatively narrow exchange rate bands imposed by the EMS exchange arrangement, most of the movements in real exchange rates are attributable either to relative price changes or to adjustments of the bilateral central parities.[2] Thus, the extent to which parity realignments have offset cumulative inflation differentials has had a critical influence on competitiveness within the system.

There have been two theoretical approaches to examining realignment magnitudes, one stressing "competitiveness" and the other stressing "discipline." While each framework is interesting in its own right, the two have very different implications for the path of real exchange rates in the EMS. Surprisingly little attention has been paid to testing the appropriateness of these frameworks in explaining the observed real exchange rate behavior. After a brief description of each framework to identify testable implications, this section empirically exam-

Table 6.1
Dates and Magnitudes of EMS Realignments (percentage changes in bilateral central rate)

	24.09. 1979	30.11. 1979	22.03. 1981	05.10. 1981	22.02. 1982	14.06. 1982	21.03. 1983	20.07. 1985	07.04. 1986	04.08. 1986	12.01. 1986
French Franc	0	0	0	-3	0	-5.75	-2.5	+2	-3	0	0
Deutschemark	+2	0	0	+5.5	0	+4.25	+5.5	+2	+3	0	+3
Irish Pound	0	0	0	0	0	0	-3.5	+2	0	-8	0
Italian Lira	0	0	-6	-3	0	-2.75	-2.5	-6	0	0	0
Dutch Guilder	0	0	0	+5.5	0	+4.25	+3.5	+2	+3	0	+3
Danish Krone	-2.9	-4.8	0	0	-3	0	+2.5	+2	+1	0	0
Belgian and Lux. Franc	0	0	0	0	-8.5	0	+1.5	+2	+1	0	+2

Note: Calculated as the percentage change against the group of currencies whose bilateral parities remained unchanged in the realignment, except for the March 21, 1983 realignment, in which all currencies were realigned. The percentages quoted here are from the official communiqué.

ines the evidence for competitiveness versus discipline in explaining realignments.

2.1 Competitiveness versus Discipline

The competitiveness view is that realignments have been "justified with reference to underlying inflation rates so as to maintain purchasing power parity."[3] The implications for the frequency and the magnitude of exchange rate adjustment have been explored more formally by Collins (1984) and Giavazzi and Pagano (1985). In an application of recent work on sticky prices,[4] these papers examine optimal exchange rate policy for a small country that pegs its currency to a relatively low inflation country.[5] (For example, the framework could be applied to France or to Italy with respect to Germany.)

The framework assumes first that there is a fixed cost to exchange rate adjustments, so that realignments occur infrequently. Second, the government is assumed to adjust the nominal exchange rate so as to minimize a loss function that depends on deviations of the real exchange rate from an optimal level. (Collins assumes that real exchange rate deviations are costly because they lead to output fluctuations.)

The very intuitive solution identifies critical levels of real exchange rate overvaluation (R_o) and undervaluation (R_u). The government will devalue the exchange rate whenever the real exchange rate appreciates enough to pass R_o, and the adjustment will be just large enough to establish a real exchange rate of R_u. Thus, devaluations will exceed the amount required to offset the cumulated inflation differential at the time of the adjustment. Because policy makers are forward looking, they add some additional devaluation to account for anticipated future inflation differentials.

In contrast, the "discipline" approach seeks to explain why exchange rate adjustments may only partially offset relative price changes, allowing the currencies of high inflation countries to appreciate. Thygesen (1981) argued that less than total offset would be necessary to provide incentives for policy convergence to narrow inflation differentials between member countries.

The discipline approach has been formalized by Giavazzi and Pagano (1988).[6] In a recent paper, they ask why high inflation countries would join the EMS, knowing that real appreciation will erode their competitiveness. In their framework, policy makers care both about the impact of the real exchange rate on output and about inflation—inflation surprises are assumed to be costly, while inflation tax receipts are assumed to be beneficial. The model assumes that realignments at most offset past inflation differentials, so that high inflation countries suffer a cost (real appreciation) from joining the system. This cost introduces a credible incentive for policy makers to reduce money growth rates and thereby slows the optimal rate of inflation.

However, Giavazzi and Pagano stress that the issue is "not whether the EMS is an effective disciplinary device but whether it is a welfare improving arrangement." They claim first that real appreciation of high inflation members is a characterizing feature of the EMS and second that these countries will have lower inflation rates inside the EMS than outside. The structure of their model assumes both of these features.

The discipline view and the competitiveness view imply very different behaviors of intra-EMS real exchange rates. In particular, if the discipline view is accurate, joining the EMS should foster convergence of inflation rates. Other things being equal, one would expect to see greater and/or more rapid convergence inside the system than outside.

Second, central parity adjustments should only partially offset cumulated price differentials for the high inflation members. Furthermore, these countries should experience consistent real appreciation until their inflation rates slow to the EMS average. Alternatively, if the competitiveness view is more appropriate, exchange rate adjustments should more than offset past appreciation, and there should be no long-run tendency to appreciation. The evidence is examined in the remainder of the section.

2.2 Inflation Differentials

Ideally, one would examine the inflation performance in the EMS by comparing actual inflation experiences with what would have happened to countries if they had not been members. Unfortunately, this analysis is beyond the scope of this chapter. Instead, I ask whether a more casual look at the data supports the widely held presumption in favor of the "discipline" model.

When the EMS was instituted in March 1979, there was a wide range of inflation rates among the members. Germany was on the low end, having averaged a 4.3 percent annual increase in its CPI during March 1972 to March 1979, while Italy was at the other extreme, with an average inflation rate of 13.0 percent over the same period. The rates for France, Belgium, Denmark, and the Netherlands ranged between 6.5 and 8.9 percent. The success of the system in maintaining its narrow bands (for all currencies except the Italian lira) with relatively infrequent adjustment was widely believed to depend on its ability to narrow the range of inflation rates.

The early prognoses were not very encouraging. Rogoff (1985), who examined the performance through March 1984, concluded that the EMS had done little to reduce inflation differentials between members. In fact, he found greater convergence outside of the system than within it. His work stressed the role of French and Italian capital controls, not convergent policies and economic performance, in explaining why realignments had not occurred more frequently.

In contrast, Ungerer et al. (1986) find more evidence of convergence through 1985. They conclude (p. 24) "that the desire for convergence of inflation rates was somewhat stronger" for countries participating in the EMS exchange arrangement. However, they note that this tendency may have preceded the EMS.

Their results are also sensitive to the time period and to the set of comparator countries.

To summarize the major developments, Table 6.2 gives CPI inflation rates for six EMS members and four non-members for four different subperiods. The last two rows present summary statistics (mean and standard deviation) for (six) EMS members and for a comparison group of five non-members. The latter group includes the United States, Britain, Japan, and Switzerland, as well as Germany.

The first column of the table shows inflation rates in the seven years preceding the formation of the system. The figures show that, on average, inflation rates were slightly higher in the EMS countries than elsewhere; however, there was less variance among members.

The second column shows that, overall, the post-EMS inflation performance has been disappointing. Although the average rate of inflation within the system declined during the first seven years of its operation (March 1979 to March 1986), it fell by only 18 percent as compared with a 30 percent decline in the average inflation rate of non-members. Furthermore, divergence (as measured by the standard deviation of average annual inflation rates) rose within the system from 2.6 to 3.4, but fell among non-members from 3.3 to 1.7. It is difficult to credit the system for reducing inflation or for promoting convergence over the entire seven-year period.

However, the seven-year average masks important differences between the early and the more recent EMS experiences. This point is made in the third and fourth columns, which show inflation performance during March 1979–82 and March 1983–86. The early EMS period, which includes the aftermath of the

Table 6.2
CPI Inflation Rates

	3/72–3/79		3/79–3/86		3/79–3/82		3/83–3/86	
Belgium	7.6		5.5		7.1		4.8	
Denmark	8.9		7.1		11.9		4.8	
France	8.7		8.3		13.4		6.0	
Germany	4.3		3.3		5.6		1.9	
Italy	13.0		12.3		18.6		9.4	
Netherlands	6.5		3.6		6.4		2.3	
U.S.	6.8		5.7		10.6		3.6	
Japan	10.8		6.2		5.5		10.5	
U.K.	12.2		7.7		14.2		5.2	
Switzerland	4.1		3.5		5.0		2.6	
	avg	std	avg	std	avg	std	avg	std
EMS	8.2	2.6	6.7	3.4	10.5	4.6	4.9	2.5
Non-EMS	7.6	3.3	5.3	1.7	8.1	4.5	4.8	3.1

second oil shock, saw larger inflation increases and more divergence among the EMS members than the non-members. Performance since 1983 has been strikingly different. Inflation rates have been reduced, so that the average within the EMS was almost identical to the average of the non-members. In addition, inflation differentials were narrowed within the system so that, again, rates diverged more outside than inside the exchange arrangement. As discussed further below, there were five realignments during the 1979–82 period, with most bilateral rates adjusted at least three times. In contrast, there was only one realignment of central parities between the end of March 1983 and 1986, and only bilateral rates involving the Italian lira were adjusted.

In summary, it remains difficult to claim that the system has reduced inflation rates and narrowed inflation differentials. This point is made most clearly by comparing the pre-EMS period with the 1983–86 period, and excluding the poor post–oil shock performance. EMS members have reduced inflation rates by only slightly more than the non-member group. Also, the divergence in inflation rates during 1983–86 is very similar to what it had been in the pre-EMS period for both groups of countries. However, following the second oil shock, there was a larger rise in average inflation rates and in inflation differentials within the EMS than among the sample of non-members. This increased divergence seems to have added to pressure for parity adjustments in the first few years of the arrangement. The return to lower inflation rates, and to smaller divergence, has helped to reduce the pressure for parity adjustments in recent years.

2.3 Disciplining High Inflation Countries?

Have exchange rate adjustments in the EMS been determined primarily to maintain competitiveness, or has concern over inflation also been important? The key feature that distinguishes the discipline model from the competitiveness model is that exchange rate adjustments will be smaller than cumulated inflation differentials in the former and larger in the latter.

Unfortunately, there are not enough realignments in the data to formally test one model against the other. However, insight can be gained from simply comparing actual exchange rate adjustments with the adjustments that would have been necessary to maintain a constant real exchange rate. This section considers bilateral real exchange rates for the high inflation countries (France, Italy, and Denmark) against the Deutschmark.[7] Multilateral real exchange rates are discussed in section 2.4.

The behavior of the franc, the lira, and the krone relative to the Deutschmark (FF/DM, LIT/DM, and DK/DM) are plotted in Figures 6.1, 6.2, and 6.3. Each plot shows the upper and lower bands for the bilateral exchange rate, the actual spot exchange rate (dotted line), and the PPP exchange rate (dashed line) that would have maintained a constant real exchange rate. For France and Denmark the real exchange rate at the beginning of the EMS (March 1979) is used as the base. As explained below, the base year chosen for Italy was March 1983.[8]

Figure 6.1
French Franc versus DM—PPP

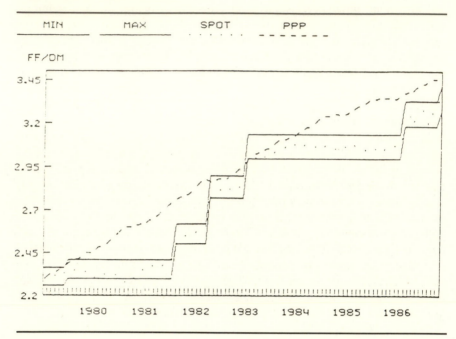

The figures show that neither model tells the whole story for any of the countries. For France and Italy the early years (1979–81) and the most recent years (1985–86) are characterized by adjustments that only partially offset cumulated inflation differentials. These periods saw real exchange rate appreciations of the FF/DM and the LIT/DM and are consistent with the discipline model of realignments.

In contrast, the intermediate period (1982–84) more closely resembles what would be expected from the competitiveness model. This is especially true for Italy, where the frequent exchange rate adjustments kept pace with the relative price changes after the initial period of real appreciation. Taking the March 1983 rate as the "target," the graph depicts authorities as following an exchange rate policy such that the actual exchange rate coincided with the target PPP rate approximately midway between realignments. Adjustments more than simply offset cumulated inflation differentials—in other words they were forward looking, as predicted by the "competitiveness" model.

In France the exchange rate adjustments during 1981–83 are even larger than would be expected from the competitiveness model. Figure 6.1 shows that not only did they include a forward-looking component to offset inflation accumula-

Figure 6.2
Italian Lira versus DM—PPP

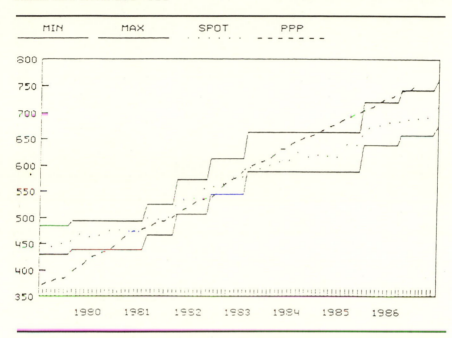

tion before the next realignment, they also included a catch-up component so that the real appreciation between 1979 and 1981 had been eroded by 1983–84.

Figure 6.3 shows that adjustments of the Danish krone during the entire 1979–85 period are better described by the competitive model than by the discipline model. It is only during 1985–86 that realignments have not offset relative price movements between Denmark and Germany.

It is interesting that in none of the countries is there a clear inverse relation between the magnitude and the frequency of adjustment. The competitiveness model breaks down as realignments become less frequent. This observation is inconsistent with considering real exchange rate deviations as the key determinant of the timing of realignments, as implied by the competitiveness model. The evidence for other models of the timing of realignments is discussed in the next section.

Overall the data do not provide strong support for either of the two models, but the evidence is more damaging for the discipline model. First, there are long periods during which central parity adjustments more than offset past inflation differentials for each of the three high inflation countries. Second, this accommodation period occurred during 1981–83, and not after the inflation rates in

Figure 6.3
Danish Krone versus DM—PPP

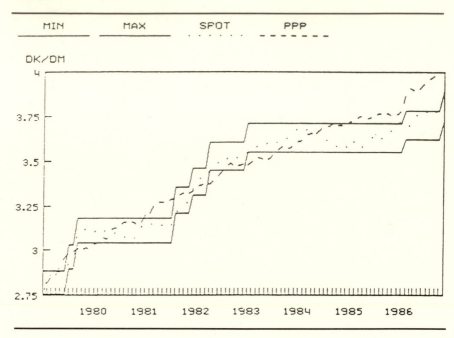

these countries decelerated. Discipline emerged after 1983 as the inflation differentials narrowed. The evidence suggests that a combination of the two models in which government objectives shift over time may be more appropriate. The failure of the simpler models presents an unfortunate tradeoff between tractability and realism.

2.4 Real Exchange Rate Behavior

The previous section discussed the behavior of bilateral real exchange rates in the EMS, identifying competitiveness as an important determinant in exchange rate management during much of the EMS period. This section uses multilateral real exchange rates to look at shifts in competitiveness within the EMS.

Figures 6.4 and 6.5 show real exchange rates for Germany, Denmark, France, and Italy. (The construction of these variables is described in the data appendix.) The figures show that the multilateral and the bilateral series have behaved quite similarly, and that there have been significant shifts in competitiveness among the EMS members.

The German and Danish currencies are shown in Figure 6.4. In real terms, the DM and the krone were within 2 percent of their March 1979 levels in December

Figure 6.4
Real Exchange Rates (Intra-EMS), Germany and Denmark

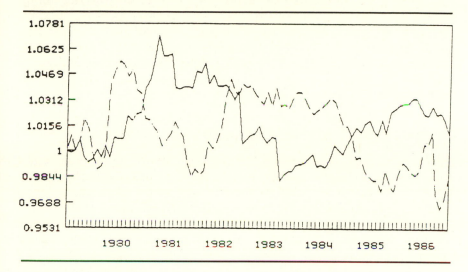

Indices: March 1979 = 1.00.

Figure 6.5
Real Exchange Rates (Intra-EMS), France and Italy

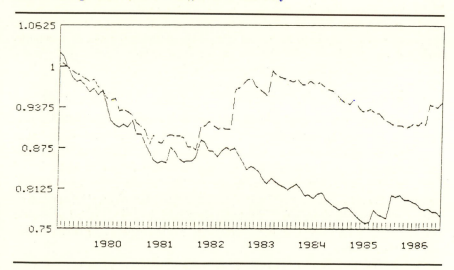

Indices: March 1979 = 1.00.

1986. However, this masks significant movements, especially of the DM, throughout the period.

Figure 6.5 documents the 1979–81 12 to 15 percent real appreciation of the French franc and Italian lira relative to the other members. From 1981 to 1984, realignments restored the franc to its 1979 level but only slowed the appreciation of the lira. Overall the franc and the lira appreciated by about 6 percent and 26 percent respectively between the beginning of the EMS and the end of 1986. Of the three high inflation countries, only Italy has consistently lost competitiveness under the EMS exchange arrangement.

3. PESO PROBLEMS: THE TIMING OF REALIGNMENTS

The previous section examined real exchange rates, focusing on the actual magnitudes of exchange rate adjustment during realignments. A second set of issues revolves around expectations of the timing of exchange rate adjustments—the so-called peso problem. The peso problem has typically been used to refer to expected devaluations in developing countries, but many of the same issues apply to realignments in the EMS. The central questions are whether market participants anticipate realignments (and if so, the determinants of their expectations) and whether these anticipations are disruptive or in some way problematic.

This section has two tasks. The first is to ask whether realignments have in fact been anticipated, and to discuss the determinants of these expectations. The second is to identify reasons why policy makers might care about exchange rate expectations and to discuss whether these potential problems are likely to be large.

3.1 Exchange Rate Expectations

As discussed in detail in Collins (1986), there is overwhelming evidence that realignments have been anticipated by market participants. One useful indicator comes from shifts in the forward exchange rate.

Consider expectations about the FF/DM rate. Under the assumption of risk neutrality,[9] the k month ahead forward exchange rate, F_{t+k}, is equal to the spot rate expected at time $t + k$, conditional on information available at time t, $_tS_{t+k}$.

$$F_{t+k} = {_tS_{t+k}} \tag{6.1}$$

There are two possibilities. Either there will be no realignment between time t and time $t + k$, in which case the expected exchange rate is $_tE_{t+k}$, or there will be a realignment,[10] in which case the expected exchange rate is $_tZ_{t+k}$. The perceived probability of a realignment between time t and time $t + k$ is denoted by $_tP_{t+k}$.

$$_tS_{t+k} = {_tE_{t+k}}\,{_tP_{t+k}} + (1 - {_tP_{t+k}})\,{_tZ_{t+k}} \tag{6.2}$$

I assume that, in the case of no realignment, the exchange rate is expected to follow a random walk.[11] Thus, a useful indicator of exchange rate expectations is the ratio between the forward exchange rate and the current spot rate, as shown in Equation 6.4.

$$_tE_{t+k} = S_t \qquad\qquad\qquad (6.3)$$

$$\frac{F_{t+k}}{S_t} = 1 + {_tP_{t+k}}\left[\frac{_tZ_{t+k} - S_t}{S_t}\right] \qquad\qquad (6.4)$$

When no realignment is expected, the ratio should equal one. Increases in the perceived realignment probability, or in the expected magnitude of adjustment if a realignment takes place, will both cause the ratio to rise above one.

Figure 6.6 plots the ratio of the one month forward premium to the current spot rate from December 1981 through December 1983. The times of two realignments (June 1982 and March 1983) are denoted by arrows. The figure shows that the ratio is slightly above one, fluctuating slightly during normal periods. In the weeks preceding realignments, however, the ratio shoots above its typical level. In the week before March 1983, for example, the forward exchange rate exceeded the spot rate by more than seven percentage points. If market participants had anticipated a realignment magnitude of 8 percent (the amount by which the FF/DM central parity was actually adjusted), this differential implied that the

Figure 6.6
Exchange Rate Expectations for FF/DM (1 Month Forward/Spot Rate)

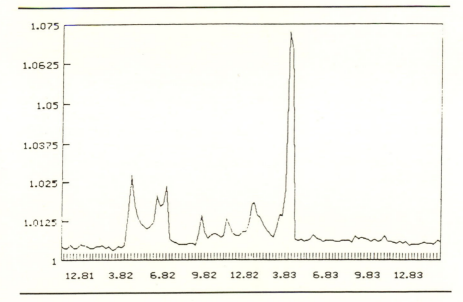

perceived probability that a realignment would occur within 30 days was in excess of 90 percent.

3.2 Interest Rate Behavior

One possible problem from anticipated devaluation is rapidly rising interest rates. This can be readily shown from the covered interest parity relationship, given in Equation 6.5. Focusing again on the French franc and the German mark, the condition says that the difference between the nominal returns on assets denominated in francs and assets denominated in marks (both of k-month maturity) is equal to the forward premium on marks. Thus, increases in the ratio of the forward rate to the current spot rate will translate into increases in the nominal interest differential.

$$i^f_{t,k} - i^g_{f,k} = F_{t+k}/S_t \tag{6.5}$$

Because nominal interest rate increases are not tied to increased inflation, they imply a rise in real rates as well. Higher domestic real interest rates may increase the fiscal burden of domestic debt and the cost of working capital, with potentially recessionary consequences.[12] These concerns provide one reason for "surprise" realignments, so as to avoid the unfavorable aspects of a long period of speculation against weak currencies.

In the EMS, capital controls in France and Italy have driven a wedge between onshore and offshore interest rates. (See Giavazzi and Pagano (1985) and Giavazzi and Giovannini (1985) for further discussion of the role of capital controls.) This has meant that offshore interest rates (for deposits denominated in currencies that are expected to be devalued) often rise dramatically in the periods preceding realignments. Although onshore rates have typically been positively correlated with offshore rates, they have risen little during these crisis periods. Thus, capital controls have mitigated one potential "peso problem."

It is too early to tell whether the gradual relaxation of capital controls in France will open this channel for potential disruption. As shown in Figure 6.7, the divergences between the onshore and offshore interest rates preceding realignments were also apparent in the two most recent episodes. The differences can be large and sustained. For instance, the offshore rates ranged from 3 percent to 8 percent above a comparable onshore rate in the two months before the April 1986 realignment.

3.3 Foreign Exchange Reserves

Another set of potential problems from anticipated devaluation are capital flight, shifts in the timing of trade payments and credits, and misinvoiced trade flows, which drain official reserves and pressure the government to devalue. In this sense, expectations of devaluation can be self-fulfilling.

Figure 6.7
Onshore versus Offshore Interest Rates, France, October 1985–March 1987

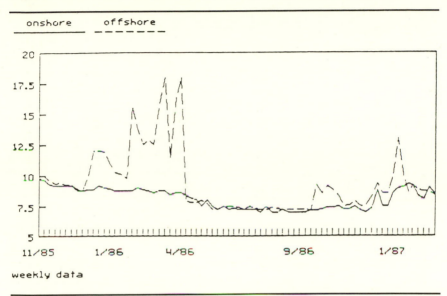

Unfortunately, it is difficult to conduct a formal test of whether expectations accelerated the decumulation of official reserves, against the alternative hypothesis that expectations were fueled by the depletion of reserves. However, a look at the data does reveal two interesting findings. First, there is a strong negative correlation between official reserves and expectations of devaluation. Figure 6.8 illustrates the point using data for France. Expectations of devaluation (measured here by the six-month forward premium) rise as reserves are depleted.

A second point is that currencies do tend to be realigned following rapid reserve decumulations. It is not necessarily true, however, that realignments occur when foreign exchange stocks are very low. (For example, French reserves were relatively high prior to the October 1981 realignment.)[13]

The previous section argued that the timing (as well as the magnitude) of realignments in the EMS cannot be adequately explained by a simple model of real exchange rate targeting, because realignments have not consistently occurred when currencies reach a critical level of overvaluation. An alternative framework for modeling the timing of devaluation assumes that the trigger is a critical level of foreign exchange reserves, and not the real exchange rate. The models are alternatively labeled "balance of payments crisis" (BOP) or "collapsing exchange rate" models, because unsustainable reserve outflows create a balance of payments crisis that results in a collapse of the current fixed exchange rate.[14]

In a recent paper, Collins (1986) extends the BOP crisis model to econometrically explore the determinants of exchange rate expectations in the EMS.

Figure 6.8
Exchange Rate Expectations and Foreign Exchange Reserves

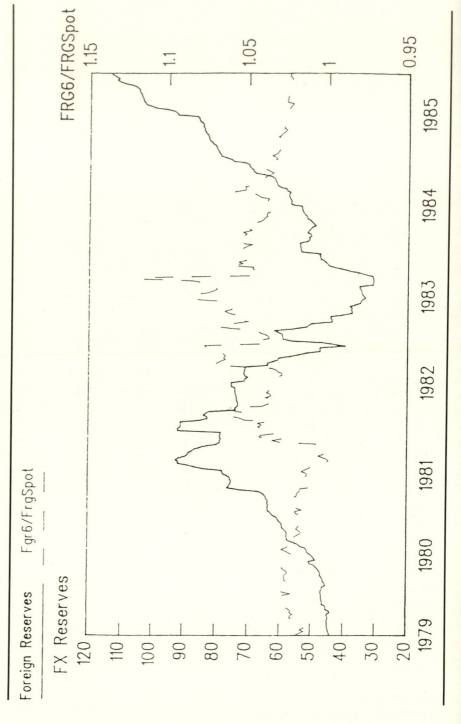

The results show that much of the shifts in exchange rate expectations can be explained by changes in economic conditions. In particular, reductions in foreign exchange reserves, deterioration of the trade balance, and depreciations of the FF/DM spot rate within the current band all reduce the expected duration of the current central parity. While it is possible to expand the model to consider the effects of other economic variables on expectations, it is quite difficult to build in a role for political factors, such as the timing of elections. The relative importance of political and economic concerns in determining the timing and magnitude of realignments remains an interesting area for research.

3. CONCLUDING REMARKS

The EMS is an interesting but complex exchange arrangement. Simplifications, often extreme, are unavoidable in developing tractable models to help explain the behavior of exchange rates in the system. This chapter was motivated by the view that these models will be useful only to the extent that they adequately capture the key features of the system. Thus, it is important to pay careful attention to the data.

The results presented here are organized around two central issues. The first is the role of intra-EMS inflation differentials in explaining the magnitudes of realignments. The analysis shows that there is little support for the hypothesis that the EMS has led to a convergence of inflation rates among members. In fact, inflation rates have also been converging outside of the system, and the within system variance of inflation rates during 1983–86 is little different from the variance before the system was instituted.

There have also been long periods of time in which exchange rate adjustments for the high inflation countries relative to Germany were enough (or more than enough) to compensate for cumulated overvaluation. Furthermore, the adjustments have become small relative to inflation differentials, as inflation rates within the system have converged. These findings are inconsistent with the view that EMS realignments are determined so as to "discipline" high inflation members. The evidence provides some support for a "competitiveness" view of realignments in which policy makers try to maintain constant (average) real exchange rates. However, this approach is also inadequate during some periods. These findings imply that additional research to explain realignments is warranted.

The second issue is that market expectations of realignments may be disruptive. There is clear evidence that central parity adjustments have been anticipated. Furthermore, many of the shifts in exchange rate expectations can be explained by changing economic conditions. One of the key variables has been the stock of foreign exchange reserves in the central bank. It is likely that depletion of foreign exchange reserves contributes to expectations of devaluation, which fuels reserve outflows (for example, through shifts in the timing of trade payments and credits). This is the same type of circle observed during balance of payments crises in developing countries.

Some of the negative consequences of expected devaluation have been mitigated in the EMS because the typically weak currencies (the French franc and Italian lira) have been subject to capital controls. Only time will tell whether relaxation of the capital controls will exacerbate the impact of exchange rate expectations of member economies, pressuring policy makers to anticipate market fears and to adjust before participants feel a realignment is imminent. The major argument against such a development, that it would relax the mechanism for "disciplining" high inflation members, becomes less convincing in light of the fact that "discipline" does not seem to have been the primary concern of policy makers or the primary explanation for the narrowing in recent intra-EMS inflation differentials.

APPENDIX

1. Spot and Forward Exchange Rates
   Weekly (Wednesday) offer rates quoted in New York, 8:30 a.m.
   Source: Data Resources, Inc.

2. Prices
   Consumer Price indices (monthly)
   Source: *International Financial Statistics.*

3. French Foreign Exchange Reserves
   Weekly (net) reserves of the Banque de France
   Source: Banque de France, *Bulletin Trimestriel,* Table 38, various issues
   Note: Net reserves were constructed to provide a measure of net foreign exchange
assets available for defense of the franc. The series was constructed as follows:
   Foreign assets   (line 1)
   − Gold   (1.25 ∗ line 1.1)
   + net position in EMCF   (line 4 −[liab] line 5)
(Lines 1, 1.1, and 4 are from the asset portion of the balance sheet. Foreign exchange assets (line 1) include gold, foreign currency, reserves, and ECUs. ECUs are held on a three-month swap basis, and are updated to represent 20 percent of gold and foreign currency holdings. Thus, the gold component of ECU holdings is subtracted to construct net reserves. The European Monetary Cooperation Fund (EMCF) provides a short-term borrowing facility for EMS members to maintain their currencies within the requisite bands.

4. Real Exchange Rates
   Intra-EMS real exchange rates were computed from monthly bilateral exchange
rates, with CPI deflators. The indices include six EMS members (Belgium, Denmark, France, Germany, Italy, and the Netherlands). The weights used are the weights of these six countries' currencies in the ECU.

5. French Interest Rates
   Offshore: one month Euro-franc deposit rate
   Onshore: one month French interbank rate
   Source: DRI

NOTES

1. Italy maintains bands of $\pm$ 6 percent.

2. Unlike the other currencies, the Italian lira's wide band has meant that exchange rate movements between realignments have had important influences on real exchange rate movements. Also, central parity adjustments have not been large enough to prevent the new bands from overlapping with the old. Thus, the EMS has served as a crawling peg without periodic discrete jumps for the lira.

3. This statement was made by Jacques Melitz in the discussion following the presentation of Giavazzi and Giovannini (1985).

4. Stiglitz and Weiss (1981, 1983).

5. Unfortunately, multi-country extensions of this problem are very complex, and to date, intractable.

6. The work extends results from Rogoff (1985b). Giavazzi and Pagano (1988) give additional references on monetary policy rules, inflationary finance, and the cooperative versus noncooperative solutions.

7. The remainder of the discussion focuses on real exchange rates among EMS members. An alternative formulation would assume that authorities are concerned about real effective exchange rates, including both members and nonmembers.

8. The discussion focuses on the relation between differential inflation rates and the rate of exchange rate adjustment. Thus, the base real exchange rate is selected so as to facilitate the comparison between the relevant slopes.

9. Most studies have rejected the hypothesis of risk neutrality because of the behavior of forecast errors—the k period ahead forward exchange rate minus the realized spot exchange rate in k periods. However, these studies maintain that there is no peso problem. They have not been successful in explaining the behavior of forecast errors using economic models of risk premia. The authors typically conclude that one explanation for their results is a peso problem with risk-neutral agents.

10. More generally, this possibility would encompass any change in the exchange regime, such as France pulling out of the EMS.

11. In a formal model one must take into account the constraints imposed by the floor and the ceiling of the bands. See Collins (1986).

12. These channels have been identified as important in the period preceding the 1980 devaluation of the Argentinian peso, for example.

13. The timing of EMS realignments might best be examined in a multilateral framework. Unfortunately, the many-country analogs of the models discussed here are extremely complex.

14. See Collins (1986) for a survey of this literature.

COMMENT BY

Francesco Giavazzi

The success of the EMS as a tool for macroecnomic convergence in Europe resulted automatically from the fact that the tool was ideally suited to the priorities of the day, which were shared by all participants. The common objective in the early 1980s was the reduction of inflation; the problem was that monetary authorities in many European

Table 6.3
Competitiveness Trends in the EMS* (Relative Unit Labor Costs, 1970–77 = 100)

Year	Germany	Italy	France	Belgium	Nether-lands	Denmark
1978	108.2	93.5	96.0	107.2	104.5	105.0
1981	98.3	90.0	95.7	86.4	88.1	85.2
1982	99.0	93.3	90.9	74.6	90.8	83.0
1986	102.6	102.0	88.6	76.4	85.0	93.1
Percentage change in competitiveness relative to Germany:						
1978 rel. to 1970–77		+14.7	+12.2	+ 1.0	+ 3.7	+ 3.2
1981 rel. to 1978		− 5.4	− 8.8	+11.7	+ 6.6	+ 7.2
1986 rel. to 1982		− 5.7	+ 6.1	+ 3.9	+10.4	−15.7

*Competitiveness is measured relative to 19 industrial partners, using an index that accounts for competition on third markets.

Source: Commission of the European Communities.

countries lacked credibility and were therefore stuck at high levels of inflation. The EMS provided an attractive way out of this deadlock. As clearly explained by Stanley Fischer (1987): "The EMS is currently an arrangement for France and Italy to purchase a commitment to low inflation by accepting German monetary policy."

The reason why the EMS brings potentially large credibility gains to central banks in inflation-prone countries, is that not only does it attach an extra penalty to inflation (in terms of competitiveness losses relative to Germany), but makes the public aware that the central bank is faced with such a penalty, and thus helps to overcome the inefficiency stemming from the public's mistrust of the authorities.

There is, however, an alternative view which suggests that the EMS has worked more like a system of pegged exchange rates and that realignments have been used to keep bilateral rates fluctuating around PPP. The problem with trying to test these two hypotheses is that they may have similar implications for the behavior of bilateral exchange rates. As explained in Giavazzi and Pagano (1988), EMS membership can yield credibility gains *even if* exchange rates fluctuate around PPP. For this to be the case, high inflation countries must be granted, at each realignment, a competitiveness "bonus" large enough to compensate for the competitiveness loss that they suffer between one realignment and the next. What is crucial is that this competitiveness "bonus" must be kept outside the control of the monetary authorities of these countries—otherwise all credibility gains vanish. Thus the only way to test the competitiveness versus the discipline view of the EMS is to ask whether the average inflation rate inside the system is lower than the inflation rate that would prevail if the exchange rate were allowed to float—an almost impossible task.

There is one case, however, in which the two models have different implications for the behavior of bilateral exchange rates. This happens when each realignment does not compensate high inflation countries for the entire loss of competitiveness suffered since the previous realignment. In this case the discipline model introduces a trend of real appreciation and is thus clearly distinguishable from the competitiveness model.[1]

What is the evidence? Since the price of credibility is a loss of competitiveness, the relative price indicator we should look at is the one that more closely mirrors a country's competitiveness. I propose to look at relative unit labor costs that more closely capture a country's underlying level of competitiveness. Table 6.3 shows relative unit labor costs for six EMS partners. It compares the level of competitiveness when the EMS started (1979) with the previous eight years, and looks at two subperiods within the system: 1979–81 and 1982–86. This is because realignments were much more frequent in the first two years of the system, relative to the subsequent period. The evidence is mixed and difficult to interpret. The behavior of unit labor costs clearly indicates that all countries, anticipating competitiveness losses relative to Germany, tried to weaken their currencies relative to the Deutschmark before entering the EMS. Inside the system the only clear cases of real appreciation relative to Germany are Italy (throughout the period) and Denmark (following the stabilization of 1982). The evidence for the other countries is mixed: France suffers a small average real appreciation (summing over the two sub-periods), while Belgium and the Netherlands tend to gain competitiveness relative to Germany.

Thus the evidence seems to be suggestive of the discipline argument only in the cases of Italy and Denmark—and the latter only after 1982. As discussed above, however, the evidence that France on average did not suffer a real appreciation relative to Germany *is not inconsistent* with the discipline argument. In the cases of Belgium and the Netherlands the evidence is in the opposite direction, suggesting that for these two countries the EMS was a vehicle of real depreciation relative to Germany.

NOTE

1. A problem with the case of trend real appreciation is that sooner or later the system will become unsustainable. Giavazzi and Pagano show, however, that even when it is unsustainable in the long run the EMS can provide (temporary) credibility gains.

7

Fiscal Policies in the EMS—A Strategic Analysis

Paul de Grauwe

Despite a significant success in stabilizing their exchange rates, EMS countries have experienced an unfavorable macroeconomic performance since 1979, compared with the rest of the industrialized world. This is illustrated in Table 7.1.

Comparing the growth rates of the GDP, one observes a strong deceleration within the EMS since 1979, which is absent from the group of non-EMS industrialized countries. As this latter group includes both European and non-European countries, we have also represented the growth rates of the European industrial countries outside the EMS. We find that the growth rate in this group of countries, although low, has not declined since 1979. Thus, the EMS stands out as a group of countries in the industrialized world that experienced a substantial decline in its growth rate during the 1980s.

A similar story can be told about the growth rate of investment. A substantial decline is observed since 1979 in the EMS. Outside the EMS we do not observe a similar deceleration of investment activity (although here also the growth rate is small in the non-EMS European countries).

As far as inflation is concerned, we observe a decline in both the EMS and the non-EMS industrial world. In 1985 inflation rates had dropped to less than half of the average during the previous 12 years. There is no evidence that the decline in the inflation rates proceeded more quickly inside than outside the EMS. Thus, the deceleration of the growth rates of output did not allow the EMS countries to achieve less inflation within the system as compared with the rest of the industrialized world.

Where does this deceleration of economic growth within the EMS come from? A first explanation can be called the "supply-side" hypothesis, and has become

Table 7.1
Macroeconomic Performance of EMS and Non-EMS Industrialized-Countries (yearly average)

Measure of performance	EMS	Non-EMS	European non-EMS
Growth of GDP			
1973–78	2.8	2.9	1.9
1979–85	1.7	2.7	1.8
Growth of investment			
1973–78	1.4	2.8	−0.2
1979–85	0.3	2.5	0.4
Inflation rate			
1973–78	9.1	9.6	12.5
1979–85	8.3	6.9	8.8
1985	4.6	3.8	5.9

Notes: (1) The *non-EMS countries* are the following: Austria, Norway, Sweden, Switzerland, Finland, Spain, Britain, Canada, the United States, and Japan. The *European non-EMS* consists of the same countries excluding the United States, Japan, and Canada. (2) The averages of each group of countries are obtained using GDP weights.

Source: OECD, *Main Economic Indicators.*

popular in explaining Europe's economic ills. It refers to phenomena like wage rigidity, lack of mobility in the labor market, and high and stifling taxes. The second (possibly complementary) explanation refers to the demand policies followed by European countries since the early 1980s (see for example, Layard et al. (1984) for a forceful statement of this hypothesis).

There can be little doubt that the supply-side hypothesis is important to explain the low-growth and high-unemployment situation now prevailing in Europe. What this hypothesis, however, does not explain very well is the more pronounced slowdown of economic growth in one part of Europe, the EMS countries, than in the other part of the continent since 1979. All the existing evidence about supply-side problems indicates that these problems are similar in most European countries, irrespective of their exchange rate regime.[1] It is, therefore, difficult to see how the existing supply-side rigidities alone can explain the slowdown of growth in the EMS. We must add the demand side to the analysis.

The most striking difference between the EMS and non-EMS countries during the 1979–85 period is the conduct of fiscal policies. This is made clear in Table 7.2. It shows the OECD measure of the cyclically corrected budgetary impulse (more precisely, the change in the structural government budget balance as a percentage of GDP) in the three groups of countries (EMS, non-EMS, non-EMS-Europe). Whereas prior to 1982 the EMS countries followed a relatively loose fiscal policy (which was mainly the result of French and Italian fiscal expansion in 1981), since 1982 the EMS countries have followed more deflationary fiscal policies than the other industrialized countries (including the other European countries).

The next question, then, is why the EMS countries tended to follow more restrictive fiscal policies (since 1982) than the rest of the industrialized world. Is it possible that the way the system operated induced the EMS member countries to react to the exogenous disturbances of the early 1980s with excessively deflationary fiscal policies? This is the question we want to analyze in this chapter. In order to do so a theoretical model is set up, and the strategic interaction between the countries is analyzed using a game-theoretic framework. We will then try to determine whether there exist institutional features that can produce such a deflationary economic policy cycle.

Table 7.2
Change in the Structural Budget Surplus, as a Percentage of GDP (yearly averages)

	EMS	Non-EMS	European Non-EMS
1979–81 :	0.10	0.34	0.74
1982–85 :	0.22	-0.48	-0.48

Note: + = contraction; − = expansion.

Sources: OECD, Economic Outlook, Dec. 1984 and May 1986. The figure for 1979 is based on unpublished information.

1. A MODEL OF STRATEGIC INTERACTIONS WITHIN THE EMS

In this section we develop a model describing the strategic interaction between two countries having a fixed exchange rate for their respective currencies, and being subjected to exogenous disturbances originating in the rest of the world.[2] Each country pursues a domestic target (say, output) and an external target, the balance of payments. They use as their instrument of economic policy the level of government spending. When changing this policy instrument each country affects not only its own output but also the output of the other country.

Let us represent this interdependent system by the following reduced-form equations:

$$y_1 = a_1 x_1 + b_1 x_2 + z_1 \tag{7.1}$$

$$y_2 = b_2 x_1 + a_2 x_2 + z_2 \tag{7.2}$$

where y_1 and y_2 are the output levels of countries 1 and 2; x_1 and x_2 are the instruments (government spending) used by countries 1 and 2; z_1 and z_2 are exogenous disturbances affecting the output levels of countries 1 and 2. These exogenous disturbances may originate from the rest of the world (for example, a worldwide recession, or changes in the exchange rates of countries 1 and 2 with the outside currency).

The signs of the reduced-form parameters depend on the underlying model structure. As will become clear from the analysis, they have an influence on the nature of the strategic interaction between the two countries. Let us first assume a Mundell-Fleming model underlying this reduced form. In addition, we assume there is relatively little capital mobility between countries 1 and 2. We make this assumption here because the empirical evidence indicates that *intra*-EMS capital mobility is relatively low (see Giavazzi and Pagano 1985). (This assumption will be relaxed in a later section to study the importance of capital movements for the strategic interaction between the two countries.) Given these assumptions, all the reduced-form coefficients in Equations 7.1 and 7.2 have a nonnegative sign— that is, increased government spending by country 1 raises domestic output and has a positive effect on country 2's output level. The latter follows from the assumption of low capital mobility, which ensures that the trade account transmission between countries 1 and 2 dominates the transmission through the capital account. As a result, more output in country 1 generates more output in country 2 due to the increased imports from country 1.

We now turn to the current account of the balance of payments. By definition we have:

$$B_1 = B_{12} + B_{13} \tag{7.3}$$

$$B_2 = B_{21} + B_{23} \tag{7.4}$$

where B_1 is the current account of country 1. It is the sum of the current accounts of country 1 with country 2 (B_{12}) and with the rest of the world (B_{13}). A similar definition holds for B_2. In addition, we must assume that

$$B_{12} = -B_{21} \tag{7.5}$$

that is, the surplus of country 1's current account with country 2 must, by definition, be equal to the deficit of country 2 with country 1.

Equations 7.3 to 7.5 are definitions. We have to add reduced-form equations describing how the current accounts are affected by the policy instruments. We then obtain

$$B_{12} (= -B_{21}) = -k_1 x_1 + k_2 x_2 \tag{7.6}$$

Equation 7.6 tells us that the current accounts of country 1 with country 2 are affected by the two policy instruments x_1 and x_2. The coefficients k_1 an k_2 are positive, that is, when country 1 expands government spending this leads to a deficit of the current account of country 1 with country 2. By the same token, an expansion of government spending in country 2 improves country 1's current account with country 2. As will be shown in a later section, the signs of k_1 and k_2 may change when we relax the assumption of capital immobility, thereby affecting the nature of the strategic interaction between the two countries.

Closing the list of reduced-form equations we have two equations describing the current accounts of countries 1 and 2 with the rest of the world:

$$B_{13} = -f_1 x_1 + c_1 z_3 \tag{7.7}$$

$$B_{23} = -f_2 x_2 + c_2 z_3 \tag{7.8}$$

The current account of country 1 with the rest of the world (B_{13}) is determined by country 1's policy instrument x_1, and by exogenous disturbances originating in the rest of the world (z_3). In addition, $f_1 > 0$, that is, an increase in government spending in country 1 increases the current account deficit of that country with the rest of the world. A similar reasoning holds for country 2.

We can now substitute Equation 7.6 and 7.7 into Equation 7.4, and 7.6 and 7.8 into 7.5, to obtain the reduced-form equations of the total current account of countries 1 and 2:

$$B_1 = -h_1 x_1 + k_2 x_2 + c_1 z_3 \tag{7.9}$$

$$B_2 = k_1 x_1 - h_2 x_2 + c_2 z_3 \tag{7.10}$$

where $h_1 = k_1 + f_1$ and $h_2 = k_2 + f_2$. It will be assumed that $h_1 > k_2$ and $h_2 > k_1$, that is, the current account of each country is more affected by its own instrument than by the instrument of the other country.

The next step in the analysis is to introduce the objective function of the authorities of the two countries. As is usual in this kind of analysis, we assume that the authorities only care about their own domestic variables (domestic output and current account). In other words, we do not assume altruistic behavior. The point of the analysis is to find out under what conditions authorities who follow purely nationalistic objectives may have an incentive to cooperate.

We will assume that each government minimizes a loss function, which is specified as follows:

$$L_1 = (y_1 - y_1{}^*)^2 + \theta_1(B_1 - B_1{}^*)^2 \tag{7.11}$$

$$L_2 = (y_2 - y_2{}^*)^2 + \theta_2(B_2 - B_2{}^*)^2 \tag{7.12}$$

that is, the authorities of country 1 set targets for output $(y_1{}^*)$ and for the current account $(B_1{}^*)$, and use their instrument x_1 to steer y_1 and B_1 as close as possible to these targets, because a deviation from the targets reduces welfare. The same is true for country 2. The weight each country attaches to the current account target is represented by θ_1 and θ_2.[3]

Substituting y_1 and y_2 from Equations 7.1 and 7.2, and B_1 and B_2 from Equations 7.9 and 7.10 yields the following expression:

$$\begin{aligned} \min L_1 = {} & (a_1 x_1 + b_1 x_2 + z_1 - y_1{}^*)^2 \\ & + \theta_1(-h_1 x_1 + k_2 x_2 + c_1 z_3 - B_1{}^*)^2 \end{aligned} \tag{7.13}$$

and

$$\begin{aligned} \min L_2 = {} & (a_2 x_2 + b_2 x_1 + z_2 - y_2{}^*)^2 \\ & + \theta_2(-h_2 x_2 + k_1 x_1 + c_2 z_3 - B_2{}^*)^2 \end{aligned} \tag{7.14}$$

Differentiating Equation 7.13 with respect to x_1 and Equation 7.14 with respect to x_2 and equating to zero yields the first-order condition for an optimum in both countries:

$$\begin{aligned} & [(a_1)^2 + \theta_1(h_1)^2]x_1 + (a_1 b_1 - \theta_1 h_1 k_2)x_2 \\ & + a_1(z_1 - y_1{}^*) - \theta_1 h_1(c_1 z_3 - B_1{}^*) = 0 \end{aligned} \tag{7.15}$$

and

$$\begin{aligned} & [(a_2)^2 + \theta_2(h_2)^2]x_2 + (a_2 b_2 - \theta_2 h_2 k_1)x_1 \\ & + a_2(z_2 - y_2{}^*) - \theta_2 h_2(c_2 z_3 - B_2{}^*) = 0 \end{aligned} \tag{7.16}$$

These two equations allow us to derive reaction functions of the two authorities. Rewrite Equations 7.15 and 7.16 as follows:

$$x_1 = \alpha_1 x_2 + \alpha_2(y_1{}^* - z_1) + \alpha_3(c_1 z_3 - B_1{}^*) \tag{7.17}$$

and

$$x_2 = \beta_1 x_1 + \beta_2(y_2{}^* - z_2) + \beta_3(c_2 z_3 - B_2{}^*) \tag{7.18}$$

where

$$\alpha_1 = -\frac{(a_1 b_1 - \theta_1 h_1 k_2)}{(a_1)^2 + \theta_1 (h_1)^2}$$

$$\beta_1 = -\frac{(a_2 b_2 - \theta_2 h_2 k_1)}{(a_2)^2 + \theta_2 (h_2)^2}$$

$$\alpha_2 = \frac{a_1}{(a_1)^2 + \theta_1 (h_1)^2}$$

$$\beta_2 = \frac{a_2}{(a_2)^2 + \theta_2 (h_2)^2}$$

$$\alpha_3 = \frac{\theta_1 h_1}{(a_1)^2 + \theta_1 (h_1)^2}$$

$$\beta_3 = \frac{\theta_2 h_2}{(a_2)^2 + \theta_2 (h_2)^2}$$

Equations 7.17 and 7.18 determine the optimal values of country 1's and country 2's instruments x_1 and x_2 for a given value of the other country's instrument, and for given values of the output targets and the other exogenous variables.

The reaction functions 7.17 and 7.18 are represented in Figure 7.1. In drawing these reaction functions, we have assumed that θ_1 and θ_2 are large enough so as to make the reaction functions positively sloped. This means that the authorities are assumed to care about their external targets. If they do not, θ_1 and θ_2 will be small, so that the reaction functions become negatively sloped. We will return to this case and analyze its implications in a later section.

The reaction functions in Figure 7.1 are drawn under the additional assumptions that are exogenous disturbances are zero ($z_1 = z_2 = z_3 = 0$), and that the authorities aim at an equilibrium of their current accounts ($B_1^* = 0$ and $B_2^* = 0$). The reaction function of country 1 is represented by the line R_1. It intersects the x-axis at the point $\alpha_2 y_1^*$. The reaction function of country 2 is represented by the line R_2, intersecting the y-axis of $\beta_2 y_2^*$.

The Nash (non-cooperative) equilibrium is obtained in point N, where the two reaction functions intersect.[4] We can now compare this equilibrium with the Pareto (cooperative) solution and the Stackelberg (leadership) solution.

The Pareto optimal points are the collection of points on the $B_1 B_2$ line. They are obtained by taking the points of tangency of the two families of indifference curves around the "Bliss points" B_1 and B_2. The latter two points represent the situations in which country 1 and country 2, respectively, achieve their two targets. Thus, in point B_1 the authorities of country 1 achieve the highest possible

Figure 7.1
Cooperative and Non-Cooperative Solutions

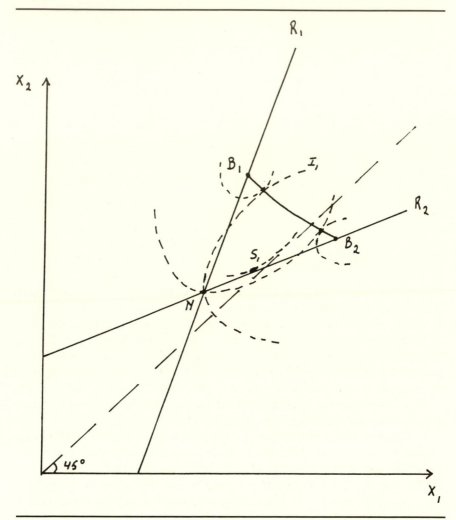

satisfaction. In B_2 country 2 achieves this "optimum optimorum." One obtains
the algebraic expression of the Bliss point of country 1 by setting $y_1 = y_1^*$ in
Equation 7.1 and $B_1 = B_1^*$ in Equation 7.9, and solving this two-equation
system for x_1 and x_2. This yields

$$x_1 = \frac{1}{a_1k_2 + b_1h_1}[k_2(y_1^* - z_1) + b_1(c_1z_3 - B_1^*)] \qquad (7.19)$$

$$x_2 = \frac{1}{a_1 k_2 + b_1 h_1}[h_1(y_1^* - z_1) - a_1(c_1 z_3 - B_1^*)] \tag{7.20}$$

Following a similar procedure one obtains the Bliss point of country 2:

$$x_2 = \frac{1}{a_2 k_1 + b_2 h_2}[k_1(y_2^* - z_2) + b_2(c_2 z_3 - B_2^*)] \tag{7.21}$$

$$x_1 = \frac{1}{a_2 k_1 + b_2 h_2}[h_2(y_2^* - z_2) - a_2(c_2 z_3 - B_2^*)] \tag{7.22}$$

It can easily be established that the Bliss point of country 1 lies above the 45° line, and the Bliss point of country 2 below the 45° line.[5] In Figure 7.1 we have drawn the two Bliss points in such a way that they are located above the Nash equilibrium point, so that it can be said that the Nash equilibrium will show a deflationary bias compared with the superior cooperative solutions on the $B_1 B_2$ contract curve. This result, however, is not necessary. It can easily be seen from Figure 7.1 that the Bliss point of country 1 can also be located to the left of the Nash equilibrium points, depending on how high the authorities of that country set their income target.

The important point to remember at this stage is that the Nash equilibrium is inferior in terms of welfare to the Pareto solutions.[6] It should be clear that these Pareto points can only be attained if the authorities agree to cooperate. Such an agreement, in turn, can come about only if a consensus exists on how the benefits of the cooperation are to be divided. We will return to this issue when we analyze the question whether the incentives to cooperate are strong enough to lead us to Pareto optimal points.

It can also be useful to interpret the Bliss points as imperialistic solutions. Suppose country 1 is an imperialistic nation in that it can impose its view on the other country, for example, by threat of an invasion or other painful experiences for country 2. Then B_1, which is the point of highest satisfaction of country 1, will be the solution of this game. (If country 2 is the imperialistic nation, B_2 will be the solution.) The Pareto points can then also be interpreted as compromise points between two antagonistic equilibria. This also makes clear that any Pareto solution will involve some "horse trading."

Finally it should be mentioned that the Nash solution can make *both* countries worse off compared with the imperialistic solutions. For example, country 2 can be better off as a victim of the imperialistic behavior of country 1 than as an independent Nash player. This will be the case if the indifference curve I_2 "embraces" the point B_1 (not shown in Figure 7.1).

The third equilibrium concept we will use here is the Stackelberg-leadership solution. If country 1 acts as a leader, and country 2 as a follower, country 1 will select the point on country 2's reaction function that maximizes its own utility.

Country 1 does this because it knows that country 2, as a follower, will always select a point on its reaction function (R_2). We can then find this Stackelberg equilibrium point in Figure 7.1 as point S_1. In S_1, country 1 achieves the highest possible indifference curve on country 2's reaction function, R_2.

The questions we will want to analyze about the characteristics of the Stackelberg solution are, first, how does it compare with the other solutions (Nash and Pareto)? Second, what are the incentives for country 1 (or possibly country 2) to act as a leader? The corollary of this question then is whether there is an incentive for country 2 to act as a follower when country 1 wishes to be a leader. As will be seen, it cannot be excluded that both countries would prefer to be leaders, or that both would like to be followers.

2. EXOGENOUS DISTURBANCES

In this section we analyze the effect of exogenous disturbances on the different equilibria. We will analyze changes in z_3, caused by disturbances originating in the rest of the world and which affect the balance of payments of the two countries. Assume this is a disturbance that deteriorates the current account of the two countries.

The effects are shown in Figure 7.2. The reaction functions of the two countries now move towards the origin. This can be seen from Equations 7.17 and 7.18. As z_3 is negative, x_1 and x_2 decline. Thus, the reaction of both countries to this exogenous disturbance is to reduce government spending.

The new Nash equilibrium point is given by N'. It is interesting to note that in N' both authorities will have reduced government spending even further, compared with their initial reaction, represented by the movement from N to I_1 for country 1 and from N to I_2 for country 2.

How does the Nash equilibrium point compare with the Pareto equilibrium points? In order to answer this question we must find out how the two Bliss points are affected. It can be shown (see Equations 7.19 and 7.20) that the Bliss point of country 1 moves in the northwest direction from B_1 to B_1'. That is, in order to attain its "optimum optimorum," country 1 wants the other country to expand, whereas it reduces its own spending. Thus if country 1 could impose its own view it would force the other country to expand. A similar reasoning leads to the conclusion that the Bliss point of country 2 has moved in the southeastern direction from B_2 to B_2'.

It is interesting to note that as a result of the exogenous disturbance, the two Bliss points move farther apart. This also means that the conflict of interest of the two partners has increased. If both were to act as imperialistic nations, each trying to impose its own interest on the other, the exogenous shock would have increased their antagonism. The interesting aspect of this increased antagonism is, as we will show immediately, the basis for larger benefits of a cooperative attitude.

It can now be established easily that the uncooperative Nash solution exhibits a

Figure 7.2
The Case of Exogenous Disturbances

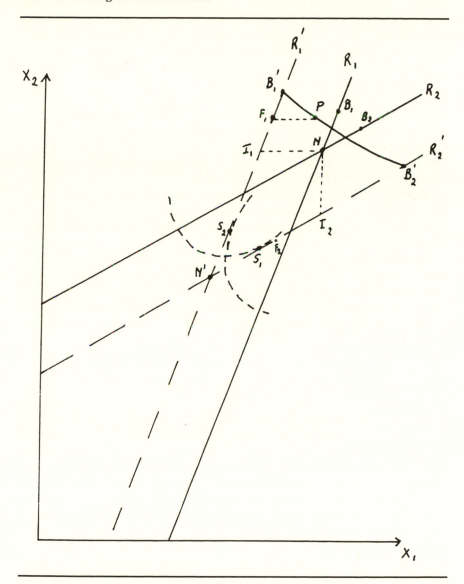

deflationary bias compared with the Pareto points. That is, the two countries will contract their spending more than they would do if they sought a cooperative response to the exogenous disturbance. They are also less well off in Nash than in the Pareto solutions.

How does the Nash solution compare with the leadership solution? The answer is also found in Figure 7.2. If country 1 acts as a leader (and country 2 as a follower) the equilibrium is given by point S_1. If the roles are reversed we obtain the equilibrium S_2. Both these equilibrium points are superior for both countries (thus also for the follower) to the non-cooperative Nash solution, and imply a less deflationary response to the exogenous disturbance.

3. INCENTIVES FOR COOPERATION

The question now becomes whether there are incentives for the two countries to move away from the non-cooperative solution. Let us analyze the incentives for cooperation first. Since both countries can gain from cooperation it seems obvious that the incentives to do so are strong. In addition, after the exogenous disturbance, the potential gains from cooperation have increased. This can be seen from the fact that the distance between the Nash point and the contract curve has increased, allowing for more beneficial trades to take place. Thus, the incentives for cooperation are present and one should observe these two countries engaging in cooperation.

Despite this potential gain from cooperation one often observes that countries do not cooperate. There are many reasons for this; here we concentrate on just a few of these. One problem that may be relevant for our discussion of the EMS has to do with difficulties of monitoring the policies of the partner once an agreement on a cooperative action has been reached.

Suppose countries 1 and 2 agree to choose point P on the contract curve and to set their fiscal policies accordingly. It is clear, however, that once this decision has been made there is an incentive for each country to cheat on the agreement, if it feels that it will be difficult for the other country to monitor its action. Country 1, for example, can by moving to point F_1 and thus by reducing its spending below the agreed level increase its welfare compared with the cooperative agreement. (Note that if there are no monitoring problems, there will be no incentive to cheat. Country 1 then realizes that its move to point F_1 will be countered immediately by country 2 by a move to F_2, and so on, leading ultimately to the Nash point. In this perfect information environment, country 1 will decide wisely to stick to the agreed solution on the contract curve.)

It is important to realize here that the two countries are in a "prisoner's dilemma" situation. We know from game theory that in such situations, cooperation will not be forthcoming if the game is played only once. If the players, however, meet repeatedly and if the rate at which they discount the future payoffs is high enough, cooperative strategies are more likely to occur (see Axelrod 1984). A major problem with fiscal policies is that the national players do not meet frequently. Decisions in fiscal policy are the result of a relatively slow democratic process, made only once a year. A typical government stays in power for only a few years, and elections are not synchronized internationally. The result is that the same national fiscal players may meet only once or twice—in any case, too infrequently to bring about cooperative strategies.

The contrast with monetary policies is important. Most decisions in monetary policy are made outside the democratic process, by agents who stay in power longer than a typical government. As a result, the same national players are likely to meet much more often in the international arena than the fiscal policy makers. This frequent international encounter of monetary authorities is conducive to cooperative strategies, and may explain why monetary cooperation within the EMS has had more success than fiscal policy cooperation.

A second problem has to do with uncertainty about the underlying model. This uncertainty may lead to a situation where countries use different models of the world. One country, for example, may use a monetarist model, the other a Keynesian model. When these national players then meet they will not easily be induced to cooperate, because cooperation may in fact not improve welfare if the true model is different from the ones used by the two players (see Frankel 1986).

Finally, the game situation analyzed here assumes that there is uniformity of preferences of the national authorities. In fact, it is more likely that game situations are encountered at different levels. Different national players (e.g., the government, trade unions, and other pressure groups) have conflicting interests. These conflicting national preferences are also likely to appear when games are played at the international level. In such a situation it is not clear that international cooperative strategies are welfare improving (see Rogoff 1985 and Vaubel 1985).[7]

We conclude that although the incentives to cooperate and thereby to avoid the deflationary bias of an uncoordinated response to the exogenous disturbance are powerful, there are several problems that make it difficult for the countries to cooperate. Some of these problems have to do with institutional features that give a low incentive to international cooperation. These problems may be particularly important in the conduct of fiscal policies, and may explain why the EMS countries have been unable to react in a cooperative way to the oil shock of the early 1980s and the worldwide recession that caused their balance of payments to deteriorate. Other problems, however, relate to uncertainty about the gains that can be expected from cooperation.

4. INCENTIVES FOR LEADERSHIP

In the absence of cooperation, do there exist incentives for countries to take a leadership (or a "followership") attitude?

One of the striking conclusions one can draw from a comparison of the two Stackelberg points S_1 and S_2 is that country 1 is better off as a follower than as a leader, and similarly that country 2 is better off as a follower than as a leader. This can be seen as follows. In S_2 (country 2 is leader and country 1 follower) country 1 attains a higher indifference curve than in S_1 (country 1 is leader and country 2 follower). The same is true when we compare S_1 and S_2 from the point of view of the welfare of country 2. Thus, following the exogenous shock, both countries have an incentive to act as followers. It follows that a leadership solution will not come about automatically. In fact, the incentive structure where-by each country prefers to be a follower makes it likely that the Nash solution will be arrived at.

All this leads to a rather dismal conclusion. The two countries have an incen-tive to cooperate, and thereby to avoid excessive deflationary policies following the exogenous deterioration of their balance of payments. However, the institu-tional environment in which fiscal policies are conducted also gives them incen-tives to cheat on any cooperative solution. As a result, cooperation may not come about. In addition, countries have an incentive to act as followers, thereby increasing the likelihood that the Nash solution will be the outcome of the game.

How can we improve on this rather uncomfortable strategic setup of the two countries? One possibility is to allow policy preferences to change. This is done in the next section.

5. CHANGING POLICY PREFERENCES

How can we change the policy environment so that the strategic interactions lead to more favorable equilibria than Nash? Here we focus on changes in preferences that make the leadership solution more likely to emerge.

Suppose country 1 decides to attach less importance to its external objective. This means that θ_1 (the weight given to the balance of payments objective in country 1's loss function) declines. Let us take an extreme situation and assume that $\theta_1 = 0$, that country 1 takes an attitude of "benign neglect" towards its balance of payments situation.

The implications for the equilibrium now are as follows (see Figure 7.3). This reaction function of country 1 is now a negatively sloped line (see Equation 7.17 where $\theta_1 = 0$). In addition, the reaction function now also defines the Bliss points of country 1.[8] This means that for any given policy of country 2, country 1 can find a value of its instrument x_1 that allows it to exactly achieve its unique objective for domestic output. As before, the Bliss point of country 2 is below the 45° line.

The contract curve is now represented by NB_2. The Nash equilibrium point is N. It is clear from this setup that cooperation will not come about. Country 1 has no incentive whatsoever to cooperate. It is perfectly happy with the Nash solution (or with any point on its reaction function). It will certainly not want to move up on the contract curve. Country 2, however, now has a strong incentive to be a leader. That is, it will select a point on the reaction function of country 1 that brings it as close as possible (in welfare terms) to its Bliss point B_2. This is represented in point S_2. Thus, in this case the leadership solution is a likely outcome.

It can now be shown that a negative balance of payments shock will not lead to a deflationary bias. This shock shifts country 2's reaction function downward. The reaction function of country 1, however, is unaffected by this disturbance ($\alpha_3 = 0$ in Equation 7.17). The new Stackelberg solution moves from S_2 to S_2' in

Figure 7.3
The Case of Benign Neglect

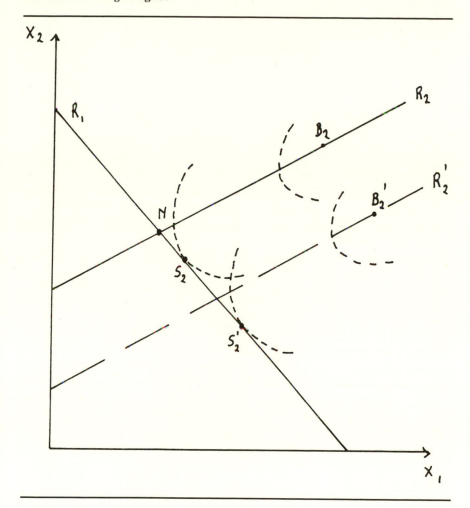

Figure 7.3. As a result, country 1 follows an expansionary, and country 2 a contractionary policy. Thus, whereas country 2 reacts by contracting its fiscal policy, country 2, which is only concerned with domestic output, reacts to this deflationary policy by expanding fiscal policy.

To conclude this discussion, it is useful to stress that the leadership solution does not imply that country 2 imposes its view on the other country. This would be characteristic of the imperialistic solution. Leadership here only implies that country 2 takes a more enlightened view of what its own interest is than in the Nash game.

The previous analysis also makes clear that there may not always be incentives for countries to behave in this enlightened way. We have constructed a case in which such enlightened behavior may emerge, that is, when one country reduces the weight it attaches to its external target to zero.[9] This policy of benign neglect toward the balance of payments was typical for the U.S. attitude and provided a pillar for the Bretton Woods system. It is absent in the present EMS arrangement, in which countries seem to attach a large weight to their external target.

6. CAPITAL MOBILITY AND STRATEGIC BEHAVIOR

The previous analysis assumed that capital mobility is small enough to guarantee a positive transmission of budgetary shocks from one country to the other. Let us now assume that capital is moving freely between countries 1 and 2. This assumption affects the structure of the model in the following way. In Equations 7.1 and 7.2 the coefficients b_1 and b_2 now have an ambiguous sign. That is, a budgetary expansion from country 1 to country 2 (and from country 2 to country 1) can positively or negatively affect output in country 2. This standard result in a Mundell-Fleming two-country model[10] can be explained as follows. A fiscal expansion in country 1 now has two opposing effects on country 2's output. The first one increases aggregate demand in country 2 through the trade account. More precisely, as imports of country 1 increase, the demand for country 2's goods and services goes up. Thus, the fiscal expansion of country 1 shifts the *IS*-curve of country 2. The second effect, through the capital account, has negative implications for aggregate demand in country 2. By increasing spending, country 1 also raises its interest rate, thereby attracting capital from country 2. This leads to a leftward movement of the *LM*-curve in country 2, so that aggregate demand is negatively affected. As a result of these opposing shifts of the *IS*- and *LM*-curves in country 2, one cannot say how the output level of country 2 will change following the fiscal expansion of country 1.

In what follows we will set $b_1 < 0$ and $b_2 < 0$. (With positive coefficients we have the same structure as in the previous sections, and the analysis made there applies.)

The reaction curves are described by the same equations (7.17 and 7.18). The coefficients α_1 and β_1 are now unambiguously positive, and are independent of the weights given to the external objectives (θ_1 and θ_2). This means that most of the analysis of the previous sections applies also to the case of high capital mobility. The difference has to do with the role of policy preferences toward the external objective. Suppose, as in the previous section, that country 1 follows a policy of benign neglect toward its balance of payments. The solution of the model is represented in Figure 7.4. Country 1's reaction function is R_1 and coincides with that country's Bliss points. Country 2's reaction function is R_2; its Bliss point is B_2. Country 2 will have a strong incentive to be a "leader." It will select the point S_2 on country 1's reaction function.

A negative current account shock shifts R_2 downward and keeps R_1 un-

Figure 7.4
The Case of High Capital Mobility

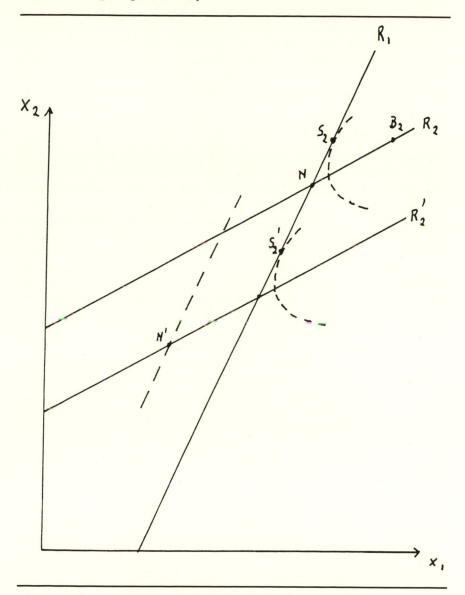

changed. The new Stackelberg solution is S_2'. We conclude that both countries will react with deflationary fiscal policies. This result has to do with the fact that when country 2 follows a contractionary policy, this leads to an expansion of output in country 1, which will then react with deflationary fiscal policies.

It can easily be shown that the deflationary spiral we obtain here will be less pronounced than in the case where country 1 gives a high weight to its external target. In that case the reaction curve of country 1 (R_1) shifts to the left (see Figure 7.4). Since the Nash solution is likely to prevail in that case, the equilibrium point will move from N to N'. Thus, we conclude that although we cannot exclude a deflationary response to a negative current account shock, the size of the deflation will be less pronounced if one country follows a policy of benign neglect toward its balance of payments.

7. SYMMETRY OF SOLUTIONS

In the previous sections we have shown that an exogenous deterioration of the balance of payments leads two countries that do not coordinate their policies to take an excessively deflationary posture. This may explain the deflationary bias that the EMS has experienced in the first half of the 1980s.

It can also easily be demonstrated that if the exogenous disturbance changes sign (i.e., if we have an exogenous improvement in the balances of payments), everything we said about excessive deflation and expansion has to be turned around. Such an exogenous shock produces too much fiscal expansion when countries choose not to coordinate their policies. The intuitive reason for this result is as follows. As the current account improves (and since we assume that each country has a fixed current account target), country 1 prefers the other country to reduce its spending so that country 1 can reduce the surplus on its current account. Thus, a positive balance of payments disturbance leads country 1 to attach a positive externality to a contraction by the other country. In an uncoordinated (competitive) policy environment this will lead to too little contraction.[11] The reader can easily check these results.

8. CONCLUSION

It is often said that more coordination of policies is the answer to the present problems concerning economic policy making in Europe. As the analysis of this chapter (and of other papers analyzing this problem) confirms, a coordinated response to exogenous disturbances generally improves welfare. This conclusion, however, is not very helpful. We have to ask the question whether the EMS provides the right incentives to coordinate policies. One of the conclusions of the theoretical analysis is that in the field of fiscal policies, the EMS countries have little incentive to cooperate.

As an alternative to cooperation, we considered leadership solutions. We found that in the present EMS arrangement, there are few incentives for one country to take a leadership position. Such an arrangement would generally be welfare improving. We showed that such an enlightened policy stance is more likely to emerge if a country is willing to take a more "benign neglect" attitude toward its balance of payments. It is probably no exaggeration to state that most countries have exhibited an obsessive attitude toward their current accounts, thereby making such an enlightened policy response an unlikely event.

This conclusion obviously leads to a dilemma. The strong weight attached by national authorities to external equilibria also explains the relative success in stabilizing intra-EMS exchange rates. At the same time this success may be responsible for the excessive deflationary policy responses following the exogenous shocks of the early 1980s. This dilemma can be resolved by recognizing that in order for exchange rate stability to be maintained, only $n - 1$ countries of the system need to have explicit balance of payments targets. An attempt by all n countries to have explicit balance of payments targets will generally not bring more exchange rate stability. It will, however, generally lead to strategic interactions that reduce the quality of economic policy making. This well-known $n - 1$ problem does not seem to have been given due consideration within the system, and may help to explain the dismal macroeconomic performance of the EMS countries since 1979.

The analysis of this chapter has many limitations. We have indicated that the institutional arrangements of the EMS make it possible that countries have reacted in an excessively deflationary manner to the large exogenous balance of payments shocks of the early 1980s. However, we have not analyzed what the quantitative importance is of this effect. Further research will be necessary to determine whether this is a theoretical effect without much quantitative importance or is a phenomenon to be reckoned with.

Another shortcoming of the chapter is that we have concentrated our attention on fiscal policies, to the exclusion of monetary policies. In addition, we have also disregarded policies regarding inflation. In further research on strategic economic interaction within the EMS, these policies should be integrated in the analysis.

NOTES

1. For a survey of empirical work on rigidities of all kinds, see Klau and Mittelstadt (1985).

2. There is now a vast literature using game-theoretic concepts to policy interactions between countries. See Hamada (1974, 1979) and Sachs (1983). Recent models of strategic interactions within the EMS are Oudiz (1985) and Melitz (1985). They emphasize the interactions of monetary policies. This approach has been criticized by Vaubel (1985). In the last section we relate some of our results to this criticism.

3. Note that the weight given to the output target has been normalized to one.

4. The exact algebraic solution is obtained by solving Equations 7.17 and 7.18 for x_1 and x_2.

5. When we set all exogenous disturbances and the balance of payments target equal to zero we find from Equations 7.19 and 7.20 that in B_1, $x_1 < x_2$. Similarly, in B_2 we have $x_1 > x_2$.

6. Note that all the points on the B_1B_2 line (the contract curve) are necessarily superior to the Nash point. It cannot be excluded that some points on the contract curve

close to the Bliss points are located on a lower indifference curve of one of the countries than in N.

7. Putnam and Henning (1986) give a fascinating account of the process that led to the cooperative agreement of the Bonn Summit 1978. It appears that the players at the summit used the agreement to strengthen their hand in domestic policy conflicts.

8. Using Equation 7.17 and setting $0_1 = 0$, we find country 1's reaction function:

$$x_1 = \frac{b_1}{a_1}x_2 + \frac{1}{a_1}(y_1{}^* - z_1)$$

Using Equation 7.1 and setting $y_1 = y_1{}^*$ yields exactly the same expression. Thus, the reaction function defines all the Bliss points of country 1.

9. See Vaubel (1985) on this issue. Vaubel argues that it is the attempt by national authorities to control an external objective (the balance of payments or the exchange rate) that is responsible for the suboptimality of a non-cooperative solution. The result obtained here is in the same vein. When the authorities reduce the weight given to the external target, the quality of policy making can be improved without explicit cooperative agreements.

10. See Dornbusch (1983) for a clear account of the transmission process in a two-country framework.

11. Note that this result depends on the assumption of a symmetrical loss function. That is, countries 1 and 2 attach the same loss in utility to a positive or a negative deviation from the balance of payments target. If, however, the authorities experience a greater utility loss from a negative than from a positive deviation from the balance of payments target, then the Nash equilibrium point is less likely to exhibit excessive expansion. Thus, if countries have "mercantilistic" preference functions, alternating positive and negative balance of payments disturbances will lead on average to excessive deflationary policies in a non-cooperative policy environment.

COMMENT BY

Alexander Swoboda

Relatively poor growth performance over 1979–85 of a number of European countries, many of them members of the EMS, as it turns out, is still a puzzle in search of an explanation. Paul de Grauwe adds one such explanation to the usual list: strategic behavior within the existing EMS institutional framework may have led to excessively deflationary fiscal policies in response to the external shocks of the early 1980s.

There are three main strands to de Grauwe's argument. First, the poor growth performance of the EMS countries over the 1979–85 period, as compared with 1973–78 and to non-EMS countries, is noted, as is the relatively restrictive turn in EMS fiscal policies after 1982. Second, a model of strategic interaction is developed which shows that given certain assumptions, fiscal policies may turn excessively deflationary (as compared with either a cooperative or leadership solution) within a fixed-rate area when an external shock produces a payment deficit. The main assumptions that are required are that the authorities of the model's two countries have two instruments (their respective fiscal policies) to achieve four targets (their respective internal and external balances) and weigh external balance targets relatively heavily in their loss functions. Third, de Grauwe examines the incentives required for the cooperative or leadership solution rather than the Nash competitive solution to emerge, and finds that they are unlikely to be present in the EMS context.

I will comment on these three parts of de Grauwe's argument in turn. I begin by asking whether strategic behavior of fiscal policies provides a convincing explanation of the low-growth puzzle and answer in the negative. I then comment briefly on de Grauwe's admirably clear model and conclude with a few remarks on the appropriateness of standard strategic behavior models for the analysis of policy coordination issues.

THE LOW-GROWTH PUZZLE

The double hypothesis that de Grauwe puts forward in the introductory part of Chapter 7 is that lower growth in the EMS over the 1979–85 period was due, at least in significant part, to the adoption of excessively restrictive fiscal policies and that, in turn, this restrictiveness was due to the way in which the EMS reacts to outside shocks. Both hypotheses seem questionable to me.

In the first place, as de Grauwe's own figures tend to show, fiscal policy in the EMS became more restrictive after 1982, after having been less so for the 1979–81 period, at least in comparison with the non-EMS or European non-EMS groups of countries. Second, one would want to have a much more detailed breakdown of the behavior of fiscal policy in individual countries, both within and outside the EMS group, to check on the hypothesis that the changes in averages for groups represent a general trend toward restrictiveness in all EMS countries (and vice-versa abroad), an observation that is crucial to the second hypothesis. Here the idiosyncratic behavior of France, for example, for at least part of the period comes to mind. Third, while the second oil price increase may indeed have represented a negative external shock for most EMS countries, the subsequent U.S. budget deficit shock represented a positive and not negative external shock, which would tend to improve the current account of EMS countries. Hence the strategic reaction should have been excessive fiscal laxity rather than restrictiveness. That such laxity did not occur is probably due to the fact that the motivation behind increased fiscal rigor in European countries in the 1980s was quite different from that suggested by de Grauwe, namely, it was partly an attempt to reduce the importance of the public sector and to limit the growth of the public debt-to-GNP ratio.

In addition, it is important to note that de Grauwe's model has countries worrying about their current account with the rest of the world (both EMS and outside countries) rather than their official settlements balance within the "fixed"-rate EMS area, and that fiscal policy is the instrument they use to approach that current account target. In fact, the logic of an EMS-type system should have them assigning monetary and not fiscal policy to fix intra-area exchange rates or, if you prefer, to maintain overall payments balance within the area at existing parities.

In brief, strategic behavior of the type outlined in de Grauwe's model does not seem to offer an adequate explanation either for the behavior of fiscal policy within the EMS or for the area's low-growth performance.

DE GRAUWE'S MODEL

My previous remarks do not detract from the interest or value of de Grauwe's model. It is carefully set up, admirably transparent, and well designed to bring out a number of important issues in the analysis of policy coordination.

As in all models of its ilk, the source of policy conflict is a shortage of instruments relative to targets. The two fiscal instruments are used to pursue four targets—two internal and two external balances. In the discussion and graphical presentation of the model, de Grauwe simplifies the problem by assuming that both countries aim at current account equilibrium. He thus can avoid the additional complication of the two countries having inconsistent goals (although the rest of the world would take up the slack anyway, as it were). There are three exogenous disturbances, only one of which plays an important role in the discussion. This is z_3, an exogenous disturbance that originates in the rest of the world and affects both countries' current accounts in the same direction. The reduced forms of the model are compatible with each country having a standard Mundell-Fleming structure, first under the assumption of low, then of high, capital mobility. Preferences are assumed to be such that the Nash equilibrium shows a deflationary bias, as compared with a cooperative solution.

Standard conclusions follow. First, the cooperative solution is preferable to the Cournot-Nash competitive solution for both countries. The reason is simple. Take a point on the contract curve; then either country can do better by moving to its reaction function, assuming the other will not change its fiscal policy. As both behave in that way, both end up worse off. Second, it is shown that the Stackelberg-leadership solution is superior to the Nash outcome, again a familiar result. Finally, de Grauwe shows that if there is a negative external shock that affects both countries, the deflationary bias increases and the cost of the Nash solution increases for both countries, which creates "the basis for larger benefits of a cooperative attitude," including the leadership solution as one special case of such an attitude.

De Grauwe uses these results to ask a number of interesting questions. First, why is it that despite the gains from cooperation countries do not cooperate? Among the possible reasons de Grauwe mentions problems of monitoring and the "non-repetitive" nature of the fiscal policy game, uncertainty about the underlying model, and conflicts within individual countries. But then, and second, should there not be incentives for one country to assume a leadership role? The problem is that, given the assumed strong bias toward external balance in the loss functions, an exogenous external shock leads both countries to prefer to be the follower rather than the leader. One solution would be, in de Grauwe's terminology, to change the policy preferences of the two countries. Assuming one country to take a benign neglect attitude toward its current account, the other now has a clear incentive to become a leader, yielding a Stackelberg solution that is superior to the Nash equilibrium. Note that this conclusion stems from the removal of one target from the loss functions, reducing the problem from one of four targets and two instruments to one of three targets and two instruments. The whole problem would disappear if both countries took a benign neglect attitude, since they could then reach their two internal targets with their two fiscal instruments.

The model, then, is an interesting and fruitful one. Still, I would like to raise two questions: First, how adequate is the model to analyze internal–external balance questions in a monetary union. Second (and I will take this up in the final section of these comments), how relevant are models of strategic behavior to the design of improved policy coordination?

As far as analyzing cooperation and conflict in an EMS-type arrangement is concerned, the model presented by de Grauwe has, as he recognizes, several shortcomings. As indicated earlier in this comment, it is not clear that the linchpin of such an arrangement, the maintenance of greater fixity of nominal exchange rates, is best analyzed, or for that matter maintained, in terms of fiscal policy. Nor, again, is overall current account equilibrium the crucial matter but, instead, the within-area official settlement balance of payments. This is quite relevant to the analysis of strategic behavior within the model as it stands. For instance, the benign neglect solution, where in response to an unfavorable external shock country 1 (the benign follower) expands fiscally and country 2 (the leader) contracts fiscally, implies a payment deficit for the first country. The Stackelberg equilibrium described by de Grauwe may thus be unsustainable in terms of the more complete underlying model, which must specify how the intra-EMS exchange rate is kept fixed. In other words, the outcome may entail reserve flows incompatible with the maintenance of fixed exchange rates—unless the first country has a very large stock of reserves and the deficit is transitory, or there is within the union a mechanism for creating additional reserves, something like the dollar standard in the later days of the Bretton Woods system.

The problems of cooperation within the EMS thus seem to me of a different nature than those analyzed by Paul de Grauwe in the present chapter. They concern, rather, the sacrifice of monetary independence, the determination of the common monetary policy and rate of inflation, the role of Germany in that respect, and the external value of the ECU. It remains true that, for good reasons or bad, countries have increasingly come to target their current accounts, and that fiscal policy is an important instrument in that respect. But this seems true whether countries are part of a regional exchange rate arrangement or their currencies float independently.

BEYOND STRATEGIC BEHAVIOR MODELS

The broader question is whether standard models of strategic interaction are a good starting point for improving policy coordination and reaping its benefits. My answer would be: "in part yes, in part no." Yes, since they do identify an important source of gains from cooperation (however small these gains appear in the simulation experiments that have been carried out so far) and can be used to raise the basic question of incentive compatibility. No, insofar as they distract attention from the importance of system reform (design of the rules of game, if you wish), take too easily as given a particular set of targets and instruments, and neglect the assignment problem or, if you prefer, neglect the importance of designing robust systems of policy response.

Of all the problems inhibiting proper coordination of policies, goal disagreement, lack of instruments, and uncertainty seem to me the most serious ones. Incompatibility of national goals concerning a shared variable (e.g., the exchange rate or the current account) can only be resolved by making these goals compatible across nations. There is no amount of coordination of instruments of economic policy that can produce a current account surplus both at home and abroad. Either the current account has to be dropped from the list of targets (by all countries or at least one residual one), or the targets must be made consistent across countries.

Supposing international consistency in targets, much more effort, it seems to me, should be put in identifying and securing an equal number of instruments of policy. The basic reason for policy conflicts of a strategic nature is in one sense always a shortage of instruments relative to targets. Before engaging in trading off the losses due to this shortage as the cooperative solution requires, one would do well to try to eliminate or reduce the shortage. This can be done either by giving up targets (the current account may be a prime candidate) or by finding and/or freeing additional instruments. Fiscal policy is one example; schemes for the international coordination of fiscal policy will remain moot as long as domestic political considerations prevent national fiscal policies from actually being changed. This brings another point to mind: one reason why the perceived gains from policy coordination appear to be much larger than those suggested by simulated comparisons between Nash and cooperative equilibrium may well be that countries are actually well below their Nash utility levels because of an inability to adjust their policy instruments.

Even with target consistency and a sufficient number of instruments, problems remain of policy coordination that cannot be analyzed with strategic behavior models. These problems stem primarily from uncertainty—more specifically, from lack of information about behavior parameters, the dynamics of adjustment, and the nature and origin of disturbances. It is here that Mundell's assignment problem and principle of effective market classification come into their own. The essential idea is to design robust systems of policy response that lead to convergence to targets in the face of uncertainty and imperfect information. This involves the design of broadly defined contingent rules of the type, "Assign monetary policy to the balance of payments under fixed exchange rates." That tradition of policy design should be revived, lest ambitious policy coordination schemes be adopted that are essentially unstable. To give but one example, Hans Genberg and I have recently shown that under flexible exchange rates, fiscal policy should be assigned to current account targets (if any) to achieve a stable system of policy response in that regime. This would contradict part of the assignment of policies to targets advocated in the "extended target zones" proposal.[1]

Finally, coherence between national policy rules and the logic of the international monetary system as a whole needs to be ensured. The $n - 1$ problem is one instance of this issue. Here incentive compatibility and strategic behavior are again relevant, and we should be grateful to Paul de Grauwe for bringing some of the issues involved to the fore.

NOTE

1. See Genberg and Swoboda (1987).

8

Causes of the Development of the Private ECU and the Behavior of its Interest Rates

Giuseppe Tullio and Francesco Contesso

The private ECU deposit and bond markets have experienced a spectacular growth that no one expected at the time of the creation of the ECU and of the EMS in March 1979. At the end of June 1986 the ECU bank deposit market had reached a volume of about 66 billion ECU (including the interbank market), while the international ECU bond issues had reached 8.9 billion in 1986. International ECU bond issues fell, however, as a percentage of the total market from 5.3 per cent in 1985 to 3.9 per cent in 1986.)[1] The reduction in the market share of ECU bond issue in 1986 was due to the competition from the strong Deutschmark, the weakness of sterling, which made the ECU less attractive for investors, and to the large volume of issues at the end of 1985, which the market needed to digest.

This chapter is divided into three parts. Section 1 deals briefly with the causes of the development of the private ECU, both in the bank deposit and bond markets. Particular attention is devoted to the role that capital controls in Italy and France have played in the development of the market. Section 2 analyzes the causes of the fluctuations of the spread between the quoted ECU interest rate and the combined Eurocurrency interest rate (or theoretical rate). In section 3 a number of very simple tests are presented, comparing the behavior of interest rates in the ECU deposit market with those in the Eurodollar, Euromark, and Europound deposit market. The first tests Meiselman's (1966) expectations theory about the term structure of interest rates. This test is admittedly rather crude

Mr. Contesso gratefully acknowledges financial support from the Italian National Science Foundation (CNR) for the period during which this research was conducted.

and is valid only under very restrictive assumptions. The second is a test suggested by Fama (1984) of the hypothesis that the observed forward interest rate contains information about the future spot rate, which allows a variable risk premium. Finally, a simple market efficiency test is performed for all four Eurocurrencies by regressing the future spot rate on the past forward rate, following Frenkel (1976).

The data used for this analysis are monthly averages of daily figures obtained from Chase Econometrics, which in turn collects them from the *Financial Times*. The data are available only from the beginning of October 1982. The last observation relates to the end of September 1985. All data are averages of bid and offer rates.

The set contains interest rates on deposits of 1, 3, 6, and 12 months' maturity. With these maturities we are able to extract from the data only forward interest rates on deposit of 3 and 6 months' maturities. All the tests mentioned above are performed with non-overlapping quarterly data, obtained by taking every third observation of the monthly data set. The use of overlapping monthly data would have generated strong autocorrelation of the residuals. Because the sample period is relatively short the degrees of freedom are only nine.[2]

1. THE CAUSES OF THE DEVELOPMENT
OF THE PRIVATE ECU MARKET

Among the causes of the private ECU's success probably the most important is its low risk–high return characteristics. Defined in terms of a basket of currencies, its value is likely to be more stable than the value of any individual component currency for an investor whose consumption basket is in third currencies (U.S. dollar, yens) or in component currencies. For the same reason, its interest rate is likely to be less volatile than that of any individual currency.[3]

The low risk–high return characteristics of the private ECU have been a cause of its development, thanks to the existence of transaction costs. With zero transaction costs investors and borrowers could have diversified their risk by forming their own preferred basket or currencies, and the private ECU would never have developed.[4]

Another cause is the favorable attitude of the Commission of the European Communities and the European Investment Bank toward the private ECU and the active role they have played in the market in the initial stages of its development.

More controversial are the roles that the European Monetary System (EMS) and the Exchange Rate Mechanism (ERM) on the one hand and the existence of capital controls on the other have played in the development of the private ECU. On the role of the EMS and the ERM there are two opposite views. One maintains that the risk diversification function of the ECU is reduced as the system becomes more coordinated and the ERM moves toward a system of fixed exchange rates. As Vaubel put it, "Any narrowing of the margins of fluctuations reduces the ECU's competitive edge in terms of short-run exchange rate stability" (Vaubel 1987). The second view holds that the declared objective of EMS member currencies to coordinate their monetary policy reinforces the private ECU. According to this view the success of the private ECU is also related to the existence of the ERM linking most ECU component currencies, which keeps the short-run volatility of exchange rates of component currencies against each other at low levels. This is especially important for ECU investors and borrowers residing in EMS member countries. They constitute the bulk of ECU primary lenders and borrowers.

In the ERM the ECU also plays the role of the pivot of the system, and this increases the confidence in the private ECU. The success of the private ECU during the period of stability of exchange rates from April 1983 to end 1985 seems to support this second view. On the other hand, the inclusion of the drachma, a high inflation currency, into the definition of the ECU in September 1984 has been perceived by market participants as a negative factor, although its weight is only about 1 per cent. If a currency with a large weight in the basket were to become unstable, this might reduce the attractiveness of the ECU as a protfolio investment, despite a low covariance of its exchange rate and interest rate with those of the more stable component currencies. The experience of 1986 is instructive in this respect. The private ECU also lost market shares because of the weakness and volatility of sterling, which is part of the definition of the ECU but does not participate in the ERM. This occurred despite the fact that sterling interest rates were very high both in nominal and in real terms. It is safe to conclude therefore that the fact that the ECU was a pivot of the ERM and that countries participating in it closely coordinate their monetary policies has contributed to the development of the private ECU, despite its reduced attractiveness as an instrument of diversification. This does not exclude, however, the possibility that in the future the balance between the confidence-creating roles of the EMS and the ERM and the diversification function of the ECU that is reduced by them may change and that further convergence may make the ECU less attractive.

There are two reasons, however, to believe that the private ECU will retain its attractiveness. First, if the private ECU succeeds in developing as a medium of exchange, it could become the European "vehicle currency," to use a term coined by Alexander Swoboda, substituting the U.S. dollar on the European side of the Atlantic. Corporations engaged in international trade would reduce their transaction and interest costs by holding one currency that is accepted in every EMS member country rather than by holding several European currencies.[5] In turn this would foster its role as a financial asset. The role of the private ECU as a medium of exchange is today virtually nonexistent. The increased use of the private ECU as a financial asset, a medium of exchange, and a currency of invoicing of European imports would also shield Europe from the instability of the U.S. dollar. Second, as the ERM moves closer to a fixed exchange rate system, the variability of short-term interest rates in member currencies will have to increase, especially if capital controls are relaxed further. Already during the period 1983–86, when the stability of exchange rates within the system was high, one has observed that national interest rates have moved in opposite directions. The smooth working of the balance of payments adjustment mechanism under pegged exchange rates requires this subordination of short-term interest rates to the external objective (Russo and Tullio 1987). It follows that the interest rate on the ECU, an average of interest rates of component currencies, will possess a greater stability than interest rates on any individual currency and will probably be characterized by a lower risk premium as well.

It follows from the above discussion that the relationship between the development of the ERM and the development of the private ECU may not be monotonic. The attractiveness of the private ECU is likely to be very small in an incohesive system with member currencies fluctuating wildly. It may increase as the cohesion of the system increases; as monetary policy coordination becomes stronger the currency diversification function of the ECU may, however, be reduced and discourage its development. As one moves closer to a fixed exchange rate system and the variability of national short-term rates increases, the private ECU may become more attractive again, especially at the short end of the market.

On the relationship between capital controls and their role in the development of the private ECU there are also two opposing views. One view favored particularly in German official circles holds that capital controls have been beneficial for the development of the private ECU market. The European Commission holds the opposite view. Those who believe that capital controls have been beneficial for the private ECU argue that Italian and French firms borrow heavily in ECUs and are stimulated to do so by exchange restrictions in their respective countries. But French and Italian firms are generally free to borrow in any currency (including their own) and would not choose ECUs if they didn't have an intrinsic appeal.

The existence of capital controls has probably contributed to making new established parities more credible after a realignment and to increasing the expected duration of new parities. Since nominal interest rates in France and Italy were so far higher than in strong currency members, French and Italian firms had an incentive to borrow abroad after realignments to take advantage of lower interest rates without incurring a large exchange rate risk. Again, if they borrowed in ECUs rather than in Deutschmarks it was because the former had an intrinsic appeal. On the contrary, the outright prohibition by the German government for German firms, banks, and households to hold ECUs in Germany and to borrow in ECUs has certainly been a negative factor for the development of the market.[6]

The Italian government has issued debt expressed in ECUs, which Italian residents were allowed to subscribe. As only the Italian government and the European Investment Bank were allowed to tap the Italian domestic market for borrowing in ECUs, they made use of their monopoly power and borrowed at a reduced cost. The yield in Italy was generally lower than the yield prevailing abroad, as arbitrage was prevented from operating. Exchange controls coupled with the granting of a monopoly power to two issuers can hardly be considered a measure fostering the private ECU. However, Italy and France have had at times credit controls on lending expressed in domestic currency and, when they were binding they have undoubtedly stimulated borrowing in foreign currencies by domestic firms and therefore indirectly, borrowing in ECUs. Credit controls accompanied by exchange restrictions my have therefore at times influenced the amount of borrowing and lending in ECUs.

Exchange controls have had a serious impact on the geographical distribution of borrowing and lending in ECUs. Borrowers typically are residents of high interest rate countries with capital controls, where they are free to borrow in any currency but not to invest in foreign currencies or ECUs, and lenders are mainly residents of the Benelux countries, where the domestic interest rate was generally lower than the one on the ECU and there are no prohibitions to hold foreign assets or ECUs. Capital controls in high interest rate countries have, however, probably implied higher transaction costs for Benelux residents interested in diversifying risk by forming their own basket. Thus indirectly capital controls may have made the private ECU more attractive than it would otherwise have been. This latter point is not likely to be very important, however.

Exchange controls have therefore had mainly negative effects on the development of the private ECU, both by limiting the access to it by German borrowers and by Italian and French investors, and by unbalancing the market geographically. This latter view finds some support in the fact that the ECU market developed considerably at a time when capital controls have been relaxed (since 1983), and its effectiveness was reduced by the willingness of countries participating in the ERM to align their real interest rates to German rates.

The difference between any Eurocurrency interest rate and the domestic interest rate on assets of equal risk and maturity has traditionally been considered a proxy of the overall degree of restriction on capital flows applied by the monetary authorities of the country in question. In the absence of capital controls and transaction costs and assuming equal reserve requirements at home and in Euromarkets, the two rates would tend to coincide, owing to the operation of arbitrageurs. Because of the restrictions on capital flows applied by the French and the Italian monetary authorities, the Eurofranc and the Eurolira interest rates have usually been significantly higher than their domestic counterparts. Table 8.1 contains the monthly interest spreads between the Euromarkets and domestic markets for three-month deposits for the ECU, the DM, the French franc, and the lira. The averages for each year are reported at the bottom of the table.[7] In 1983 the average spread was 3.68 for the French franc and 2.05 for the lira. However, these figures are heavily influenced by expectations of the March 1983 realignment. From April to December 1983 the average was 1.54 for the French franc and 1.14 for the Italian lira. For the French franc the spread fell to 0.81 in 1984 and 0.41 in the first nine months of 1985. For the lira the average was 1.54 in 1984 and 0.76 in the first nine months of 1985.

For the Deutschmark the average spread has been negative but negligible (in

Table 8.1

Spread between European and Domestic Three-Month Interest Rates (Monthly Averages)*

		ECU	DM	FF	·LIT
1982	October	1.1878	-0.42	5.3936	3.83
	November	1.4705	-0.1731	5.3889	6.1266
	December	2.4676	-0.2323	9.762	6.965
1983	January	2.1918	-0.2666	8.7687	5.4896
	February	2.206	-0.1294	9.1341	4.4427
	March	2.8635	-0.3256	12.4149	4.3844
	April	0.1864	-0.1769	1.2035	-0.0262
	May	0.0724	-0.2213	1.3418	-0.4808
	June	0.2708	-0.142	1.8204	1.0048
	July	0.111	-0.3483	1.4644	0.7176
	August	0.4862	-0.1663	2.723	1.563
	September	0.5015	-0.1216	2.0012	1.7461
	October	0.3538	-0.2863	1.6355	2.8422
	November	0.178	-0.1526	0.6436	1.4525
	December	0.2789	-0.1482	1.0041	1.4425
1984	January	0.244	-0.0875	0.8265	1.4675
	February	0.7381	-0.0814	3.1065	2.34
	March	0.687	-0.1525	2.7181	3.2344
	April	0.1178	-0.1293	0.6967	1.4469
	May	0.1474	-0.0935	0.4249	1.2715
	June	0.0846	-0.2362	0.5375	1.1219
	July	0.144	-0.2578	0.2312	2.0687
	August	-0.0241	-0.3653	0.0806	0.69
	September	0.1758	-0.2141	0.2094	1.1966
	October	0.2178	-0.1435	0.4181	1.81
	November	0.1203	-0.1556	0.5125	1.1312
	December	0.0353	-0.133	-0.0359	0.7287
1985	January	0.2381	-0.0341	0.0606	1.45
	February	0.4177	0.0714	0.3415	1.8312
	March	0.4487	-0.1722	0.1656	2.2469
	April	0.1716	-0.1189	0.1195	1.4737
	May	-0.1072	-0.1386	-0.0231	-0.555
	June	0.0421	-0.1237	0.1062	0.3031
	July	0.0789	-0.2045	0.5102	-0.14
	August	0.3489	-0.1551	1.673	0.3437
	September	0.1651	-0.085	0.7458	-0.1167
1983	Mean	0.8083	-0.2071	3.6796	2.0482
1984	Mean	0.2240	-0.1708	0.8105	1.5423
1985	Mean	0.2004	-0.1068	0.4111	0.7597

*Differences between combined Eurocurrency and combined domestic three-month interest rates.

the order of 10 to 20 basis points), with the domestic rate systematically exceeding the Euromark rate, probably because of reserve requirements on bank deposits held in Germany by nonresidents. Also, for the DM the absolute value of the spread has tended to fall over time, but the changes are probably too small to attach great significance to them.

The spread between the combined ECU interest rate calculated in the Euromarkets and the combined ECU rate calculated in national markets gives a synthetic view of changes in capital market restrictions within the EMS and/or their effectiveness during the sample period. It has fallen from 81 basis points in 1983 to 22 in 1984 and to 20 in the first nine months of 1985.

Figure 8.1 shows the spreads reported in Table 8.1. Even disregarding the period before March 1983, which is disturbed by the general realignment, a downward trend in the spread for the ECU, the French franc, and the lira is visible.

Figure 8.1
Spread between European and Domestic Interest Rates

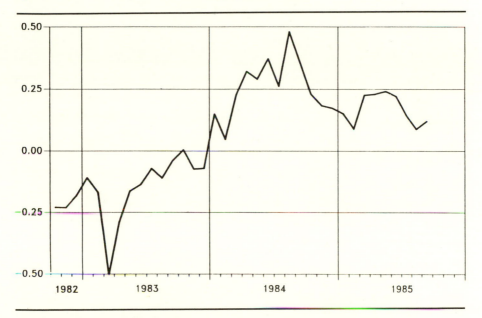

2. THE SPREAD BETWEEN THE QUOTED ECU INTEREST
RATE AND THE COMBINED EUROCURRENCY RATE

Figure 8.2 shows the difference between the quoted ECU deposit rate at the three-month maturity and the combined Eurocurrency interest rate.[8] Table 8.2 contains the same difference for deposits of maturity of 1, 3, 6, and 12 months. The spread reached a minimum negative value of 50 basis points at the time of the March 1983 general realignment and a maximum positive value of 47 basis points in August 1984, the last full month prior to the mid-September change in the weights. The data reported in the table seem to suggest that the spread was more sensitive to expectations of realignments at the one-month maturity, while it was more sensitive to expectations of changes in the weights at the longer end of the market. Expectations of realignments and of changes in the weights must be clearly important factors to explain changes in the spread.

Figure 8.2
Spread between Quoted ECU Three-Month Deposit Rate and Combined Eurocurrency Three-Month Interest Rate

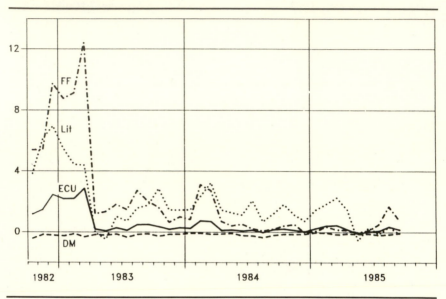

During the same period there was only one general realignment in March 1983,[9] and only one change in the definition of the basket, in September 1984, when the quantity of the member currencies was changed and the Greek drachma was introduced into the basket.

That expectations of realignments and of changes in the ECU weights should lead to changes in the spread is due to following. The influence of expectations of realignments on the spread is related to the existence of transaction costs in arbitraging between the ECU market and Euromarkets and to the fact that these costs change as expectations of realignments change. The difference between bid and ask prices normally increases when a realignment approaches, both in the foreign exchange market and in the Eurodeposit market. Arbitrage operations therefore become more costly, and this should explain why the spread can reach the levels observed during and before March 1983. Consider the case of an imminent devaluation of the French franc. The Eurofranc interest rate starts reflecting the expectations of the devaluation and goes up, giving rise to the possibility of making profits by borrowing in ECUs and investing in Eurofrancs and in other component currencies of the ECU, without incurring an exchange risk. However, the possibility of making profits is limited by (a) the widening of the spread between bid and ask rates in the ECU deposit market, (b) the widening

Table 8.2
Difference between Quoted ECU Deposit Rate and Combined Eurocurrency Rates (monthly averages)*

		MATURITY			
		1 Month	3 Months	6 Months	12 Months
1982	October	-0.1704	-0.2299	-0.1918	-0.1943
	November	-0.1866	-0.2316	-0.2057	-0.1968
	December	-0.1224	-0.1826	-0.1612	-0.1563
Average		-0.1598	-0.2147	-0.1862	-0.1825
1983	January	-0.1701	-0.1094	-0.1155	-0.1501
	February	-0.2571	-0.1678	-0.1574	-0.0928
	March	-1.3971	-0.5048	-0.1998	-0.1515
	April	-0.2326	-0.2892	-0.1477	-0.1617
	May	-0.1909	-0.1633	-0.1705	-0.1617
	June	-0.1203	-0.1362	-0.1477	-0.256
	July	-0.2501	-0.0723	-0.0644	-0.0556
	August	-0.0647	-0.1106	-0.0576	-0.0729
	September	-0.0492	-0.0406	-0.0194	-0.0591
	October	-0.0232	4.114E-03	-0.0369	-0.0528
	November	0.0166	-0.0735	-0.0525	-0.0602
	December	0.1047	-0.0705	-0.0473	-0.0796
Average		-0.2195	-0.1445	-0.1014	-0.1128
1984	January	1.07	0.1485	0.1396	0.1206
	February	0.2864	0.0474	0.0403	0.0544
	March	0.3357	0.2262	0.1692	0.2999
	April	0.3786	0.32	0.3392	0.4604
	May	0.3818	0.2894	0.2343	0.2262
	June	0.4223	0.3708	0.381	0.187
	July	0.2703	0.261	0.2805	0.1337
	August	0.4981	0.4697	0.6742	0.6504
	September	0.3649	0.354	0.5717	0.5533
	October	0.2414	0.2295	0.2185	0.2952
	November	0.2488	0.1824	0.2629	0.4015
	December	0.1402	0.1726	0.1934	0.2621
Average		0.3865	0.2560	0.2921	0.3037
1985	January	0.2019	0.1505	0.1275	0.0831
	February	0.3397	0.0891	0.0117	-0.1926
	March	0.2322	0.2251	0.1917	-0.0233
	April	0.2193	0.2293	0.2448	0.2851
	May	0.176	0.2404	0.3005	0.2901
	June	0.1735	0.2197	0.2165	0.1159
	July	0.1178	0.1435	0.1063	-0.0279
	August	0.0799	0.0884	0.0838	0.0415
	September	-0.0974	0.1202	0.1347	0.054
Average		0.1603	0.1674	0.1575	0.0696
Standard Dev.		0.3710	0.2185	0.2178	0.2293

*Quoted ECU rate minus combined rate.

of the spread between bid and ask rates in the foreign exchange market, where the borrowed ECU has to be transformed into its component currencies, and (c) the widening of the spread in the Eurodeposit markets of the component currencies.

Expectations of changes in the weights have led to a large increase in the spread in the months preceding the September 1984 change because the weight of weak (high interest) currencies was expected to be increased and those of strong (low interest currencies) was expected to be reduced. In addition, the Greek drachma was expected to be introduced into the definition of the basket. Table 8.3 shows the weights of the member currencies before and after the change. As the ECU is defined in terms of a fixed number of each member currency, the weight of currencies that tend to depreciate falls in time. Member countries can, according to the EMS agreements, reassess the weights every five years or every time that the weight of one currency changes by more than 25 per cent. The quoted ECU interest rate was already incorporating the expected increase in the combined interest rate prior to the September 17 change in the weights.

There are other factors influencing the spread as well. First, in equilibrium and in the presence of transaction costs, the ECU deposit rate would not necessarily be equal to the combined rate; it would be lower if ECU deposits diversify the risk and higher if the interest rates are positively correlated. This risk factor would not be constant through time; as interest rates and inflation rates of component currencies move closer together and they become closer substitutes, the risk diversification element would become smaller, as discussed in the previous section. In a world without transaction costs private agents wanting to diversify the risk would form their own basket and the ECU would lose its diversification function. If the ECU existed in such a world the combined and the quoted interest rate could not diverge. Second, especially in the early part of the sample period, the ECU market could be considered to be in its infancy. Two possible scenarios can be envisaged. One is that banks involved in ECU lending could have fixed interest rates at below competitive levels to attract customers and as a result they could offer correspondingly low interest rates on deposits. A second scenario is that the banks, being new in the business, are demanding a very large spread between borrowing and lending rates, which depresses the borrowing rates substantially below the combined Eurocurrency rate and possibly raises lending rates above the combined Eurolending rates. This behavior would have also been justified by the initially higher transaction costs due to the large disequilibrium between primary ECU liabilities and assets of Eurobanks and the ensuing costs of "bundling" the ECU. As the market becomes less unbalanced, as a result of economies of scale setting in and as banks become more familiar with the new instrument, the spread between deposit and lending rates may fall, moving the quoted ECU deposit rate closer to the combined Eurocurrency deposit rate. Unfortunately, there is no direct way to test this hypothesis, since homogeneous time series on the spread between ECU deposit and lending rates are not

Table 8.3
Weights of the ECU before and after the September 1984 Changes in the Weights

Currency	Amount of national currency in the basket		Percentage weights of currencies in the basket			
	March 13 1979	September 17 1984	March 13 1979[a]	September 14 1984[b]	September 17 1984[c]	
Deutschmark	0.828	0.719	33.0	36.9	32.0	
French franc	1.15	1.31	19.8	16.7	19.0	
Pound sterling	0.0885	0.0879	13.3	15.1	15.0	
Italian lira	109	140	9.5	7.9	10.2	
Dutch guilder	0.286	0.256	10.5	11.3	10.1	
Belgian franc	3.66	3.71	9.3	8.1	8.2	
Luxembourg franc	0.14	0.14	0.4	0.3	0.3	
Danish krone	0.217	0.219	3.1	2.7	2.7	
Irish punt	0.00759	0.00871	1.1	1.0	1.2	
Greek drachma		1.15			1.3	

[1]Initial currency weights in the ECU, calculated with central parity rates on March 13, 1979.
[2]Pre-redefinition currency weights, calculated with market exchange rates on September 14, 1979.
[3]Post-redefinition currency weights, calculated with market exchange rates on September 17, 1979.

Source: EC Commission and ECU Newsletter, based on EC Commission data.

available. However, a very crude attempt was made to test for a significant effect of the ratio of bank ECU deposits to bank ECU assets, as a proxy for the disequilibrium in the market and the potential implications for transaction costs of banks, on the spread between the quoted and the combined ECU interest rate. No significant influence was detected. However, the proxy used for disequilibrium in the market is available for only part of the sample period and only on a quarterly basis; the series was interpolated linearly to obtain monthly figures.

For completeness it should be observed that the spread was again negative at the time of writing[10] and that in 1986 the disequilibrium between primary bank borrowing and lending in ECUs was substantially reduced.

3. THE TERM STRUCTURE OF ECU DEPOSIT RATES, TESTS OF MARKET EFFICIENCY AND COMPARISONS WITH OTHER EUROCURRENCIES

In the previous section the factors affecting the behavior of the spread between the quoted and the combined ECU deposit interest rate have been analyzed. In this section three separate tests will be presented for ECU, Eurodollar, Euromark, and Europound interest rates. The tests are first a test of Meiselman's expectations theory about the term structure of interest rates, a test of the hypothesis that the observed forward interest rate contains information about the future spot rate suggested by Fama (1984), and finally a simple market efficiency test that consists of regressing the future spot interest rate on the past forward interest rate (Frenkel 1976).

The sample period is October 1982 to September 1985. The data set used is monthly averages of daily figures purchased from Chase Econometrics, which in turn collects them from the *Financial Times*. All the data are averages of bid and ask rates.

The data set contains interest rates on deposits of 1, 3, 6, and 12 months' maturity. The interest rate on deposits of nine months' maturity was obtained by geometric interpolation. With these maturities we are able to extract from the data only forward interest rates on deposits of three- and six-month maturities. All the tests mentioned above are performed with non-overlapping quarterly data obtained by taking every third observation of the monthly data set. The use of overlapping monthly data would have sharply increased the numbers of degrees of freedom but would have led to strong autocorrelation of the residuals. Because the sample period is relatively short, the degrees of freedom are only nine. Thus all the results have to be interpreted with some caution.

A test of Meiselman's expectations theory about the term structure of interest rates will be presented first. This test shows to what extent innovations in interest rates are significantly correlated with changes in the forward rate. The innovation is defined as the difference between the spot rate and the past forward rate. This difference is the forecasting error made by using the forward rate as the predictor of the future spot rate. The test suggests to what extent the information contained in the current spot rate is incorporated into the revision of the forward interest rates implicit in the term structure. To explain the tests made, the following symbols are used: R = Actual rate of interest prevailing in the market, annualized. An interest rate of 10 percent is expressed as 0.10. r = Forward rate of interest.

The subscript on the left refers to the month or week in which the rate becomes applicable (e.g., $t + n$ stands for n weeks or months from week or month t). The first subscript on the right refers to the time until maturity of the deposit, generally expressed in months. The second subscript on the right refers to the month or week during which the expectation of the future interest rate is held by the market.

Definitions Relevant for Meiselman's Model

Pure expectations theory:

$$(1 + R_{n,t})^n = (1 + R_{1,t})(1 + {}_{t+1}r_{1,t}) \cdots (1 + {}_{t+n-1}r_{1,t})$$

Hicksian formulation of the forward rate:

$${}_{t+n}r_{1,t} = \frac{(1 + R_{n+1,t})^{n+1}}{(1 + R_{n,t})^n}$$

where $R_{n,t}$ is the observed rate at time t with maturity n.

The Meiselman Model

Three-Month Forecasting Horizon

forecasting error

$$
{}_{t+3}r_{3,t} - {}_{t+3}r_{3,t-3} = F({}_{t}R_3, {}_{t-t}r_{3,t-3})
\tag{8.1}
$$

$${}_{t+3}r_{3,t} = \frac{(1 + R_{6,t})^2}{(1 + R_{3,t})} - 1$$

$${}_{t+3}r_{3,t-3} = \frac{(1 + R_{9,t-3})^3}{(1 + R_{6,t-3})^2} - 1$$

$$r_{3,t-3} = \frac{(1 + R_{6,t-3})^2}{(1 + R_{3,t-3})} - 1$$

where ${}_{t+3}r_{3,t}$ is the forward interest rate on a three-month deposit expected at time t for time $t + 3$; ${}_{t+3}r_{3,t-3}$ is the forward interest rate on a three-month deposit expected at time $t - 3$ for time $t + 3$. Hence the difference ${}_{t+3}r_{3,t-t}$ +

$_3 r_{3,t-3}$ is the revision of the forward interest rate on a three-month deposit that the market makes at time t with respect to time $t - 3$. $_t r_{3,t-3}$ is the forward interest rate on a three-month deposit that the market had expected at time $t - 3$ for time t. Equation 8.1 states that at time t the market revises its opinion about the forward rate on a three-month deposit relating to time $t + 3$ on the basis of the forecasting error it makes at time $t - 3$.

Six-Month Forecasting Horizon

$$_{t+6} r_{3,t} - {_{t+6}} r_{3,t-3} = F(_t R_{3,t} - {_t} r_{3,t-3})$$ (8.2)

$$_{t+6} r_{3,t} - 3 = \frac{(1 + R_{9,t})^3}{(1 + R_{6,t})^2} - 1$$

$$_{t+6} r_{3,t-3} = \frac{(1 + R_{12,t-3})^4}{(1 + R_{9,t-3})^3} - 1$$

where $_t r_{3,t-3}$ and $_t R_{3,t}$ are defined above.

Table 8.4 contains estimates of a linear version of Equations 8.1 and 8.2. For each currency the first line reports the estimates of a linear version of Equation 8.1 and the second line the estimate of the linear version of Equation 8.2.

Before we interpret the results presented in Table 8.4, a word of caution is in order. From the test presented one can infer that the market revises the forward rate on the basis of the forecasting error only under certain restrictive assumptions. If the risk (liquidity, time) premium is zero or time invariant and if the interest rate follows a univariate stationary process whose innovations are orthogonal to the history of publicly available information, then the optimal forecasts of future interest rates will be updated exactly as Meiselman's model predicts (Melino 1986). These are quite restrictive assumptions. Another reason for interpreting the results of Table 8.4 with caution is that the interest rate on deposits of nine months' maturity was obtained by geometric interpretation.

For the Eurodollar and the Euromark the estimates of the parameter b fall within the value of 1 ± 2 standard deviations. For these two Eurocurrencies the estimates of b for the six-month forecasting horizon are not significantly below the estimate of b for the three-month horizon. For both horizons these markets seem to make strong use of the information contained in the interest rate innovation. For Eurosterling and the quoted ECU one observes that the estimates of b are significantly below 1, suggesting a less than complete incorporation of the new information into the forecast of the future interest rate. For the quoted ECU the estimates of b are the lowest.

It has already been mentioned that a problem of Meiselman's tests is the existence of a risk premium that changes through time. There is unfortunately not much agreement in the literature on how to measure the liquidity premium. Nevertheless, in Table 8.5 an attempt was made to measure the liquidity premium

Table 8.4

Meiselman's Model: Quarterly Non-overlapping Data with Quarterly Error Adjustment (Period: January 1983–September 1985)*

| | | EURODOLLAR | | |
n	a	b	R^2	D.W.
3	0.003	1.06	0.95	1.49
	(2.77)	(14.58)		
6	0.002	1.08	0.92	1.69
	(1.36)	(10.50)		

| | | EURODEUTSCHMARK | | |
n	a	b	R^2	D.W.
3	0.003	1.13	0.88	2.38
	(2.56)	(8.00)		
6	0.002	1.06	0.73	2.21
	(1.01)	(4.88)		

| | | EUROSTERLING | | |
n	a	b	R^2	D.W.
3	-0.0009	0.80	0.85	1.84
	(0.78)	(7.24)		
6	-0.0008	0.78	0.86	2.06
	(0.70)	(7.42)		

| | | E C U | | |
n				
3	-0.0004	0.44	0.36	1.90
	(0.21)	(2.23)		
6	-0.003	0.18	0.07	2.43
	(1.35)	(0.80)		

*Numbers in parentheses are *t*-statistics.

Revision of Forward Rate = a + b. Forecasting Error + Epsilon.

Table 8.5

Liquidity Premium (monthly data; averages for period October 1982–August 1985)

PREMIUM FOR THREE MONTH HOLDING PERIOD

Currency	6 months	Asset maturity 9 months	12 months
USD	0.770 (1.219)	1.301 (2.553)	1.948 (3.956)
DM	0.526 (0.543)	0.878 (1.175)	1.298 (1.849)
STG	-0.166 (1.286)	-0.166 (2.215)	-0.186 (3.107)
ECU	0.717 (0.688)	1.009 (1.065)	1.422 (1.377)
ECU*	0.688 (0.676)	1.057 (1.068)	1.502 (1.487)

PREMIUM FOR SIX MONTH HOLDING PERIOD

Currency	Asset maturity 12 months
USD	1.123 (1.981)
DM	0.652 (0.725)
STG	-0.064 (1.146)
ECU	0.840 (0.497)
ECU*	0.942 (0.576)

*Combined Eurocurrency ECU interest rate.
Standard deviations are in parentheses.

on the four Eurocurrencies for deposits of up to 12 months, following Santomero (1975).[11]

The liquidity premia are quite high for all currencies except the pound sterling. According to the calculations investors seem to require a premium of about 80 basis points on an annual basis to hold dollar deposits for six months rather than for three months. The premium amounts to almost 200 basis points for 12-month dollar deposits. For the DM the premium is about 50 basis points for six-month deposits and 130 for 12-month deposits. For the quoted ECU it is about 70 basis points for six-month maturity and about 140 for 12-month maturity.

The liquidity premia for holding a deposit for 12 rather than six months have the same ranking by currency as those calculated for three-month holding periods.[12] The highest premium was recorded for the U.S. dollar and the lowest for the DM and the pound. The variability of the liquidity premia, as measured by their standard deviations, was also quite high.[13] It is worth noting that for the ECU it is among the lowest of all maturities and for all holding periods.

In a recent article Fama (1984) presents a generalization of Meiselman's model that allows for time-varying risk premia and which incorporates Meiselman's pure expectations theory as a special case. Fama considers the following regressions (where the error terms have been omitted for simplicity):

$$P_{3,t} = a_1 + b_1({}_{t+3}r_{3,t} - {}_tR_{3,t}) \tag{8.3}$$

$${}_{t+3}R_{3,t+3} - {}_tR_{3,t} = a_2 + b_2({}_{t+3}r_{3,t} - {}_tR_3) \tag{8.4}$$

He calls the term in parentheses the current forward–spot differential. This differential is different from the forecasting error of Equations 8.1 and 8.2. Equations 8.3 and 8.4 imply that changes in the current forward–spot differential influence both the risk premium $P_{3,t}$ and the future change in the spot rate ${}_{t+3}R_{3,t+3} - {}_tR_{3,t}$. Evidence that b_1 is reliably positive means that the current forward rate contains information about the premium. Evidence that b_2 is reliably positive means that the current forward rate has power as predictor for the spot rate at time $t + 3$. Under Meiselman's pure expectations theory the coefficient b_1 is equal to zero (there is no premium or the premium is time invariant), and the coefficient b_2 is equal to 1.0. In this case it follows from Equation 8.4 that

$${}_{t+3}R_{3,t+3} = a_2 + {}_{t+3}r_{3,t} + \text{Error term} \tag{8.5}$$

which says that the forward rate is an unbiased predictor of the future spot rate, if in addition a_2 is equal to zero.

Table 8.6 contains tests of Equation 8.4 with non-overlapping quarterly data. The most satisfactory results are obtained for the Deutschmark and the ECU, for which the estimate of the coefficient b_2 is reliably positive and not significantly different from 1. For both of these currencies the D.W. statistics indicate the absence of significant autocorrelation of the residuals, and the R^2 is satisfactory.[14]

To test whether the forward interest rate is an unbiased predictor of the future spot interest rate, the following regression has been estimated, following Frenkel (1976):

$$R_{3,t} = a + b\, r_{3,t-3} + \text{Error term} \tag{8.6}$$

Table 8.6
Changes in the Spot Rate on the Current Forward Spot Differential (Period: January 1983–September 1985)*

	a_2	b_2	R^2	D.W.
Eurodollar	0.86 (1.11)	-1.89 (1.54)	0.21	2.10
Eurodeutschmark	-0.58 (2.27)	1.18 (2.01)	0.31	1.74
Eurosterling	0.20 (0.56)	0.44 (0.56)	0.03	2.53
Ecu	-0.87 (2.73)	1.26 (2.90)	0.48	2.22

Estimates of Equation 8.4. Quarterly non-overlapping data.
*Numbers in parentheses are t-statistics.

where $R_{3,t}$ is the current three-month rate and $r_{3,t-3}$ is the three-month forward rate observed at time $t - 3$.

If the constant in this regression doesn't differ significantly from zero and the coefficient on the forward rate doesn't differ from unity, the latter is an unbiased predictor of the former.

Table 8.7 contains the estimates of Equation 8.6 for the four Eurocurrencies, performed with non-overlapping quarterly data. While all the regressions have a relatively weak R^2, the D.W. statistics indicate the absence of autocorrelation for Eurosterling and the ECU. In addition the estimates of the coefficient b for these two currencies are not significantly different from 1, and the estimates of the coefficient a are not significantly different from zero. For the private ECU and for Eurosterling the tests presented in Table 8.7 seem to indicate that the market is efficient.

On the basis of the tests presented in Table 8.6 and 8.7 one can conclude that the ECU deposit market compares quite well with the other Eurocurrency deposit markets considered here, both as far as the predictive power of the 3-months forward rate is concerned (Table 8.6) and as far as the efficiency of the market is concerned (Table 8.7). On the other hand the ECU fares badly as far as the pure expectations theory of the term structure of interest rates is concerned (Table 8.4). This may be due to the fact that expectations of realignments and of changes in the ECU weights have significantly altered the term structure of interest rates in the ECU deposit market. For the tests of Table 8.4 interest rates on deposits of up to 12 months maturity were used, while for the tests of Tables 8.6 and 8.7 interest rates on deposits of only up to 6 months maturity were used.

Table 8.7
Tests of Market Efficiency (Period: January 1983–September 1985)*

	a	b	R^2	D.W.
Eurodollar	5.21 (1.65)	0.43 (1.43)	0.19	1.13
Eurodeutschmark	4.21 (3.13)	0.23 (1.04)	0.11	1.23
Eurosterling	3.91 (0.86)	0.65 (1.49)	0.20	1.76
Ecu	2.78 (0.73)	0.66 (1.79)	0.26	2.25

Quarterly non-overlapping data.
*Numbers in parentheses are t-statistics.

APPENDIX 1: METHODS TO CALCULATE THE COMBINED ECU INTEREST RATE

The theoretical ECU interest rate can be calculated in four ways.

The first two methods lead under certain conditions to identical results; the same holds for the other two. The difference between these two groups of computing formulas lies in the kind of exchange rate used to compute the weight of the interest rate of each component currency—spot in the first two methods, forward in the last two.

Method A

In this chapter the following formula to compute the theoretical ECU interest rate has been used:

$$\text{Combined ECU interest rate} = \sum_{i=1}^{n} \frac{CU_i}{EX_i} \cdot I_i$$

where n is the number of component currencies in the ECU; CU_i is the units of currency i in the ECU basket definition; EX_i is the spot exchange rate of currency i against ECU, defined as a number of units of currency i per ECU; and I_i is the currency interest rate i.

Method B

This method relies on the interest rates of member currencies obtained from the interest rate of one of the member currencies or of a third currency by using the assumption of interest rate arbitrage. The spot exchange rate is used to compute the component currency weight in the ECU, as in Method A.

This method can be viewed as the same as the first, but only if the interest parity condition holds perfectly:

$$\text{Theoretical ECU interest rate} = \sum_{i=1}^{n} \frac{CU_i}{EX_i} \cdot (I_x + FP_i)$$

where I is the interest rate on base currency x; and FP is the forward premium or discount for component currency i against the base currency x, expressed in annual percentage terms.

Method C

This formula is a variant of Method A, obtained by replacing the spot exchange rate by the forward exchange rate.

$$\text{Theoretical ECU interest rate} = \sum_{i=1}^{n} \frac{CU_i}{FX_i} \cdot I_i$$

where FX_i is the forward exchange rate of a currency i against the ECU, defined as units of component currency i per ECU.

Method D

This method, called the commercial bank method, uses an outright forward exchange rate against the ECU. We know that the forward exchange rate of currency i against the ECU, under covered interest rate parity, is given by

$$FX_i = EX_i + EX_i \cdot \left[\frac{(1 + \frac{I_i}{100})}{(1 + \frac{I_{ECU}}{100})} - 1 \right]$$

The theoretical rate is computed by solving the above equation for I_{ECU}:

$$\text{ECU interest rate} = \left[\frac{(1 + \frac{I_i}{100}) \cdot EX_i}{FX_i} - 1 \right] \cdot 100$$

The resulting ECU interest rate is lower than the rate generated using spot exchange rates. This is due to the fact that high interest rate currencies are at a discount under covered interest parity, and consequently these currencies have a lower percentage weight in the basket than when spot exchange rates are applied to the fixed currency units, as in Methods A and B.

APPENDIX 2: DESCRIPTION AND SOURCES OF THE DATA USED

Eurorates

The Euromarket interest rates (supplied by Chase Econometrics Interactive Data Corporation) are weekly averages of daily market closing rates (source: *Financial Times*).

The data used are middle rates between bid and ask quotations.

The maturities are 1 month, 3 months, 6 months, and 12 months.

The nine-month rate has been obtained by calculating the geometric mean between six- and twelve-month rates.

The period covered is from the 40th week of 1982 until the 39th week of 1985.

The data are available for the following Eurocurrencies: U.S. dollar, Deutschmark, Dutch guilder, Belgian franc, Danish krone, French franc, Italian lira, ECU.

For the Irish punt and the Greek drachma, the corresponding domestic interest rates have been used to calculate the combined Eurocurrency ECU interest rates.

For the Irish punt the 1-, 3-, and 6-month maturities are available. The six-month rate has been used as a proxy for the 12-month rate.

For the Greek drachma, only the interest rate at three-month maturity is available; this has been used as a proxy for all the other maturities.

Domestic Interest Rates

The domestic interest rates used are:

For the Deutschmark, the three-month interbank bid rate, weekly (Wednesday quotation).

For the Irish punt, the three-month deposit middle rate, weekly average.

For the pound sterling, the three-month commercial paper ask rate, weekly (Wednesday quotation).

For the Italian lira, the 79-day Treasury Bill middle rate, weekly (Wednesday quotation).

For the French franc the three-month interbank paper rate was used, ask rate (Wednesday quotations).

For the Dutch guilder, the three-month large bank deposit middle rate, weekly (Wednesday quotation).

For the Belgian franc, the 120-day Treasury Bill middle rate, weekly (Wednesday quotation).

For the Danish krone, the short-term bill rate, monthly.

For the Greek drachma, the three-month money market offered rate for convertible drachma, weekly average.

The source for the drachma is the Bank of Greece; for all the other currencies, the source is Chase Econometrics Interactive Data Corporation.

Exchange Rates

The exchange rate data are national currencies against the ECU. They are weekly averages of middle rates. The source is the *Financial Times* (data collected by Chase

Econometrics), except for the Greek drachma exchange rate, the source for which is the Commission of the European Communities.

NOTES

1. The loss in market share was even more pronounced for syndicated bank credits: from 6.2 percent in 1985 to 1.7 percent in 1986.

2. If we had interest rates on deposits of two months' maturity, we could calculate forward rates for the one-month maturity and we could have performed the tests with monthly data, without overlapping the period.

3. This does not exclude the fact that, for instance, for a Dutch investor, the Deutschmark may be more stable than the ECU in terms of Dutch florins, nor that the German interest rate may be more stable than the ECU interest rate.

4. This important point was suggested by Hermann-Josef Dudler.

5. Swoboda (1968).

6. The ban was lifted in June 1987.

7. These spreads have to be interpreted with some caution, first because the interest rates are not exactly comparable in terms of risk characteristics, and second because the Euro interest rates are averages of daily figures, while most national interest rates are averages of Wednesday quotations.

8. The method used to compute the combined Eurocurrency interest rate is Method A, which is illustrated in Appendix 1.

9. The realignment of July 1985 was minor, since it involved only a change in the central rate of the lira and was largely unexpected.

10. May 1987.

11. The premium is calculated as follows. First one computes the asset return as

$$A_{n,t} = \frac{(1 + {}_tR_{n,t})^n}{(1 + {}_{t+1}R_{n-1,t+1})^{n-1}} - 1$$

The premium is

$$P_{n,t} = A_{n,t} - R_{1,t}$$

where $R_{n,t}$ stands for the market interest rate on an asset of maturity n observed at time t.

12. See the bottom half of Table 8.5.

13. They are reported between parentheses in Table 8.5.

14. No attempt was made to estimate Equation 8.3 because of the difficulties in extracting reliable time series of the risk premium from the data.

COMMENT BY

Manfred J. M. Neumann

The private use of ECUs has made considerable headway during recent years. Though still rather small by comparison, the ECU deposit and loan markets may have passed the state of infancy sufficiently to warrant academic attention. The primary purpose of the chapter by Tullio and Contesso is to discuss why private interest in the ECU has grown during recent years and to compare the behavior of the interest rate in the ECU deposit market with those of other Euro deposit markets.

WHY PRIVATE ECUs?

The private ECU is a currency cocktail that permits the investor to diversify his or her portfolio in a standardized fashion in order to improve the return/risk distribution. Although it seems that even for European investors the ECU is below the efficiency frontier (von Moltke 1986), it is a fact that the ECU deposit and loan markets have grown remarkably during recent years.[1]

Tullio and Contesso provide a useful discussion on why these markets may have taken off. In their view the private ECU has profited from the fact that the official ECU serves as a pivot of the European exchange rate mechanism. Indeed, this is an important aspect that may explain why of all private currency cocktails only the ECU has made headway. The private SDR, for comparison, is a complete failure.

In my view, additional important factors in favor of the ECU have been (1) the massive support of these markets by the EC authorities, who have a vested interest in developing this unit, and (2) the credit and capital controls instituted by weak currency countries like Italy and France. The geographical imbalance in ECU borrowing and lending is quite telling in this respect. Whether it will change because German residents are free now to borrow in ECUs remains to be seen.

It is by no means clear, however, that the private ECU will become an important instrument should the member countries of the EMS improve on policy coordination and abolish the still substantial restrictions on the free flow of capital within the EMS area. After all, the productivity of the private ECU, and hence its attractiveness, will decrease the closer the national rates of interest and inflation move together (Neumann 1983). Of course, matters would be different if the ECU were to become a medium of exchange, as Tullio and Contesso speculate. But that would require a European union with joint monetary policy—the end of the tunnel to some, a nightmare to others.

ON THE SPREAD BETWEEN THE QUOTED ECU DEPOSIT RATE AND THE COMBINED EUROCURRENCY RATE

In section 2 of their chapter Tullio and Contesso present computed spreads between ECU deposit rates quoted by banks for various maturities and corresponding combined Eurocurrency rates (see their Table 8.2). They observe that these spreads were negative until the end of 1983 and positive threrafter. This is a peculiar observation that requires explanation. Consequently, the authors advance several suggestions with special emphasis on the role of expectations of realignments and of official redefinitions of the ECU basket. However, very likely their observation is just a statistical artifact. To substantiate this surmise I will first offer a theoretical and then an empirical argument.

Consider a bank that arbitrages between ECU deposits and Euromarkets. The bank will invest funds in the Euromarkets at the combined rate i_E and cover them by supplying ECU deposits at the quoted rate i_Q, provided the interest differential matches the bank's transaction cost c_B.

$$i_Q - i_E \leq -c_B \tag{8.7}$$

It follows that the spread $i_Q - i_E$ cannot be nonnegative, though it may fall numerically with increasing competition, diminishing capital controls, and improvements in banking technologies. Also, the negative interest rate spread will rise numerically during periods of increasing uncertainty in response to rising bid/ask spreads in Eurocurrency markets, which raise c_B temporarily.[2]

The theory of arbitraging implies that the spreads considered by Tullio and Contesso must be negative. Observations to the contrary indicate a serious data problem. I suggest that the combined Eurocurrency rates computed by the authors[3] are not comparable to the deposit rates quoted by banks. In the computation of the combined rates the authors apply weights based on the official currency composition of the ECU. This amounts to assuming a closed basket. Most banks, in contrast, treat ECU deposits as open ECU baskets in order to facilitate trading (Lomax 1983). As a result, the deposit rates quoted by banks will take expected changes in the currency composition into account, as the authors realize themselves. It follows that the inconsistent construction of the interest spreads precludes any insight into the interdependence of ECU deposit and Eurocurrency markets.

ON THE TERM STRUCTURE AND MARKET EFFICIENCY

In the final section of their chapter Tullio and Contesso present regression work. To judge from the last paragraph of that section the implicit idea is to demonstrate "that the ECU deposit market compares quite well with the other Eurocurrency deposit markets" in terms of the predictive power of the three-month forward rate and of market efficiency. If the estimates presented and the data used are reliable, however, one might equally well conclude that all these markets are defective because none of them passes a simple efficiency test.

The authors estimate first Meiselman's error learning model of the term structure. According to that model expectations about future interest rates are systematically adjusted (by a constant factor) to the most recent forecast error:

$$_{t+3}r_{3,t} - {_{t+3}}r_{3,t-3} = a + b(R_{3,t} - r_{3,t-3}) + \epsilon_t \tag{8.8}$$

where $a = 0$ and $1 > b > 0$, $_{t+3}r_{3,t}$ denotes the three-month rate expected at t for $t + 3$, and $R_{3,t}$ is the actual rate at t. Of the authors' estimates only the one for the three-month ECU rate is in line with Meiselman's model, exhibiting a zero intercept and a positive slope coefficient that is significantly below unity (see the authors' Table 8.4).

The authors, in contrast, give more prominent attention to their estimates for the Eurodollar and the Euromark, which produce slope coefficients of unity. The latter property is unwarranted, however, because it implies market inefficiency. If $b = 1$, Equation 8.8 can be written as

$$_{t+3}r_{3,t} = R_{3,t} + a + (_{t+3}r_{3,t-3} - r_{3,t-3}) + \epsilon_t \tag{8.9}$$

This says that the three-month rate expected today for $t + 3$ equals today's actual rate plus a constant plus the future change of this rate as it was expected at $t - 3$. Clearly, this is not a property of an informationally efficient market. Hence, if we accept the estimates of the authors' Table 8.4 we have to conclude that the Euromarkets for dollar, mark, and sterling are inefficient.

But note that Tullio and Contesso provide further estimates that cast doubt on the efficiency of the ECU deposit market, too. They estimate the following regression, taken from Fama (1984):

$$_{t+3}R_{3,t-3} - R_{3,t} = a_2 + b_2(_{t+3}r_{3,t} - R_{3,t}) + v_t \tag{8.10}$$

The actual change in the interest rate is regressed on its expectation. If expectations are rationally formed and the market is competitive, the intercept a_2 should be zero, the slope b_2 unity, and the error term white noise. None of the estimates, presented in the authors' Table 8.6, passes this test. The estimates for Eurodollar and Eurosterling do not reach the 5 percent level of significance, while the estimates for Euromark and ECU yield significant non-zero intercepts.

These damaging results are confirmed by a final test, where the authors regress spot interest rates on past forward rates (see the authors' Table 8.7). None of the estimates reaches the 5 percent level of significance.

In sum, the empirical results presented by Tullio and Contesso may lead us to conclude that none of the Euromarkets examined complies with the requirements of informational efficiency.[4] However, on the consideration that the authors' data base consists of no more than 11 observations, we must not be too concerned.

NOTES

1. But note that the ECU's market share is still small. At the end of 1986 no more than 2.1 percent of total foreign assets and 1.8 percent of total foreign liabilities of the BIS-reporting banks were ECU dominated.

2. But note that changes in bid/ask spreads cannot show up in the empirical measures presented by Tullio and Contesso because their data are averages of bid and offer rates.

3. The authors report four different methods of computing combined Eurocurrency rates but do not explain why the method actually used is to be preferred.

4. But note that the authors themselves do not draw this conclusion.

9

Currency Unification, Currency Competition, and the Private ECU: Second Thoughts

Roland Vaubel

1. THE PRETENSE OF KNOWLEDGE

One Money for Europe?

Should there be only one money in Europe? I used to think so. I am no longer sure. I believe that we do not know.

There is no such thing as a costless currency union. The costs concern the price-level target for the union as a whole and for the individual member states.

First of all, currency unification is likely to raise the average rate of inflation in Europe. There are several reasons for this:

1. Currency substitution, which acts as a check on the monetary policies of the national central banks, is no longer possible within the union (Hayek 1976).

2. Not only "exit" but also "voice"[1] (i.e., the protest of voters) becomes less effective as a corrective feedback mechanism:

(i) Voters in the inflation-ridden countries cannot point as easily to the example of superior central banks nearby.

(ii) The causal nexus between monetary policy and inflation becomes less transparent (Johnson 1970: 105). The price level reacts with a longer lag in a currency union because an immediate depreciation relative to other member currencies is no longer possible.

More generally, currency unification is the substitution of a union money monopoly for an oligopoly of partly competing national suppliers. The degree of competition within the oligopoly depends on the extent of exchange rate flexibility and of exchange controls. The smaller the degree of competition among money producers, the larger is the price (opportunity cost) of holding money (i.e., the nominal interest rate and inflation) and the smaller is output (i.e., real balances). Empirical research by de Grauwe (1985 and chapter 7 of the present book), Collins (chapter 6) and myself (1978c) supports this theoretical conclusion with regard to monetary policy collusion in the European Community.[2] The extent to which these results would also apply to an EC money monopoly may depend on the degree of extra-union competition. If currency unification increases worldwide competition among *major* currencies more than it reduces competition among *minor* currencies, its effect on currency competition and world inflation could even be beneficial. We must confess: we do not know.

But even if the average inflation rate in the EC and elsewhere was not affected by currency unification, national price levels in the member states could no longer be kept stable in the presence of intra-union real exchange rate changes.[3] To see this, note that, between two countries,

$$S \equiv \frac{P}{P*} \cdot R$$

or, in rates of change,

$$\hat{S} \equiv \hat{P} - \hat{P}* + \hat{R}$$

where S is the spot exchange rate in units of the domestic currency; P is the domestic price level to be stabilized; $P*$ is the foreign price level to be stabilized; and R is the real exchange rate between the commodity baskets for which P and $P*$ are calculated. If the real exchange rate varies (i.e., $\hat{R} \neq 0$), and if the nominal (spot) exchange rate is fixed at 1 as a result of currency unification (i.e., $\hat{S} = 0$), it follows that $\hat{P}$ and $\hat{P}*$ cannot both be equal, for example, to zero:

$$-\hat{R} = \hat{P} - \hat{P}* \neq 0$$

For this reason, Vaubel (1978a) has suggested that the extent of intra-union real exchange rate variations is a criterion of the desirability of currency unification for a given group of countries.[4]

Table 9.1 shows the extent of long-run real exchange rate changes between the EC member states (excluding Luxembourg), if the consumer price index (CPI) is used. The maximum real exchange real change, 1.95 per cent per annum, occurred between the Danish and the Greek consumer baskets. Thus, if Denmark and Greece had been members of an EC currency union and if the Greek price level had been kept stable, Denmark would have had to suffer an inflation rate of about 2 per cent. Probably few economists would consider real exchange rate changes a very serious obstacle to currency union, as long as they are of this

Table 9.1
Compound Average Rates of Real-Exchange-Rate Appreciation Relative to Greece on CPI Basis, 1959–85 (percent per annum)

Denmark	1.95
Netherlands	1.91
Portugal	1.79
Spain	1.54
Ireland	1.51
FR Germany	1.31
UK	1.11
Italy	0.99
Belgium	0.81
France	0.70

Source: Calculated from IMF International Financial Statistics.

magnitude, but the criterion as such is clearly relevant. Moreover, real exchange rate changes have been much larger over subperiods such as 1959–76 (3.35 per cent p.a. between the Netherlands and Britain) or 1971–76 (7.34 per cent p.a. between the Netherlands and Italy).[5] The shorter the period, the larger tends to be the part of intra-Community real exchange rate changes that is due to intra-Community differences in money supply shocks or to parity adjustments and that would cease to exist in a European currency union. But as the oil price shocks have shown, there are also reversible real exchange rate variations that are not due to differential monetary policies or parity changes.[6] In a currency union, there are bound to cause price level changes and price level risk in at least some member states.

If these are the costs of currency union, at least from a classical perspective,[7] what are the benefits? Currency unification eliminates various types of information cost, transaction cost and risk: the cost of being informed about current exchange rates and exchange controls, the transaction cost of changing monies and of passing exchange controls, and the exchange rate and convertibility risks or the cost of protection against them.[8] The existence of these costs is well known but they cannot be quantified. We do not even know whether the exchange rate risk, which currency unification eliminates, generates smaller or larger costs than the price level risk, which currency unification renders inevitable. Is the exchange rate risk less costly because

- it is cheaper to organize a forward market for a homogeneous good like foreign exchange than for a heterogeneous basket of commodities, or because

- international transactors have a comparative advantage over domestic transactors in dealing with risk in general?

There is no operational scientific method of measuring and comparing the costs and benefits of currency unification for a given group of countries. For the same reasons, as we shall see, there is no operational scientific method of defining optimum currency areas.

A Modern Classical Theory of Optimum Currency Areas

So far we have enquired whether a given group of countries, the European Community, ought to form a currency union. The question posed by the theory of optimum currency areas is a different one: Which countries or regions should join which currency union, if global welfare is to be maximized?

I used to argue that the extent of real exchange rate changes between the potential members of such currency unions is a comprehensive criterion for the determination of optimum currency areas (Vaubel 1978a). I calculated the variance of real exchange rate changes with respect to a common numeraire to find the optimal combination of EC countries for each number of union members. Table 9.2 contains an updated version of this exercise. It is based on the figures of Table 9.1.

Table 9.2
Minimum Variances of Real-Exchange-Rate Changes for Different Numbers of Members, 1959–85

EC member country	10	9	8	7	6	5	4	3	2
Denmark	X	X	X	X	X	X		X	
Netherlands	X	X	X	X	X	X		X	
Portugal	X	X	X	X	X	X		X	
Spain	X	X	X	X	X	X			X
Ireland	X	X	X	X	X	X			X
FR Germany	X	X	.X	X	X				
UK	X	X	X	X			X		
Italy	X	X	X				X		
Belgium	X	X					X		
France	X						X		
Greece									
Minimum Variance	0.203	0.168	0.129	0.098	0.064	0.042	0.033	0.007	0.00045

Table 9.2 shows that, from the point of view of real exchange rate performance, Greece, France, Belgium, Italy, Britain, and the Federal Republic of Germany—in this order—would have been the least appropriate members of an EC currency union of declining membership, but that, for example, the optimal four-member currency area would have comprised Britain, Italy, Belgium, and France.

The real exchange rate criterion is comprehensive from a classical perspective in that it allows for, and attributes appropriate weights to, the traditional criteria of the theory of optimum currency areas, such as diversification (Kenen 1969), factor mobility (Mundell 1961), openness (McKinnon 1963), fiscal integration (Kenen 1969), and so on. These criteria are of two types:

1. characteristics determining the size and frequency of changes in demand and supply conditions that require real international adjustment (e.g., diversification), and

2. characteristics that reduce the real exchange rate effect of such changes (e.g., labor mobility).

Thus, whereas the first group of characteristics determines the need for real international adjustment, the second affects the extent to which real international adjustment takes the form of real exchange rate adjustment, hopefully, as the least costly adjustment mechanism.

The need for international adjustment is smaller, the more diversified the country's international transactions with the other potential members of the currency union. To the extent that the need for international adjustment is unanticipated, the insurance principle will operate more effectively, and the smaller is the correlation of disturbances between transactions. Since unexpected price level changes are more costly than expected ones, the cost of international adjustment also depends on its predictability. What matters in a classical framework is not the diversification of production but the diversification of international trade, transfers, and capital movements. While it is true that "a country that engages in a number of activities is also apt to export a wide range of products" (Kenen 1969: 49), its imports are likely to be less diversified, the more products it produces itself.

There are other factors determining the need for real international adjustment that have generally been overlooked in the theory of optimum currency areas. For example, the need for real international adjustment is smaller, the more similar are (1) the patterns of production, (2) the tastes, and (3) the supply-side policies of the potential member countries. One way of reducing the need for policy-induced real international adjustment is to complete the common market for goods, services, and factors of production before the national currencies are merged (Yeager 1958: 420). This consideration may justify Germany's present insistence that restrictions on capital movements ought to be abolished prior to any further exchange rate commitments. The transition to the origin principle of value-added taxation should also precede currency unification (Christie and Fratianni 1978; Laidler 1978).

The extent to which international adjustment requires real exchange rate adjustment (most directly, terms of trade adjustment)[9] is smaller, the higher the international mobility of labor (Mundell 1961), because labor mobility increases the national price elasticity (or real exchange rate elasticity) of supply. International capital mobility can have the same effect but it can also augment the required real exchange rate change. If, for example, the world demand for goods shifts from the products of country A to those of country B and thereby increases B's terms of trade, capital movements from A to B would initially require an additional increase in B's terms of trade in order to reduce B's current account balance.

The effects that fiscal integration exerts on the need for real exchange rate adjustment are also ambiguous.[10] If A and B are fiscally integrated, the shift in world demand, it is true, leads to public transfer payments from B to A, which reduce the increase in B's terms of trade. But if the deterioration in country A is due to a supply-side shock (say, a permanent deterioration of industrial relations in A), A's terms of trade tend to increase and the transfer payments from B would reinforce this terms of trade increase.

Mutual openness can also reduce the real exchange rate effect of a given need for real international adjustment in a currency union (McKinnon 1963). If, as in the small-country case, the terms of trade are invariable and if the union central bank stabilizes the prices of tradable goods as a proxy for the union price level, changes in a country's relative prices between tradables and non-tradables have a smaller impact on its consumer price index and on its CPI-related real exchange rate, the larger the share of tradable goods in its CPI basket, that is, the more open it is with respect to trade. However, if the country's terms of trade are variable and if the central bank stabilizes the union price level, the result is the opposite: the country's price level is less stable, the larger is the share of tradable goods in its consumer price basket (and the greater is its terms of trade change).

Since the traditional criteria of optimum currency areas are mostly ambiguous, difficult to measure, and not commensurable in any other way, the availability of a comprehensive and operational measuring stick, the real exchange rate criterion, is important. But it is not comprehensive enough. It ignores the other cost of currency unification: the weakening of currency competition; and it does not take full account of the benefits of currency unification: the reduction of information costs, transaction costs, and risks in international transactions between the member countries (though this benefit is positively correlated with the degree of mutual openness).

There is widespread agreement that the small and central member countries would reap the largest benefits from currency unification. But Table 9.2 does not indicate that these countries (except for the Netherlands) would also suffer the smallest costs in terms of price level instability. We do not know which EC member countries are the most suitable candidates for currency unification.

2. A DISCOVERY PROCEDURE

Free Currency Competition

The classical criteria for optimum currency regimes and optimum currency areas concern the price level behavior and the transaction domain of money. The behavior of the price level determines a money's usefulness as a standard and a store of value. The most informative and least risky standard of value is a money whose purchasing power is stable in terms of the basket of goods and services that the individual money user wants to buy or sell. With respect to the store-of-value function, the optimal money offers as high a yield, and as low a (portfolio) risk, as possible. The size of a money's transaction domain determines its usefulness as a medium of exchange and as a contractual standard of value; in this respect, the optimum currency area is the world.

All this is well known, but its implication for the question of currency unification is rarely spelled out. The implication is that the classical criteria of optimum currency areas and regimes are identical with the microeconomic criteria that a rational user of money employs in choosing among currencies. Each money user weighs the advantages of a large transaction domain against the disadvantages of an unstable and rising price level.[11] He also knows his purchase and sales plans (the relevant basket and transaction domain) and his yield-risk indifference curves. Thus, individual money users, not politicians or economists, have a comparative informational advantage in determining the optimal number and pattern of currency domains.[12] Unlike politicians and their economic advisers, individual money users also have a sufficient incentive to make use of this information.

I used to believe that the desirability of a European currency union was a foregone conclusion and that currency competition would merely show us the optimal path to that end (Vaubel 1977). I now realize that the end itself has to be questioned[13] and that currency competition is not only the optimum currency unification process, if currency union is desirable, but also the optimal procedure of finding out whether currency union is desirable. If several currencies survive in free and unbiased competition,[14] we know at the same time their optimal transaction domains. If a single currency prevails, we know at the same time what sort of money is optimal (for instance, whether a money of stable or increasing purchasing power is preferable). The optimum may vary over time.

Ultimately, free choice in currency is a procedure of selecting the best central bank constitution. To the extent that instrumental decisions should be left to central bankers, free choice in currency is also a way of selecting the optimal monetary policy rule and the best personnel to execute it, though the best monetary policy under currency competition may not be the best monetary policy for a currency union.[15]

Economic integration can mean market integration or policy integration. Monetary integration is usually interpreted as a case for policy integration; such policy integration is advocated because it is thought to improve market integration. Monetary market integration is considered to be perfect if, and only if, a single money is used.

But this conclusion is premature and incompatible with our other notions concerning market integration. Perfect integration in the market for goods and services does not require that all consumers demand the same basket of goods and services, nor that they buy it from the same supplier. Perfect integration of capital markets does not require that all savers hold identical portfolios of assets, or that they hold the liabilities of only one issuer. If tastes differ[16] or if the use and production of money are not natural monopolies, monetary market integration can be perfect in the presence of multiple currencies. Exchange controls, not multiple currencies, are necessarily inconsistent with monetary market integration.

The Parallel Currency Approach to Monetary Integration

If free and unbiased competition among existing currencies—and possibly with new, perhaps even private, currencies—is politically infeasible, the parallel currency approach can be viewed as a second-best solution to increase choice and competition among currencies. Instead of choosing among all EC currencies, each money user would be free to choose between his or her national and one common European currency, the parallel currency. The private ECU may be considered a parallel currency in this sense, even though it is not privileged in this way in all member countries,[17] and even though its exchange rate with the national member currencies is not freely flexible.[18]

Opponents of the private ECU, especially in Germany, tend to argue that a European parallel currency must not be permitted to gain ground unless there is agreement about the monetary end state to be attained and about the policy actions to be taken on the way to it.[19] Such reasoning reveals a complete misunderstanding of the rationale of the parallel currency approach. As we have seen, currency competition is a discovery procedure. If we knew the desirable end state and the optimal patter of transition, the case for the parallel currency would be much less convincing.

The parallel currency approach and the EMS exchange rate arrangement are widely regarded as complements rather than substitutes. This view has to be qualified. It is true that a European parallel currency like the ECU can contribute to stabilizing intra-EMS exchange rates. By serving as a substitute for the dollar, the ECU might reduce the intra-EMS tensions that are caused by currency substitution toward and away from the dollar (though it increases currency substitution within the EMS). By exerting competitive pressure on the more inflation-prone EMS central banks, it might induce them to bring their currencies in line with the others. Exchange rate stability, or more generally, price equalization, can result not only from collusion but also from competition. But if the parallel currency contributes to intra-EMS exchange rate stability, the exchange rate agreement of the EMS becomes increasingly superfluous for this purpose. Thus, collusion and competition are substitutes in this respect.

Conversely, we may ask whether the EMS exchange rate arrangement improves the prospects for the private ECU. The ECU benefits from the fact that it serves as a pivot for the EMS. This implies that the margins of fluctuation between the ECU and the EMS currencies are on average only half as large as the margins of fluctuation between any pair of EMS currencies. As a currency basket the ECU has also benefited from the lack of convergence as manifested in the repeated parity adjustments. But if the Community pursues its exchange rate strategy (the "Werner Plan") further, it weakens the ECU's competitive position in both respects.

Any narrowing of the margins of fluctuation reduces the ECU's competitive edge in terms of short-run exchange rate stability. Moreover, any reduction of the margins of fluctuation or of parity adjustments tends to increase the expected covariance of yields on assets denominated in different currencies[20] and thereby reduces the ECU's attractiveness as an instrument of currency diversification. In terms of expected yield, ECU deposits are only preferable to deposits in "weak" member currencies—provided, of course, that money does not bear interest or is subject to non-interest-bearing reserve requirements or that capital gains from exchange rate changes are not fully taxed. If parity adjustments were expected to decrease, the incentive to hold ECU balances rather than the weaker EMS currencies would diminish. Thus, the EMS exchange rate strategy tends to reduce the attractiveness of the private ECU.[21] Moreover, as Girton and Roper (1980: 158) point out, "the formation of a central bank cooperative will reduce pressure to provide holders of monies with a desirable alternative money, such as an attractive and available parallel currency."

To sum up, the EMS exchange rate strategy undermines the parallel currency approach, while the parallel currency approach tends to render the exchange rate strategy redundant. The Community's decision to try both approaches at the same time reveals, therefore, that it expects little from the parallel currency approach and that it expects more from the EMS approach.

Nevertheless, there is a sense in which the parallel currency approach and EMS exchange rate strategy are complementary. For the EC Commission, the parallel currency approach is primarily a fallback position in case the EMS approach fails. The private ECU serves as a diversifying device not only for portfolio owners but also for European policy makers. It is part of the portfolio of policy instruments that uncertainty has led them to resort to.

3. THE PRIVATE ECU AS A PARALLEL CURRENCY

I used to believe that "a basket-type European Currency Unit is not a suitable starting point for a strategy of currency unification because, as a currency, it would not offer a sufficient yield to be able to outcompete all national member currencies" (Vaubel 1978b: 418).[22] I am no longer sure about the first part of this statement. The private ECU has obtained a larger market share than I expected, especially in the Dutch and Belgian market for deposits and in the French and Italian credit market. I now believe that there are methods—short of indexing the ECU[23]—that might enable it to displace all but the strongest member currency and to merge with the latter in a unified currency.[24] It would merely be necessary to alter the procedure by which the ECU weights are adjusted to market developments.

How to Reform the ECU

At present, the weights that the EC member currencies are given in the ECU currency basket depend on the member countries' shares in Community GNP and intra-EC trade and in the short-term monetary support mechanism. It is left to the Council of Ministers to weigh these shares, but the currency weights must stay within the range set by these three criteria. The currency weights are to be reexamined every five years or on request, if the weight of one component currency has changed by at least 25 percent. Some such requests have been turned down. The weights are adjusted in such a way that the external value of the ECU does not change as a result.

Even if the ECU is not viewed as a vehicle of European currency unification, the current weight adjustment procedure has three disadvantages:

1. It leaves unnecessary room for discretion to European policy makers. It exposes the users of ECUs to avoidable policy risk. Some private contractors have protected themselves against this risk by using an ECU of immutably fixed currency composition (so-called closed ECUs). But this means that more than one type of ECU is employed in the markets if official weight adjustments occur.

2. Since the official weights depend on the countries' shares in intra-Community trade and since the small member countries are most open with respect to intra-Community trade, their currencies receive larger weights in the ECU basket than would be justified by their monetary base shares (and by their GNP shares). As I have explained in some detail elsewhere (Vaubel 1980a: 189–92), this distorts the choice of intervention currencies for intra-marginal interventions in favor of the small currencies, because intervention in the "overweighted" currencies has a stronger impact on the domestic currency value of the ECU than intervention in the "underweighted currencies." This distortion is aggravated if the central bank is buying foreign currencies and acquires an ECU-denominated claim to settlement.

3. The official weight adjustments prevent the appreciating and more stable member currencies from increasing their ECU weights in the longer run. Between the official weight adjustments, it is true, the individual member currencies can enlarge their ECU weight through revaluation. But the official adjustments of the currency weights reverse this effect. The ECU cannot become better than the average.

My proposal would eliminate these defects and open the way for a competitive process of currency unification.

The basic idea is that the weights that the member currencies are assigned in the ECU basket should be permitted to respond permanently to the currency preferences of European money holders. In the simplest case, the ECU currency weights would be equal to the share that each member currency occupies in the EC money supply at market exchange rates. It might be advisable to use the monetary aggregate that would have yielded the smallest rate of ECU inflation in the past (e.g., since March 1979). The weights would be adjusted automatically and at regular intervals (say, annually) on the basis of a moving average. To the extent that a national member currency was displaced by the ECU, its weight in the ECU would diminish. Since the ECU is likely to displace primarily the weakest (high inflation) currencies, the weight adjustments would strengthen the ECU. Even if all member currencies that are weaker than the ECU at the beginning dropped out completely, the weight adjustments would ensure that the ECU basket is always stronger than at least one of the remaining member currencies. Only if the ECU had displaced all but the strongest member currency (i.e., if it had ceased to be a basket) would the process of currency substitution have come to an end. At this final stage, the ECU would be identical with the strongest national member currency.

For political reasons, it might be necessary or even desirable to adjust the nationality composition of the board(s) of the surviving central bank(s) so as to allow for the effects that their decisions have on ECU users in other member countries. If the quality of monetary policy depends on the constitution, rather than the personnel, of the central bank (as the theory of public choice would predict), the economic cost of such a political compromise is likely to be small.

Ideally, the proportional representation (or voting power) of country j on the central bank board of currency i (v_{ij}) would be determined according to the following formula:

$$v_{ij} = \frac{M_{ij}/S_{i/e} + w_i^e \cdot M_j^e}{\sum_j (M_{ij}/S_{i/e} + w_i^e \cdot M_j^e)}$$

with $\sum_j v_{ij} = 1$ and $\sum_i w_i^e = 1$,

where the subscript i denotes the *currency* or the central bank issuing it, respectively; the subscript j denotes the *nationality* of the money holder or the board member, respectively; $S_{i/e}$ is the ECU exchange rate of currency i (units of i per ECU); M_{ij} is the money supply in currency i held by residents of country j; M_j^e is the ECU money supply held by residents of country j; and w_i^e is the current weight of currency i in the ECU. If the central bank board responsible for currency i has n_i members and if each is to have one vote of equal weight, representation of foreign country j on the board of i might usefully require that $v_{ij} \geq 1/n_i$.

If the cost of collecting information about M_{ij} and M_j^e is taken into account, the calculation of v_{ij} may have to be simplified. For example, the distribution of currency in circulation (notes and coins) should be ignored in calculating the voting weights. It might be sufficient to distinguish only deposits held (1) by domestic residents, (2) by residents of other EC countries, and (3) by other foreigners, and to allocate the deposits held by residents of other EC countries to these member countries in fixed proportions or according to their money supply shares.

Ideally, the governments of the member countries would take an entirely neutral attitude in the process of currency competition. This implies that they would let their own currency choice be guided by the currency preferences of private EC money holders as represented by the ECU. Thus, the ECU would have to be receivable in payment of taxes and be usable in all government payments. Legal tender laws would have to be abolished or adjusted so as to avoid any discrimination against the ECU. Although such a neutral attitude would be desirable, it need not, however, be indispensible for the parallel currency approach to succeed.

The proposed method of calculating the ECU weights offers a number of important advantages:

1. Unlike the present procedure, it is completely automatic and minimizes policy risk.

2. Unlike the present procedure, it does not distort the choice of intervention currencies for intra-marginal interventions.

3. Unlike the present procedure, it would be responsive to the revealed currency preferences of the EC money holders. It would enable the preferred member currencies to irreversibly enlarge their ECU weights, and to do so not only through exchange rate changes but also as a result of money supply responses to increased foreign money demand. It would indirectly simulate generalized currency competition: each member currency would compete with each other member currency through its ECU weight.

4. If European currency union is optimal and if the ECU can overcome its infant currency problem, the ECU would bring about currency union in a more or less gradual process. There would be no need for an "institutional leap"; in particular, there would be no discontinuity in the transition to the final stage of currency union.[25]

5. The proposed method would enable us to find out which is the best central bank constitution and to select it for the European Community.

6. Both as a parallel currency and as a divergence indicator, the proposed ECU would exert a stronger disciplinary effect on the national central banks than the present ECU ever could.

However, there is a problem of transition from the present ECU to the proposed ECU. As Table 9.3 indicates, the M_1 and M_2 weights, for example, differ

Table 9.3
Alternative Weighting Schemes for the European Currency Unit (at central rates)

	present method			M_1 weights*		M_2 weights*	
	amounts since 17.09.1984	percentage weights on 17.09.1984	percentage weights on 12.01.1987	percentage weights on 17.09.1984	percentage weights on 12.01.1987	percentage weights on 17.09.1984	percentage weights on 12.01.1987
bfr	3.71	8.2	8.7	4.0	3.5	5.7	5.4
lfr	0.14	0.3	0.3	0.1	0.3	0.6	0.7
DM	0.719	32.0	34.9	22.2	21.4	19.3	17.5
hfl	0.256	10.1	11.0	5.5	5.4	4.7	4.5
£	0.0878	15.0	11.9	13.1	12.3	16.7	13.8
dkr	0.219	2.7	2.8	2.6	3.5	2.5	3.1
FF	1.31	19.0	19.0	23.0	25.6	22.0	29.0
Lit	140.00	10.2	9.4	28.1	26.9	25.5	23.7
Ir £	0.00871	1.2	1.1	0.5	0.4	0.9	0.7
Dr	1.15	1.3	0.8	1.0	0.7	1.9	1.6

[a]For computational facility, the money stock averages relate merely to the beginning-of-quarter values in the preceding year. To facilitate comparison with the current method of computing weights, the money stock figures have also been converted at the official central rates.
Note: bfr = Belgian franc; lfr = Luxembourg franc; DM = Deutschmark; hfl = Dutch guilder; £ = English pound; dkr = Danish krone; FF = French franc; Lit = Italian lira, Ir£ = Irish punt; Dr = Greek drachma.

Sources: Money stocks (except Luxembourg): OECD, *Main Economic Indicators;* for Luxembourg: *IMF International Financial Statistics.* ECU composition and exchange rates: Deutsche Bundesbank, *Statistische Beihefte zu den Monatsberichten, Reihe 5: Die Währungen der Welt.*

considerably from the present ECU weights. Moreover, they are larger for high inflation currencies like the Italian lira and the French franc and smaller for low inflation currencies like the Deutschmark and the Dutch guilder. The main reason is that velocity differs enormously between some member countries (in some cases by more than 3 : 1).

There may be monetary aggregates for which this is not the case. If not, the proposal may have to be modified for practical purposes. One way would be to partially adjust for velocity differences; however, this would lead us back to GNP or GDP weights. Another solution might be to retain the present ECU definition until it yields a higher annual rate of inflation than at least one of the money supply baskets; at this moment, the ECU would be redefined as the money supply basket that would have yielded the lowest rate of ECU inflation over the preceding year. But there are also procedures that would render the ECU immediately responsive to currency preferences without requiring a major and perverse initial adjustment of weights. For example, the percentage point changes of the money supply weights could be added to, or subtracted from, the present ECU weights, respectively (subject to the provision that no member currency can receive an ECU weight that is larger than 1 or smaller than 0). However, Table 9.3 demonstrates that at least if central rates and lagged annual averages of M_1 and M_2 had been used, this method would have yielded a reduction of the weights of the strongest currencies (DM, hfl, or Dutch guilder) from September 1984 to January 1987, whereas the present method yielded an increase. Such effects could be avoided if present weights (or simply GNP weights) were adjusted in proportion to the extent that the domestic currency had been displaced by the ECU (and possibly by other member currencies) in the money holdings of domestic residents. The ECU weights that the domestic currency loses would then be taken up by the ECU in its new composition (or if the domestic currency had been displaced by another national member currency, by that currency).

How Not to Reform the ECU

There remains the question of whether the official ECU ought to be redefined in the same way and whether the private and the official ECU ought to be "linked" in such a manner that central banks could use their ECU holdings with the European Monetary Cooperation Fund (EMCF) for ECU interventions in the foreign exchange market.[26] Allen (1986: 51–53), for example, has proposed that, instead of depositing a certain proportion of their gold and dollar reserves with the EMCF, the member central banks should pay subscriptions in their own currencies, each in accordance with the ECU weight of its own currency.

The official ECU has its place, if at all,[27] in the EMS exchange rate strategy. It does not belong to the parallel currency approach, although ECU interventions would promote the private use of the ECU. Thus, like myself, who doubt the wisdom of intervening in exchange markets, will not see a useful role for the official ECU, however defined. But even the advocates of foreign exchange interventions should have their doubts about these proposals for at least three reasons:

1. If central banks want to obtain foreign exchange for intervention purposes, they ought to be obliged to borrow it in the market, that is, on market terms. The terms offered by official international organizations are not market terms, even if a so-called market rate of interest is charged, because they are invariant with respect to the creditworthiness of the borrower and the size and term of the loan.

2. Whereas the present practice of creating official ECUs is no more than a redenomination of existing reserves, official international liquidity would expand, if the central banks could pay their subscriptions in their own currencies.

3. It is not efficient to intervene with a currency basket that partly consists of the domestic currency.[28] Within the framework of the EMS strategy, interventions should not be diversified at all; they ought to be conducted in the member currency that is "at the other end" (Vaubel 1980a: 187–89).

But this advice—almost all of it—is unlikely to be heeded.

NOTES

1. This is the terminology of Albert Hirschmann (1970).

2. Vaubel (1978c) has shown that, in 1968–78, the average rate of monetary expansion in Western Europe was higher, the smaller the differences among the national rates of monetary expansion across countries. De Grauwe (1985) has found that the average inflation rate of the EMS countries has fallen less from 1979 to 1984, and was higher, than the average inflation rate of the other major OECD countries.

3. However, real exchange rate changes do not pose a problem if the price level target is derived from the so-called theory of the optimum quantity of money. Real exchange rate changes are perfectly consistent with zero nominal interest rates in all member states of the currency union. A price level problem does not arise because the theory of the optimum quantity of money does not consider money as a standard of value but merely as a store of value (Mussa 1977).

4. In the meantime, I have discovered the same idea in Pearce (1974). It also plays a role in McKinnon's derivation of his openness criterion (1963). Mundell (1961), too, views regional inflation as a cost of currency unification, and Friedman (1953) notes that the size of real exchange rate changes affects the number of price changes in a currency union.

5. See Vaubel (1978a). Figures for the period 1959–79 can be found in Lehment (1984: 252). Vaubel has also shown that, in 1959–76, the maximum real exchange rate changes have been much smaller in existing currency unions such as the United States (0.65 per cent p.a.), FR Germany (0.76 per cent p.a.), and Italy (1.29 per cent p.a.).

6. This has been overlooked in Daniel's recent test for monetary and real causes of real exchange rate changes (Daniel 1986).

7. Keynesian economists, who believe that national governments would do a useful job when asked to stabilize output and employment (and to do so not by stabilizing, but at the expense of stabilizing, the price level), will see additional costs of currency union. The same is true for those who expect that, owing to currency unification, international wage differentials would narrow more than international differentials of labor productivity and that undesirable capital movements from the periphery to the agglomeration centers would occur. Moreover, there are those who regard seigniorage from inflation as part of an optimal tax structure and expect the optimal inflation rates to vary from country to country. All these authors are even more inclined to doubt the desirability of currency unification.

8. In this respect, currency union must not be confused with an EMS-type adjustable peg system. The latter does not eliminate these information and transaction costs; it is likely to reduce exchange rate risk but also to increase the average level, and the unexpected variations, of exchange controls.

9. In the following I shall assume that an increase in the terms of trade generates a

real exchange rate appreciation on a CPI basis because each country's products occupy a larger share in its own consumer price basket than in foreign consumer price baskets.

10. The capital mobility criterion and the fiscal integration criterion have also been questioned by Fleming (1971), but on the basis of a different analysis.

11. Keynesians might object that the analysis that has led to this conclusion did not allow for undesirable output fluctuations. However, if economic agents are concerned about output fluctuations, they also have a sufficient incentive to reduce them by choosing an appropriate standard of value in their contracts. Free choice among currencies would permit us to discover the weight that economic agents attach to the target of output stabilization as compared with other targets.

12. This is also the view of Hayek (1976: 17, 21), Girton and Roper (1980: 153, 158f.), and Claassen (1984: 57; 1986: 45). *The Economist's* (1978) The All Saints' Day Manifesto is ambivalent on this point. On the one hand, it states that "it is for the people themselves to decide whether they want monetary union or not" (1978: 37). On the other hand, it predicts that "our proposal offers the best way of achieving a monetary system which will be not only European-wide in scope but stable as well" (1978: 37).

13. Chen (1975) reports a case in which two currencies, one based on silver, the other on copper, circulated side by side at variable exchange rates for two centuries. The silver currency was mainly used in the cities, whereas the copper currency prevailed in the rural areas. The terms of trade between the two currency areas were subject to large fluctuations.

14. One might object that individual choice among currencies generates Pareto-relevant transaction cost externalities. However, as I have argued elsewhere (1984: 41–44), in competitive markets each money user has a sufficient incentive to choose the currency that minimizes social transaction costs.

15. In conditions of currency competition and currency substitution, fixed rates of monetary expansion are less likely to be optimal than they are under money monopolies. They are not likely to prevail under free currency competition (Vaubel 1977: 451; Girton and Roper 1980: 153).

16. As has been pointed out, differences in tastes with respect to goods and services or with respect to risk can cause differences in currency preferences. Since different portfolio owners evaluate risk in terms of different commodity bundles, Tobin's separation theorem does not hold in the real world.

17. Until recently the French government had liberalized ECU transactions to a greater extent than transactions in foreign member currencies. The German Bundesbank pursues the opposite policy.

18. The nineteenth-century writers (Mill, Jevons, etc.) reserved the term "parallel standard" for the flexible exchange rate case. The fixed exchange rate case was called a "double standard."

19. *Die Parallelwaehrungsstrategie* "ist nur denkbar und möglich, wenn sie von dem politisch gewollten Integrationsziel initiiert und getragen wird; nur so erhält sie auch ihren Sinn und Inhalt" (Graumann 1979: 166). "Eine Conditio sine qua non für jedes weiterführende integrationspolitische Handeln ist Klarheit über das künftige Prozedere" (Kloten 1985: 462). "Es ist daher . . . zunächst erforderlich, zu klareren Vorstellungen über die längerfristige Rolle der ECU zu kommen" (Stoltenberg 1985: 2).

20. As Guiseppe Tullio has pointed out at the conference, this forecast rests on the assumption that the reduction of exchange rate variability is not completely offset by an increase in nominal interest rate variability.

21. This conclusion can be found in Vaubel (1980b: 64), Thygesen (1980: 21), Neumann (1983: 324), Abraham and Lacroix-Destree (1984: 25), Burrett (1982: 168), von Moltke (1986: 87), Allen (1986: 25). For the opposite view see Keyzer (1983: 319) and Masera (1986).

Masera points out that "the period of relative stability in exchange rates in the past three years has been the one which showed the most significant expansion in the (ECU) market" (p. 17). He concludes from his portfolio analysis that

the ECU can find its place in efficient portfolios for European residents . . . even more so in a perspective of increasing monetary cohesion in the EMS. With the risk of significant movements in intra-EEC exchange rates declining, EEC residents are likely to perceive the ECU as an increasingly closer substitute for the domestic currency than other foreign currencies. (p. 32)

But his mean-variance analysis is marred by the fact that he measures risk in terms of the domestic currency rather than in terms of a representative basket of goods and services; in other words, he commits the error (noted in Vaubel 1978b: 123) of measuring only nominal (balance sheet) risk instead of real (purchasing power) risk. The same effect can be found in Micossi's analysis (1985: 338) and in Edison's attempt (1986) to construct a currency basket that is optimal for Germany portfolio owners and to compare it with the ECU. Unfortunately, the domestic currency is not a riskless asset. Von Moltke (1986), by contrast, compares the expected rates and variances of real yields on financial assets dominated in ECU and major national currencies.

22. De Grauwe and Peeters (1979: 42) even predicted that "it is not to be expected that the ECU can be used as a symbol and as an instrument of European monetary integration, because the ECU itself will remain less attractive than the existing alternatives, i.e., national currencies."

23. A European parallel currency defined as an indexed currency basket has notably been proposed by the signatories of the All Saints' Day Manifesto (*Economist* 1978). Vaubel (1978b) contains a detailed analysis of this proposal. The current period of relatively low European inflation rates offers an ideal occasion to permit and introduce indexed monetary and financial contracts. This is because, at the present time, such a move would hardly generate inflation expectations. On the contrary, by reducing the output and employment effects of unexpected inflation, indexation diminishes the political temptation to reinflate.

24. For a discrete and rudimentary version of this method see the last paragraph in Vaubel (1980b: 64).

25. The other proposals for a basket-type parallel currency suffer from such a discontinuity problem; see Vaubel (1978b: 178f.), and Gebauer (1986: 171f.). The problem is not limited to the parallel-currency approach. As far as I can see, free currency competition and my proposal for adjustment of ECU weights are the only exceptions to Micossi's rule (1985: 342) that "it is not possible to proceed to a common currency world without an 'institutional leap' setting up a central authority to manage it."

26. Such a link has notably been suggested by Masera (1986) and Allen (1986). For a critique see Kloten (1985: 459) and Vaubel (1987: 99f.).

27. "Man kann . . . mit Fug und Recht konstatieren, daß das EWS nicht schlechter funktioniert haette, wenn es die offizielle ECU nicht gäbe" (Scharrer 1984: 1087).

28. This drawback is recognized by Masera (1986: 15) and Allen (1986: 63, n. 85).

COMMENT BY

Peter B. Kenen

Roland Vaubel covers a wide range of issues in this stimulating and provocative chapter. I will resist the temptation to comment on all of the issues so as to focus on the most controversial.

I must start by pointing out that the conference in Florence was attended by people from two planets. Some of us came from a world in which prices are sticky, monetary policies have real effects (including effects on real exchange rates), and the reallocation of resources can be painful. In that world, governments have wide-ranging responsibilities, and while they may fail to discharge them effectively, some of us continue to believe that we should try to help them improve their performance. Other participants, including Roland Vaubel and Pascal Salin, appear to come from a world in which markets are cleared instantaneously by perfectly flexible prices, monetary policies can affect the price level but do nothing else, good or bad, and adjustment costs are low if not negligible. In their world, moreover, governments appear to be incorrigibly incompetent and should therefore do as little as possible in order to minimize the number of things they do wrong.

Because we come from different planets, we sometimes look at different sides of the same equation, and that is true of the equation that figures so importantly in the first part of Vaubel's chapter. It is his definition of the real exchange rate, $R = SP^*/P$, where R is the real exchange rate, S is the nominal exchange rate in units of home currency, P^* is the consumer price index in the foreign country, and P is its domestic counterpart.

Vaubel appears to believe that the stability of P is the overriding objective of monetary policy, because unanticipated fluctuations in the price level introduce noise into information about relative prices, while systematic variations in the price level reduce the usefulness of the national currency as a standard and store of value. If two governments are good at stabilizing their price levels, it is therefore possible to peg the nominal exchange rate between their currencies. If one government does better than the other, the nominal exchange rate should be allowed to float. The argument assumes, of course, that there is no intrinsic need to change the real exchange rate. A change in R has thus to be interpreted as an indication that monetary policies differ in quality, and any such change in R must be offset eventually by a change in S.

Those of us who come from the other planet are inclined to wonder about the intrinsic stability of the real exchange rate and may be inclined to attach less importance to the absolute stability of P, compared with other policy objectives. To sort out the issues, let us look at P more carefully, using a simple two-product framework. Let

$$P = p_1^a p_2^{1-a} = p_2(p_1/p_2)^a = Sp_2^*(p_1/p_2)^a$$

where p_1 is the price of the first country's export measured in that country's currency and a is its share in domestic consumption, p_2 is the price of the second country's export measured in the first country's currency, and p_2^* is the price of that same good measured in the second country's currency. My formulation concedes the validity of the Law of One Price, which I do for the sake of maintaining civility between the delegations from the two planets. Analogously,

$$P^* = p_2^*(p_1/p_2)^{a^*},$$

where $a*$ is the share of the first country's good in the second country's consumption. By implication,

$$R = (p_1/p_2)^{a* - a},$$

which says that Vaubel's measure of the real exchange rate has to change whenever there is a change in the terms of trade and the two countries consume different baskets of goods.

Vaubel knows all this but does not seem to care. He calls attention to one implication in the footnote, which asks us to assume that a is larger than one-half and $a*$ smaller than one-half. He does not bother to point out, however, that the calculations in his Table 9.1 and the country groupings in Table 9.2 may say more about the values of the shares, a and $a*$, than they say about the compatibility of countries' monetary policies, and they may say nothing at all about the need for real adjustment—the need for changes in relative prices—reflecting the size and character of real shocks, the degrees of internal and international factor mobility, the extent of trade flow or output diversification, and all of the other criteria usually cited in the currency area literature. Far from being a comprehensive criterion for currency unification, Vaubel's R may be a statistical artifact reflecting the weights assigned to goods in the two countries' consumer price indexes.

I will go farther. Measured changes in the terms of trade do not even tell me what I want to know about the problems of my planet. Before I can decide whether an exchange rate should be pegged or allowed to float, I want to know about the need for adjustment, *ex ante,* and the degree of price flexibility. If prices are sticky and exchange rates are pegged, measured changes in the terms of trade may understate the need for adjustment or, turning the argument on end, the need for exchange rate flexibility. And then there is the matter of capital mobility, which can lead to very large changes in the measured terms of trade because floating exchange rates may be quite volatile. This volatility occurs on both planets.

Let me turn now to other matters and start with the story of the two economists who met on the street. "How are you?" asked one. "Compared to what?" asked the other. When Vaubel discusses the costs of a currency union I had to ask whether he is comparing one money for Europe with the present European Monetary System or with some hypothetical system of freely floating exchange rates. It was not until I reached his conclusion, where he confessed doubts about the wisdom of intervening in exchange markets, that I came to my own conclusion about his frame of reference. He is comparing one money for Europe with freely floating rates.

The standard of comparison matters. If we are comparing one money for Europe with freely floating rates within Europe, the relevant question is the one that Vaubel raises: Will the threat of currency substitution between Europe's currency and, say, the dollar curb the inflationary proclivities of a European central bank more effectively than the threat of substitution between two European currencies curbs the corresponding proclivities of the existing national central banks? If, instead, the standard of comparison is the present pegged-rate arrangement, the question must be posed differently: Would a single European central bank react more strongly to the prospect of currency depreciation against the dollar than the Banque de France reacts today to the prospect of losing reserves within the EMS?

A similar problem arises when we come to competition between national currencies and an ECU functioning as a parallel currency. The performance of the ECU as an endogenously generated, unmanaged parallel currency, competing with officially issued national currencies, may be a very poor predictor of its performance as the officially managed currency of a European central bank.

This objection is not central to Vaubel's own argument, however, because he would use the ECU as an instrument for fostering Darwinian competition among the central banks, until only one of them remained and its national currency became indistinguishable from the ECU. To change the metaphor, it would be the function of the ECU to self-destruct once it had completed its search for the best-managed national currency—a proposal that is no doubt designed to persuade the Bundesbank to look with more favor upon the ECU, since it is the most probable survivor of Vaubel's Darwinian process. Even so, it is not clear that a Bundesbank board that gradually co-opted members from other EC countries would be the same Bundesbank board we know and love so well. Or, to change the metaphor once again, Vaubel's proposal looks like a way of making a regime change without confronting the Lucas critique, and that may not be possible.

Next, an objection to Vaubel's view of currency competition. The notion that national currencies can compete freely for the allegiance of individual users of money seems to me a simplistic doctrine. It flies in the face of strong evidence that the production of money is indeed a natural monopoly. On both of our planets, monetary history has featured the centralization of the currency-creating function. The convenience of profligate governments played a role in the process, but the gradual extinction of competing bank notes that took place everywhere says something about informational economies and the importance of transaction costs, which speak in turn to the case for having and using a single currency. As a practical matter, it may be very difficult for households and firms to use a foreign or parallel currency for day-to-day transactions. They may be able to diversify their portfolios but not the contents of their billfolds. This says, incidentally, that M-1 is the wrong number for Vaubel to use in his imaginative scheme for redefining the ECU and determining national representation on the board of the surviving central bank.

Finally, a question. On my planet, governments that have had the most experience with indexed contracts have been trying hard to get rid of them. Why does Vaubel want them on his planet?

Bibliography

Abraham, Jean-Paul, and Yvonne Lacroix-Destree (1984). "EMS, ECU and Commercial Banking." *Revue de la Banque* (February): 5–35.

Adams, Charles, and Daniel Gros (1986). "The Consequences of Real Exchange Rate Rules for Inflation: Some Illustrative Examples." *IMF Staff Papers,* 33, no. 5: 439–76.

Allen, Polly Reynolds (1986). *The ECU: Birth of a New Currency.* New York: Group of Thirty, *Occasional Papers,* no. 20.

Armington, Paul (1985). "Towards Understanding Major Fluctuations of the Dollar." Mimeo.

Artus, Jacques R. (1978). "Methods of Assessing the Long-Run Equilibrium Value of an Exchange Rate." *Journal of International Economics* 8: 275–99.

Asikoglu, Yaman (1986). "Macroeconomic Asymmetries and Policy Interdependence Between Europe and U.S." Ph.D. thesis. Kingston: Queen's University.

Axelrod, R. (1984). *The Evolution of Cooperation.* New York: Basic Books.

Balassa, Bela (1964). "The Purchasing-Power Parity Doctrine: A Reappraisal." *Journal of Political Economy* 72 (December): 1258–67.

———— (1984). "Adjustment Policies and Development Strategies in Sub-Saharan Africa, 1973–78." In Moshe Syrquin, Lance Taylor, and Larry E. Westphal (eds), *Economic Structure and Performance. Essays in Honor of Hollis B. Chenery.* New York: Academic Press, pp. 317–40.

———— (1985). "Policy Experiments in Chile, 1973–83." In Gary M. Walton (ed.), *National Economic Policies of Chile.* Greenwich, CT: JAI Press, pp. 203–38. Reprinted as Essay 8 in Bela Balassa, *Change and Challenge in the World Economy.* London: Macmillan, pp. 157–84.

Balassa, Bela, Gerardo M. Bueno, Pedro-Pablo Kuczynski, and Mario Henrique Simonsen (1986). *Toward Renewed Economic Growth in Latin America.* Mexico

City: El Colegio de Mexico, Rio de Janeiro: Fundacao Getulio Vargas, and Washington, D.C.: Institute for International Economics.

Balassa, Bela, and John Williamson (1987). *Adjusting to Success: Balance of Payments Policies in the East Asian NICs*. Washington, D.C.: Institute for International Economics.

Baldwin, Richard, and Paul Krugman (1986). "Persistent Trade Effects of Large Exchange Rate Shocks." Mimeo.

Barro, Robert J. (1974). "Are Government Bonds Net Wealth?" *Journal of Political Economy* 82: 1095–1117.

Bergsten, C. Fred (1986). "Crisis and Reform of the International Monetary System." The Ernest Struc Memorial Lecture, delivered at the School of Advanced International Studies of the Johns Hopkins University, November 13.

Black, Stanley W (1976). *Exchange Policies for Less Developed Countries in a World of Floating Rates. Essays in International Finance*, no. 11. Princeton University, Princeton, NJ (December).

Blanchard, Oliver (1979). "Speculative Bubbles, Crashes and Rational Expectations." *Economic Letters* 3: 386–89.

Branson, William H. (1979). "Exchange Rate Dynamics and Monetary policy." In Assar Lindbeck (ed.), *Inflation and Employment in Open Economies*. Amsterdam." North-Holland. pp. 189–224.

————— (1985). "Causes of Appreciation and Volatility of the Dollar." In The Federal Reserve Bank of Kansas City (ed.), *The U.S. Dollar—Recent Developments, Outlook, and Policy Options*. Kansas City, pp. 33–63.

————— (1986). "The Limits of Monetary Coordination as Exchange Rate Policy." *Brookings Papers on Economic Activity*, no. 1: 175–94.

Branson, William H., and W.J. Buiter (1983). "Monetary and Fiscal Policy with Flexible Exchange Rates." In J.S. Bhandari and B.H. Putnam (eds), *Economic Interdependence and Flexible Exchange Rates*. Cambridge, MA: MIT Press.

Brodsky, David A., and Gary S. Sampson (1983). "Exchange Rate Variations Facing Individual Industries in Developing Countries." *Journal of Development Studies* (April): 349–67.

————— (1984). "The Sources of Exchange Rate Instability in Developing Countries: Dollar, French Franc and SDR Pegging Countries." *Weltwirtschaftliches Archiv*, no. 1: 133–54.

Bruce, Neil, and Douglas Purvis (1985). "The Structure of Factor and Goods Markets in Open Economy Macroeconomic Models." In Ronald W. Jones and Peter Kenen (eds), *Handbook in International Economics*, vol. 2. Amsterdam: North-Holland.

Buiter, William H. (1985). "A Guide to Public Sector Debt and Deficits." *Economic Policy* 1: 14–79.

Buiter, William H., and Richard C. Marston (eds) (1985). *International Economic Policy Coordination*. Cambridge, MA: MIT Press.

Burrett, Mario (1982). *Rechnungseinheiten als Instrument der monetären Integration. Empirischer Befund, Theoretische Grundlagen und Währungspolitische Effizienz am Beispiel der Europäischen Gemeinschaft*. Freiburg.

Canarella, G., and S. Pollard (1986). "The 'Efficiency' of the London Metal Exchange. A Test with Overlapping and Non-Overlapping Data." *Journal of Banking and Finance* 10 (December): 575–93.

Chen, Chau-nan (1975). "Flexible Bimetallic Exchange Rates in China, 1650–1850: A Historical Example of Optimum Currency Areas." *Journal of Money, Credit, and Banking* 7: 359–76.

Christie, Herbert, and Michele Fratianni (1978). "European Monetary Union: Rehabilitation of a Case and Some Thoughts for Strategy." In M. Fratianni and Th. Peeters (eds), *One Money for Europe*. London: Basingstoke, pp. 3–34.

Claassen, Emil-Maria (1983). "Comments on Paul de Grauwe's 'What are the Scope and Limits of Fruitful International Monetary Cooperation in the 1980s?' " In: George M. von Furstenberg (ed.), *International Money and Credit: The Policy Roles*. Washington, D.C.: International Monetary Fund, pp. 409–19.

———— (1984). "Monetary Integration and Monetary Stability: The Economic Criteria of the Monetary Constitution." In P. Salin (ed.), *Currency Competition and Monetary Union*. The Hague: Nijhoff, pp. 47–58.

———— (1986). "The Optimum Monetary Constitution: Monetary Integration and Monetary Stability." In W. Meihofer (ed.), *Noi si mura. Selected Working Papers of the European University Institute*. Florence: European University Institute, pp. 399–429.

Claassen, Emil-Maria, and M. Krauss (1986). "Budget Deficits and the Exchange Rate." Florence: European University Institute, *Working Paper* no. 86/212.

Collins, Susan M. (1984). "Fixed Exchange Rates, Devaluations and Credibility Crisis." Ph.D. dissertation, MIT, Cambridge, MA.

———— (1985). "Expectation of Devaluation: An Inverse Gaussian Model of Realignment in the European Monetary System." Cambridge, MA: Harvard University. Mimeo. October.

———— (1986). "The Expected Timing of Devaluation: A Model of Realignment in the European Monetary System." Cambridge, MA: Harvard University. Mimeo.

Connolly, Michael (1985). "On the Optimal Currency Peg for Developing Countries." *Journal of Development Economics* (August): 555–59.

Cooper, Richard N. (1984). "Economic Interdependence and Coordination of Economic Policies." In R. Jones and P. Kenen (eds), *Handbook of International Economics*, vol. 2. Amsterdam: North-Holland.

———— (1986). "International Cooperation in Public Health as a Prologue to Macroeconomic Cooperation." *Brookings Discussion Papers in International Economics* (Washington, D.C.), no. 44.

Corden, W. Max (1981). "Exchange Rate Protection." In R. N. Cooper et al. (eds), *The International Monetary System under Flexible Exchange Rates: Global, Regional and National. Essays in Honor of Robert Triffin*. Cambridge, MA: Ballinger.

———— (1986). "Fiscal Policies, Current Accounts and Real Exchange Rates: In Search of a Logic of International Policy Coordination." *Weltwirtschaftliches Archiv* 122: 423–38.

Daniel, Betty C. (1986). "Empirical Determinants of Purchasing Power Parity Deviations." *Journal of International Economics* 21: 313–26.

De Grauwe, Paul (1983). "What are the Scope and Limits of Fruitful International Monetary Cooperation in the 1980s?" In George M. von Furstenberg (ed.), *International Money and Credit: The Policy Roles*. Washington, D.C.: IMF, pp. 375–408.

———— (1985). "Memorandum." In *Memoranda on the European Monetary System*.

House of Commons, Treasury and Civil Service Committee, *The Financial and Economic Consequences of UK Membership of the European Communities*. London, pp. 5–11.

De Grauwe, Paul, and Michele Fratianni (1985). "Interdependence, Macro-economic Policies and All That." *World Economy* 8: 63–76.

De Grauwe, Paul, and Theo Peeters (1979). "The EMS, Europe and the Dollar." *The Banker* (April): 39–45.

De Grauwe, Paul, and Marc Rosiers (1984). "Real Exchange Rate Variability and Monetary Disturbances." *International Economic Research Paper*, no. 44. Louvin: Centruum voor Economische Studien.

Deutsche Bundesbank (1979). *Monthly Report* (April).

Devereux, M., and D. Purvis (1986). "Fiscal Policy and the Real Exchange Rate." *Queen's University Discussion Paper*, no. 963. Kingston.

Dewes, L.D. (1986). "Mechanics of the Short-Term Interbank ECU Market." Conference on the ECU Market. New York: Salomon Brothers Center for the Study of Financial Institutions, January.

Diba, B.T., and H.I. Grossman (1985). "Rational Bubbles in Stock Prices?" *NBER Working Paper*, no. 1779.

Dornbusch, Rüdiger (1976). "Expectations and Exchange Rate Dynamics." *Journal of Political Economy* 84: 1161–76.

———— (1982). "Equilibrium and Disequilibrium Exchange Rates." *Zeitschrift für Wirtschafts- und Sozialwissenschaften*, no. 6: 573–99.

———— (1983). "Flexible Exchange Rates and Interdependence." *IMF Staff Papers* 30.

———— (1986). "Flexible Exchange Rates and Excess Capital Mobility." *Brookings Papers on Economic Activity*, no. 1: 209–26.

Duffey, G., and I. Giddy (1978). *The International Monetary Market*. Englewood Cliffs, NJ: Prentice-Hall.

The Economist (1978). All Saints' Day Manifesto for European Monetary Union, November 1. Reprinted in M. Fratianni and Th. Peters (eds), *One Money for Europe*. London: Basingstoke, pp. 37–43.

Edison, Hali J. (1986). "Is the ECU an Optimal Currency Basket?" *International Finance Discussion Papers*, no. 282 (May). Washington, D.C.: Board of Governors of the Federal Reserve System.

Edison, Hali J., Marcus Miller, and John Williamson (1987). "On Evaluating and Extending the Target Zone Proposal." *Journal of Policy Modeling*.

Edwards, Sebastian (1986). "Real Exchange Rate Variability: An Empirical Analysis of the Developing Countries Case." *NBER Working Paper*, no. 1939.

Evans, George W. (1986). "A Test for Speculative Bubbles and the Sterling–Dollar Exchange Rate: 1981–84." *American Economic Review* 76: 621–36.

Fama, E.F. (1976). "Forward Rates as Predictors of Future Spot Rates." *Journal of Financial Economics* 3 (October): 361–77.

———— (1984). "The Information in the Term Structure." *Journal of Financial Economics* 13 (December): 509–28.

Feldstein, Martin (1986). "The Budget Deficit and the Dollar." *NBER Working Paper*, no. 1898.

Findlay, M.C., and E.J. Kleinschmidt (1975). "Error Learning in the Eurodollar Market." *Journal Financial and Quantitative Analysis* 15 (September): 429–46.

Fischer, Stanley (1983). "The SDR and the IMF: Towards a World Central Bank?" In

G.M. von Furstenberg (ed.), *International Money and Credit: The Policy Roles.* Washington, D.C.: IMF, pp. 179–99.

———— (1987). "British Monetary Policy." In R. Layard and R. Dornbusch (eds.), *The Performance of the British Economy.* Oxford: Oxford University Press.

Fleming, J. Marcus (1962). "Domestic Financial Policies under Fixed and Floating Exchange Rates." *IMF Staff Papers* 9: 369–79.

———— (1971). "On Exchange Rate Unification." *Economic Journal* 81: 467–88.

Flood, Robert, and P. Garber (1983). "A Model of Stochastic Process Switching." *Econometrica* (May).

———— (1984). "Gold Monetization and Gold Discipline." *Journal of Political Economy* 92: 90–107.

Flood, Robert P., R.J. Hodrick, and P. Kaplan (1986). "An Evaluation of Recent Evidence on Stock Market Bubbles." *NBER Working Paper,* no. 1971.

Frankel, Jeffrey A. (1985). "Six Possible Meanings of 'Overvaluation': The 1981–85 Dollar." *Essays in International Finance,* no. 159 (December): Princeton University.

———— (1986). "The Sources of Disagreement Among the International Macro Models and Implications for Policy Coordination." *NBER Working Papers,* no. 1925 (May).

Frenkel, Jacob A. (1976). "A Monetary Approach to the Exchange Rate: Doctrinal Aspects and Empirical Evidence." *Scandinavian Journal of Economics* 78, no. 2: 200–224.

———— (1981). "The Collapse of Purchasing Power Parities During the 1970s." *European Economic Review* 16: 145–65.

———— (1986). "Commentary on 'Causes of Appreciation and Volatility of the Dollar.' " In Federal Reserve Bank of Kansas City (ed.), *The U.S. Dollar—Recent Developments, Outlook, and Policy Options.* Kansas City, pp. 53–63.

Frenkel, Jacob A., and Assaf Razin (1985). "Government Spending, Debt and International Economic Interdependence." *Economic Journal* 95: 619–36.

———— (1986a). "Fiscal Policies in the World Economy." *Journal of Political Economy* 94, no. 3: 564–94.

———— (1986b). "Real Exchange Rates, Interest Rates and Fiscal Policies." *Economic Studies Quarterly* 37, no. 2: 99–113.

———— (1986c). "Fiscal Policies and Real Exchange Rates in the World Economy." *NBER Working Paper,* no. 2065.

———— (1986d). "Deficits with Distortionary Taxes: International Dimensions." *NBER Working Papers,* no. 2080.

———— (1987). *Fiscal Policies and the World Economy.* Cambridge, MA: MIT Press.

Friedman, Milton (1953). "The Case for Flexible Exchange Rates." In M. Friedman (ed.), *Essays in Positive Economics.* Chicago, IL: Chicago University Press pp. 157–203.

Gandolfo, G. (1986). *International Economics.* Berlin: Springer-Verlag.

Gandolfo, G., P.C. Padoan, and M.L. Petit (1986). "Optimal Exchange Rate Management via Pontryagin's Principle in the Italian Economy." Proceedings of the 25th IEEE Conference on Decision and Control, Athens, December 10–12.

Gandolfo, G., and M.L. Petit (1987). "Dynamic Optimization in Continuous Time and Optimal Policy Design in the Italian Economy." *Annales d'Economie et de Statistique.* no. 6–7, 311–33.

Gebauer, Wolfgang (1986). "Ecunomics: Perspektiven einer europäischen Geldver-
    fassung." *Kredit und Kapital* 11: 159–77.
Genberg, Hans (1978). "Purchasing Power Parity under Fixed and Flexible Exchange
    Rates." *Journal of International Economics* 8: 247–76.
———— (1981). "Purchasing Power Parity as a Rule for a Crawling Peg." In J. William-
    son (ed.), *Exchange Rate Rules: The Theory, Performance and Prospects of the
    Crawling Peg*. London: Macmillan.
———— (1984). "On Choosing the Right Rules for Exchange-Rate Management." *The
    World Economy* 7: 391–406.
Genberg, Hans, and Alexander K. Swoboda (1983). "Fixed Exchange Rates, Flexible
    Exchange Rates, or the Middle of the Road: A Reexamination of the Arguments in
    View of Recent Experience." *Discussion Papers in International Economics*
    (Geneva), no. 830.
———— (1987). "The Current Account and the Policy Mix under Flexible Exchange
    Rates." *IMF Working Paper,* WP 87/70 (October 15).
Giavazzi, F., and A. Giovannini (1985). "European Currency Experience." *Economic
    Policy* (October).
Giavazzi, F., and M. Pagano (1985). "Capital Controls and the European Monetary
    System." In F. Giavazzi (ed.), *Capital Controls and Foreign Exchange Legisla-
    tion, Occasional Paper* no. 1 (February). Milano: Euromobiliene.
———— (1988). "The Advantage of Tying One's Hands: EMS Discipline and Central Bank
    Credibility." *European Economic Review.* 32, no. 5: 1055–75.
Girton, Lance, and Don Roper (1980). "The Theory of Currency Substitution and Mone-
    tary Unification." *Economie Appliquée,* 23, no. 1: 135–60.
Graumann, Dieter (1979). *Die Parallelwährung als Europäische Integrationsalternative*.
    Frankfurt/M.
Guillaumont, Patrick (1986). "L'ouverture commercial sur l'extérieur mesurée à partir du
    taux d'exportation." Paper presented at the Conference Strategies de Développe-
    ment Comparées (zone franc et hors zone franc), Clermont-Ferrand, France,
    November.
Guillaumont, Sylviane (1984). "Les raisons du choix de leur regime des changes par les
    pays en voie de développment." Paper presented at the Congrès International des
    Economistes de Langue Française, Clermont-Ferrand, France, May.
Halm, G.N. (1965). "The 'Band' Proposal: The Limits of Permissible Exchange Rate
    Variations." *Special Papers in International Economics,* no. 6. Princeton, NJ:
    Princeton University, International Finance Section.
Hamada, K. (1974). "Alternative Exchange Rate Systems and the Interdependence of
    Monetary Policies." In R. Aliber (ed.), *National Monetary Policies and the Inter-
    national Financial System*. Chicago, IL: Chicago University Press.
———— (1979). "Macroeconomic Strategy and Coordination under Alternative Exchange
    Rates." In R. Dornbusch and J.A. Frenkel (eds.), *International Economic Pol-
    icies*. Baltimore: The Johns Hopkins University Press.
Hayek, Friedrich A. (1976). "Choice in Currency. A Way to Stop Inflation." *Occasional
    Papers*, no. 48. London: Institute of Economic Affairs.
Helleiner, Gerald K. (1981). "The Impact of the Exchange Rate System on the Develop-
    ing Countries. A Report to the Group of Twenty-Four." New York: UNDP/
    UNCTAD Project INT/75/015, April.

Henderson, Dale W. (1984). "Exchange Market Intervention Operations: Their Role in Financial Policy and Their Effects." In J.F.O. Bilson and R.C. Marston (eds), *Exchange Rate Theory and Practice*. Chicago, IL: The University of Chicago Press, pp. 359–98.

Hirschmann, Albert O. (1970). *Exit, Voice and Loyalty*. Cambridge, MA: MIT Press.

International Monetary Fund (ed.) (1985). *Users' Guide to the SDR*. Washington, D.C.

——— (1987). "The Role of the SDR in the International Monetary System." *Occasional Paper*, no. 51. Washington, D.C.

Istituto Bancario San Paolo di Torino (1984). "Expectation of an ECU Basket Re-Definition." *ECU Newsletter* (June): 12–16.

Johnson, Harry G. (1970). "The Case for Flexible Exchange Rates, 1969." In G.N. Halm (ed.), *Approaches to Greater Flexibility of Exchange Rates*. Princeton, NJ: Princeton University Press, pp. 91–111.

Jurgensen, Philippe (1983). *Report of the Working Group on Exchange Market Intervention*. Paris: Ministry of France.

Kenen, Peter B. (1969). "The Theory of Optimum Currency Areas: An Eclectic View." In R.A. Mundell and A.K. Swoboda (eds.), *Monetary Problems of the International Economy*. Chicago, IL: Chicago University Press, pp. 41–60.

——— (1983). "Use of the SDR to Supplement or Substitute for other Means of Finance." In G.M. von Furstenberg (ed.), *International Money and Credit: The Policy Roles*. Washington, D.C.: IMF, pp. 327–60.

——— (1986). "Financing, Adjustment, and the International Monetary Fund." *Studies in International Economics*. Washington, D.C.: The Brookings Institution.

Keyzer, Marinus (1983). "Comment on 'International Monies and Monetary Arrangements in Private Markets' by D.F. Lomax." In G. von Furstenberg (ed.), *International Money and Credit: The Policy Roles*. Washington, D.C.: International Monetary Fund, pp. 319–22.

Kiguel, Miguel A., and Jose Saul Lizondo (1986). "Theoretical and Policy Aspects of Dual Exchange Rate Systems." *Discussion Paper* no. 201 (October). Washington, D.C.: World Bank Development Research Department.

Klau, F., and A. Mittelstadt (1985). "Labour Market Flexibility and External Price Shocks." *Working Papers*. OECD, Economics and Statistics Department.

Kloten, Norbert (1985). "Die ECU: Perspektiven Monetarer Integration in Europa." *Europa-Archiv* 15: 415–66.

Krueger, Anne O. (1974). "The Political Economy of a Rent-Seeking Society." *American Economic Review* (June): 291–303.

Krugman, Paul R. (1986). "Is the Strong Dollar Sustainable?" In Federal Reserve Bank of Kansas City (ed.), *The U.S. Dollar—Recent Development, Outlook, and Policy Options*. Kansas City.

Laidler, David (1978). "Difficulties with European Monetary Union." In M. Fratianni and Th. Peeters (eds.), *One Money for Europe*. London: Basingstoke, pp. 52–63.

Layard, R., G. Basevi, O. Blanchard, W. Buiter, and R. Dornbusch (1984). "Europe: The Case for Unsustainable Growth." *Centre for European Policy Studies Papers*, no. 8/9.

Lehment, Harmen (1984). "Freely Flexible Exchange Rates or a Common Currency?" In P. Salin (ed.), *Currency Competition and Monetary Union*. The Hague: Nijhoff, pp. 247–60.

Levich, Richard M. (1978). "Tests of Forecast Models of Market Efficiency in the International Money Market." In J.A. Frenkel and H.G. Johnson (eds.), *The Economics of Exchange Rates*. Reading, MA: Addison-Wesley.

—— (1986). "Gauging the Evidence on Recent Movements in the Value of the Dollar." In Federal Reserve Bank of Kansas City (ed.), *The U.S. Dollar—Recent Development, Outlook, and Policy Options*. Kansas City.

Liviatan, N. (1980). "Anti-Inflationary Monetary Policy and the Capital-Import Tax." *Warwick Economic Research Papers*, no. 171.

Lomax, D.F. (1983). "International Moneys and Monetary Arrangements in Private Markets." In G.M. von Furstenberg (ed.), *International Money and Credit: The Policy Roles*. Washington, D.C.: IMF, pp. 261–318.

Lumsden, M.A. (1985). "The Level and Structure of Interest Rates on SDR-Denominated Financial Assets." Washington, D.C.: International Monetary Fund, Treasurer's Department, DM/85/27, May.

Marris, Robin, and Steven Martin (1985). "New Light on the Trend of Real Exchange Rates." *Financial Times*, October 30.

Marris, Stephen (1985). "Deficits and the Dollar: The World Economy at Risk." *Policy Analyses in International Economics* (Washington, D.C.), no. 14.

Marston, Richard C. (1980). "Cross-Country Effects of Sterlization, Reserve Currencies and Foreign Exchange Intervention." *Journal of International Economics* 10: 63–78.

—— (1985). "Exchange Rate Unions as an Alternative to Flexible Rates: The Effects of Real and Monetary Disturbances." In J. Bilson and R.C. Marston (eds.), *Exchange Rate Theory and Practice*. Chicago, IL: The University of Chicago Press.

Masera, Rainer S. (1986). "An Increasing Role for the ECU." *Temi di Discussione*, no. 65 (June). Rome: Banca d'Italia.

McKinnon, Ronald I. (1963). "Optimum Currency Areas." *American Economic Review* 53: 717–25.

—— (1982). "Currency Substitution and Instability in the Dollar World Standard." *American Economic Review* 72: 320–33.

—— (1984). *An International Standard for Monetary Stabilization*. Washington D.C.: Institute for International Economics.

—— (1986). "Commentary on 'Is There a Case for More Managed Exchange Rates?' " In Federal Reserve Bank of Kansas City (ed.), *The U.S. Dollar—Recent Developments, Outlook, and Policy Options*. Kansas City, pp. 213–15.

—— (1986a). "Monetary and Exchange Rate Policies for International Financial Stability: A Proposal." Stanford, CA. Mimeo. September.

Meese, Richard A. (1986). "Testing for Bubbles in Exchange Markets: A Case of Sparkling Rates?" *Journal of Political Economy* 94: 345–73.

Meese, Richard, and K. Rogoff (1983a). "The Out-of-Sample Failure of Empirical Exchange Rate Models: Sampling Error or Misspecification?" In J.A. Frenkel (ed.), *Exchange Rates and International Macroeconomics*. Chicago, IL: The University of Chicago Press.

—— (1983b). "Empirical Exchange Rate Models of the Seventies: Are Any Fit to Survive?" *Journal of International Economics* 14.

—— (1985). "Was It Real?" The Exchange Rate–Interest Differential Relation, 1973–

1984." *International Finance Discussion Papers*, no. 268. Washington, D.C.: IMF.

Meiselman, D. (1966). *The Term Structure of Interest Rates*. Englewood Cliffs, NJ: Prentice-Hall.

Melino, A. (1986). "The Term Structure of Interest Rates: Reform, Evidence and Theory. University of Toronto, Department of Economics and Policy Analysis. Mimeo.

Melitz, Jacques (1985). "The Welfare Case for the European Monetary System." *Journal of International Money and Finance* 4, no. 4: 485–506.

Micossi, Stefano (1985). "The Intervention and Financing Mechanisms of the EMS and the Role of the ECU." *Banca Nazionale del Lavoro, Quarterly Review* (December): 327–45.

Moltke, Albrecht von (1986). "Die Private Verwendung von ECU." Reutlingen: Institut für Europäische Wirtschaftsfragen, Beiträge zu Internationalen Wirtschaftsfragen, April.

Morgan Guaranty (1978). *World Financial Markets* (May).

Mundell, Robert A. (1961). "A Theory of Optimum Currency Areas." *American Economic Review* 51: 657–65.

———— (1963). "Capital Mobility and Stabilization Policy under Fixed and Flexible Exchange Rates." *Canadian Journal of Economics and Political Science* 29: 475–85.

———— (1968). *International Economics*. New York: MacMillan.

Mussa, Michael (1977). "The Welfare Cost of Inflation and the Role of Money as a Unit of Account." *Journal of Money, Credit, and Banking* 9: 276–86.

———— (1981). "The Role of Official Intervention." *Occasional Paper*, no. 6. New York.

———— (1986). "Nominal Exchange Rate Regimes and the Behavior of Real Exchange Rates: Evidence and Implications." *Carnegie-Rochester Conference Series on Public Policy* 25: 117–213.

Neary, J.P., and D.D. Purvis (1983). "Real Shocks and Exchange Rate Dynamics." In Jacob A. Frenkel (ed.), *Exchange Rates and International Macroeconomics*. Chicago, IL: The University of Chicago Press.

Neumann, Manfred J.M. (1983). "Comment on 'International Monies and Monetary Arrangements in Private Markets' by D.F. Lomax." In G. von Furstenberg (ed.), *International Money and Credit: The Policy Roles*. Washington, D.C.: International Monetary Fund, pp. 322–26.

Nurkse, Ragnar (1944). *International Currency Experience. Lessons of the Interwar Period*. Princeton, NJ: Princeton University Press.

Obstfeld, Maurice (1982). "Can We Sterlize? Theory and Evidence." *American Economic Review, Papers and Proceedings* 82: 45–50.

———— (1983). "Exchange Rates, Inflation, and the Sterilization Problem: Germany 1975–1981." *European Economic Review* 21: 161–89.

———— (1985). "Floating Exchange Rates: Experience and Prospects." *Brookings Papers on Economic Activity*, no. 2: 369–450.

———— (1986). "Rational and Self-Fulfilling Balance-of-Payments Crises." *American Economic Review* 76: 72–81.

Officer, Lawrence H. (1976). "The Purchasing-Power-Parity Theory of Exchange Rates: A Review Article." *IMF Staff Papers* (March): 1–60.

Oppenheimer, P.M. (1974). "Non-Traded Goods and the Balance of Payments: A Historical Note." *Journal of Economic Literature* 12, no. 3: 882–88.

Oudiz, Gilles (1985). "European Policy Coordination: An Evaluation." *CEPR-Discussion Paper Series,* no. 81 (October).

Paraire, Jean-Luc (1986). "L'instabilité des taux de change." Paper presented at the Conference Strategies de Développement Comparé (zone franc et hors zone franc), Clermont-Ferrand, France, November.

Pearce, Ivor Frank (1974). "Some Aspects of European Monetary Integration." In H.G. Johnson and A.R. Nobay (eds.), *Issues in Monetary Economics.* London: Oxford University Press, pp. 75–97.

Poole, William (1970). "Optimal Policy Choice of Monetary Policy Instruments in a Simple Stochastic Macro Model." *Quarterly Journal of Economics* 84: 197–216.

Purvis, Douglas D. (1985). "Public Sector Deficits, International Capital Movements, and the Domestic Economy: The Medium-Term is the Message." *Canadian Journal of Economics* 18 (November): 723–42.

Putnam, R., and C.R. Henning (1986). "The Bonn Summit of 1978: How does International Economic Policy Really Work?" *Discussion Papers in International Economics* (October). Washington, D.C.: The Brookings Institution.

Rogoff, K. (1985). "Can International Monetary Policy Cooperation be Counterproductive?" *Journal of International Economics.* 18, no. 3–4: 199–218.

———— (1985a). "Can Exchange Rate Predictability be Achieved Without Monetary Convergence? Evidence from the EMS." *European Economic Review* 28 (June–July): 93–116.

———— (1985b). "The Optimal Degree of Commitment to an Intermediate Monetary Target." *Quarterly Journal of Economics* 100. no. 4: 1169–89.

Russo, M., and G. Tullio (1987). "Monetary Rules for Price Stability and for the Smooth Balance of Payments Adjustment Under Different Exchange Rates Systems: The Lesson for the EMS." Brussels: Commission of the European Communities. July. Mimeo.

Sachs, Jeffrey D. (1983). "International Policy Coordination in a Dynamic Macroeconomic Model." *NBER Working Paper,* no. 1166.

———— (1984). "Real Exchange Rate Effects of Fiscal Policy." *NBER Working Paper,* no. 1255.

———— (1985). "The Policy Mix and the Dollar: 1985." *Brookings Papers of Economic Activity,* no. 1.

———— (1986). "Is There a Case for More Managed Exchange Rates?" In Federal Reserve Bank of Kansas City (ed.), *The U.S. Dollar—Recent Developments, Outlook, and Policy Options.* Kansas City, pp. 185–211.

———— (1986a). "The Uneasy Case for Greater Exchange Rate Coordination." *American Economic Review, Papers and Proceedings* 76: 336–41.

Sachs, Jeffrey D., and Charles Wyplosz (1984). "La Politique Budgétaire et le Taux de Change Réel," *Annales de L'INSEE,* no. 53.

Santomero, A.M. (1975). "The Error-Learning Hypothesis and the Term Structure of Interest Rates in Eurodollars." *Journal of Finance* 30 (June): 773–84.

Scharrer, Hans-Eckart (1984). "Europe und die ECU." *Zeitschrift für das Gesamte Kreditwesen* 37: 1086–91.

Seidel, H. (ed.) (1984). *Geldwertstabilität und Wirtschaftswachstum.* Gottingen: Vandenhoeck & Ruprecht.

Sengupta, A. (1986). "Allocation of SDRs Linked to Reserve Needs: A Proposal." *Finance and Development* 23, no. 3.

Sjaastad, Larry A. (1983). "Liberalization and Stabilization Experiences in the Southern Cone." In Nicolas Ardito Barletta, Mario I. Blejer, and Luis Landau (eds.), *Economic Liberalization and Stabilization Policies in Argentina, Chile and Uruguay.* Washington, D.C.: World Bank, pp. 87–103.

Stiglitz, Joseph E., and Andrew Weiss (1981). "Credit Rationing in Markets with Imperfect Information." *American Economic Review* 71: 393–411.

—— (1983). "Incentive Effects of Terminations: Applications to the Credit and Labor Markets." *American Economic Review* 73: 912–27.

Stoltenberg, Gerhard (1985). "Die ECU—Diskussion geht am Kern vorbei." *Handelsblatt,* May 31. Reprinted in Deutsche Bundesbank, *Auszuge aus Presseartikeln,* no. 37: 1–2.

Swoboda, Alexander (1968). *The Euro-Dollar Market: An Interpretation.* Essays in International Finance, Princeton: Princeton University Press.

Takagi, Shinji (1984). "Testing the Performance of the SDR Peg in Jordan, 1975–83." Washington, D.C.: International Monetary Fund. Mimeo.

—— (1986). "Pegging to a Currency Basket." *Finance and Development* (September): 41–44.

Thygesen, Niels (1980). "Some Economic and Financial Issues." In R. Triffin and A.A.L. Swings (eds.), *The Private Use of the ECU.* Brussels. Kredietbank, pp. 9–24.

—— (1981). "The European Monetary System—An Approximate Implementation of the Crawling Peg?" In J. Williamson (ed.), *Exchange Rate Rules: Theory, Performance and Prospects of the Crawling Peg.* London: Macmillan Press.

Tobin, James (1982). "A Proposal for Monetary Reform." In J. Tobin (ed.), *Essays in Economic Theory and Policy.* Cambridge, MA: MIT Press.

Triffin, Robert (1963). *Gold and the Dollar Crisis.* New Haven: CT: Yale University Press.

Tryon, Ralph W. (1983). "Small Empirical Models of Exchange Market Intervention." *Staff Studies,* no. 134. Washington, D.C.: Board of Governors of the Federal Reserve System.

Ungerer, H., O. Evans, T. Mayer, and P. Young (1986). "The European Monetary System: Recent Developments." *IMF Occasional Paper,* no. 48.

Ungerer, H., O. Evans, and P. Nyberg (1983). "The European Monetary System: The Experience, 1979–82." *IMF Occasional Paper,* no. 19.

Vaubel, Roland (1977). "Free Currency Competition." *Weltwirtschaftliches Archiv* 113: 435–61.

—— (1978a). "Real Exchange-Rate Changes in the European Community: A New Approach to the Determination of Optimum Currency Areas." *Journal of International Economics* 8: 319–39.

—— (1978b). "Strategies for Currency Unification." *Kieler Strudien* (Tübingen) 156.

—— (1978c). "The Money Supply in Europe: Why EMS May Make Inflation Worse." *Euromoney* (December): 139–42.

—— (1980a). "The Return to the New European Monetary System: Objectives, Incentives, Perspectives." In K. Brunner and A.J. Meltzer (eds.), *Monetary Institutions and the Policy Process. Carnegie-Rochester Conference Series on Public Policy,* 13, Amsterdam, pp. 173–221.

––––––– (1980b). "Discussion of Governor de Strycker's Paper." In R. Triffin and A.A.L. Swings (eds.), *The Private Use of the ECU*. Brussels: Kredietbank, p. 64.

––––––– (1984). "The Government's Money Monopoly: Externalities or Natural Monopoly?" *Kyklos* 37: 27–58.

––––––– (1985). "International Collusion or Competition for Macroeconomic Policy Coordination? A Restatement." *Recherches Economiques de Louvain* 51.

––––––– (1987). "Review of 'The ECU: Birth of a New Currency' by Polly Reynolds Allen." *The World of Economy* 10 (March): 98–100.

Wickham, Peter (1985). "The Choice of Exchange Rate Regime in Developing Countries." *IMF Staff Papers* (June): 248–88.

Williamson, John (1982). "A Survey of the Literature on the Optimal Peg." *Journal of Development Economics* (August): 39–62.

––––––– (1984). "A New SDR Allocation." Washington, D.C.: Institute for International Economics.

––––––– (1985a). *The Exchange Rate System*. Rev. edn. Washington, D.C.: Institute for International Economics.

––––––– (1985b). "On the System in Bretton Woods." *American Economic Review* (May).

––––––– (1986). "Target Zones and Indicators as Instruments for International Economic Policy Coordination. A Report to the Group of 24." Institute for International Economics, Washington, D.C.

––––––– (1986a). "Target Zones and the Management of the Dollar." *Brookings Papers on Economic Activity*, no. 1: 165–74.

––––––– (1987). "Exchange Rate Policy for Developing Countries: A Case for Collective Action." *Journal of Foreign Exchange and International Finance*.

Woo, Wing T. (1984). "Speculative Bubbles in the Foreign Exchange Markets." *Brookings Discussion Papers*, no. 13.

Yeager, Leland B. (1958). "Exchange Rates Within a Common Market." *Social Research* 25: 415–38.

Name Index

Subject Index

About the Editor and Contributors

EMIL-MARIA CLAASSEN is a Professor of Monetary Economics and International Economics at the University of Paris-Dauphine. Professor Claassen has a Ph.D. from the University of Cologne (Germany) and from the University of Paris (France). He has passed the German *Habilitation* (University of Cologne) and the French *Concours d'Agrégation* (University of Paris). He has been post-doctoral fellow at the University of Chicago and held academic positions at INSEAD (Fontainebleau, France), at the European University Institute (Florence, Italy), and as Bundesbank Stiftungsprofessur at the Free University of Berlin (Germany). He was Visiting Professor at Queen's University, Stanford University, and New York University. He is consultant of the World Bank and of the FAO. Professor Claassen is author or co-author of 18 books and 70 journal articles. His current research interests focus on development economics.

BELA BALASSA is Professor of Political Economy at Johns Hopkins University and Consultant to the World Bank. He holds a doctor's degree in law and political science from the University of Budapest (1951) and a Ph.D. in Economics from Yale University (1959). He has taught at the Universities of California (Berkeley), Columbia, Paris, and Clérmont-Ferrand and at the Institut d'Études Politiques. Dr. Balassa has been consultant to U.S. governmental agencies, UN organizations, and governments of developing countries. He has more than 250 publications to his credit in professional journals and collective volumes and is the author, co-author, or editor of 24 books.

ULRICH CAMEN is Researcher at the Geneva Graduate Institute of International Studies from which he received his Ph.D. in 1975. His main research fields are international trade and international finance.

MARCELLO DE CECCO is Professor of Economics at the University of Roma, La Sapienza, Faculty of Economics and Commerce. Previously he taught at the European University Institute in Florence and at the University of Siena. He has been visiting professor in various European Universities, including Oxford, Edinburgh, the London School of Economics, and the École National d'Administration, Paris. He has held the Chair of Italian Culture at the University of California, Berkeley, and has been a Fellow of the Institute for Advanced Study, Princeton University. For several years a director of the Monte dei Paschi di Sien and of the Italian International Bank, he is the author of *Saggi di Politica Monetaria*, 1968, and *Money and Empire*, 1974. He is editor of the following works: *International Adjustment*, 1983 (with J. P. Fitoussi); *Changing Money*, 1987; *Economic Theory and Economic Institutions*, 1985; and *A European Central Bank?*, 1989 (with A. Giovannini).

SUSAN M. COLLINS is an Associate Professor of Economics at Harvard University and a Faculty Research Fellow at the National Bureau of Economic Research. She received her B.A. in economics from Harvard University and her Ph.D. from the Massachusetts Institute of Technology. She teaches courses in international trade and open economy macroeconomics. She is the author of numerous articles. Her current research has focused on exchange rate management, macroeconomic policy and performance in South Korea, and the developing country debt crisis.

FRANCESCO CONTESSO is Country Analyst at the Commission of the European Communities in Brussels. He has degrees in economics (University of Naples and University of Paris IX) and international finance (University of Paris XIII).

GIANCARLO GANDOLFO is Professor of International Economics at the Faculty of Economics and Commerce, University of Rome, La Sapienza. He holds degrees from the University of Rome. He has been on the staff of the research department of the Bank of Italy and Professor of Mathematical Economics at the Faculty of Economics and Banking of Siena. He is the author or co-author of 15 books, over 80 articles, including *Aggiustamento della bilancia dei pagamenti ed equilibrio macroeconomico* (1970); *Economic Dynamics: Methods and Models* (1971 and 1980); *Qualitative Analysis and Econometric Estimation of Continuous Time Dynamic Models* (1981); *International Economics I* and *II* (1987); *Modelli econometrici in tempo continuo e politiche economiche ottimali* (1989).

HANS GENBERG is a Professor of Economics at the Graduate Institute of International Studies in Geneva, Switzerland. Holder of a B.A. in mathematics from Macalester College and M.A. and Ph.D. degrees in economics from the University of Chicago, Dr. Genberg has been a Visiting Professor at the Graduate School of Business of the University of Chicago a Visiting Scholar at the International Monetary Fund. He is the author of two books and numerous journal articles dealing with international monetary economics. His most recent research has dealt with exchange-rate management, international interdependence of stock markets, and the determinants of current account imbalances under floating exchange rates.

FRANCESCO GIAVAZZI is Professor of Economics at the University of Bologna, a Research Associate of the National Bureau of Economic Research in Cambridge (Mass.), and Co-Director of the International Macroeconomics program at the Centre for Economic Policy Research in London. He has a Ph.D. from Massachusetts Institute of Technology and has taught at Essex University, the University of Padova, and the University of Venice. He is a member of the CEPS Macroeconomic Policy Group, an advisory group to the Directorate General for Economic and Financial Affairs at the EC, and of the Treasury Advisory Committee on the Management of the Public Debt in Rome. His monograph *Limiting Exchange Rate Flexibility: the EMS,* co-written with Alberto Giovannini of Columbia University) has been published by MIT Press in April 1989.

PAUL DE GRAUWE is a Professor of Economics at the University of Leuven, Belgium, and also a research fellow at the Centre for European Policy Studies, Brussels. He earned his Ph.D. from Johns Hopkins University and has worked as an economist at the International Monetary Fund (1973–74). He has been a visiting professor at the University of Paris, the University of Michigan, the University of Pennsylvania, the University of Brussels, the University of Kiel. He has published 5 books and more than 90 articles. His research interests focus on international monetary problems.

PETER B. KENEN is Walker Professor of Economics and International Finance and Director of the International Finance Section at Princeton University. He earned his Ph.D. at Harvard and taught at Columbia, where he was chairman of the Economics Department and Provost of the University. He has been a fellow of the Center for Advanced Study in the Behavioral Sciences and of the Royal Institute of International Affairs and has held visiting appointments at the Hebrew University, and Stockholm School of Economics, the Australian National University, and the University of California, Berkeley. His recent publications include *Managing Exchange Rates* (1988), *The International Economy* (1989), and *Exchange Rates and Policy Coordination* (1989).

MANFRED J.M. NEUMANN is a Professor of Economics at the University of Bonn. He holds the Dr. rer. pol. from the University of Marburg. He has held positions at the Deutsche Bundesbank, the University of Konstanz, and the Free University of Berlin. He is an organizer of the Konstanz Seminar on Monetary Theory and Monetary Policy and serves on the editorial boards of several journals, including the Journal of International Money and Finance. Dr. Neumann is the author or co-author of over 60 articles and book chapters on monetary economies.

DOUGLAS D. PURVIS is Professor and Head of the Department of Economics at Queen's University in Kingston, Canada. He is the author of numerous academic articles for professional journals, is co-author of a widely used principles of economics textbook, and has written extensively in the public press on economic policy. Previous positions he has held include Director of the John Deutsch Institute for the Study of Economic Policy and Clifford Clark Visiting Economist at the Department of Finance, Ottawa.

PASCAL SALIN is a Professor of Economics at the University Paris-IX-Dauphine. He has published numerous articles and books, among which are *L'ordre monétaire mondial* (1982) and *L'arbitraire fiscal* (1985), and he has edited several books, including *Currency Competition and Monetary Union* (1984). He is presently preparing a book on the theory of monetary systems.

JÜRGEN SCHRÖDER is Professor of Economics and International Economic Relations at University of Mannheim. Since 1985 he is Managing Director of the Institute for Post Graduate Studies in International Economics at the University of Mannheim. He has been a Visiting Professor at the University of California in Santa Cruz, the University of Hong Kong, Stanford University, and most recently at the European University Institute in Florence. He was a Visiting Scholar at the Hoover Institution, Stanford University (1984–85). He is the author of more than 30 articles on economic theory, economic policy, and international economics and the author or co-author of two books on international economics.

ALEXANDER SWOBODA is a Professor of Economics at the Graduate Institute of International Studies and Director of the International Center for Monetary Banking Studies in Geneva. A Yale graduate, Dr. Swoboda has been Post-Doctoral Fellow in Political Economy at the University of Chicago (1966–67), visiting assistant professor at the Chicago Graduate School of Business, and visiting professor at John Hopkins University's Bologna Center, the London School of Economics and Political Science, and Harvard University. He also teaches monetary analysis at the University of Geneva. An occasional consultant to private banks, central banks and international organizations such as the IMF and World Bank. Dr. Swoboda is chiefly interested in international monetary economics, macroeconomics, and international banking and finance.

GIUSEPPE TULLIO is Professor of Economics at the University of Cagliari (Italy). A University of Chicago Ph.D. (1977), he has been Economist at the International Monetary Fund, Senior Economist at the Research Department of the Bank of Italy, Economic Adviser of the Italian Minister of the Budget (1981–1983), and Economic Adviser at the Commission of the European Communities (1984–1987). He has published *The Monetary Approach to External Adjustment: A Case Study of Italy* (1981), and, with A. Sommariva, *German Macro-economic History: 1880–1979* (1987). He has also published several articles on applied monetary economics in the leading journals in the field.

ROLAND VAUBEL is a Professor of Economics at the University of Mannheim, West Germany. He has a B.A. in Philosophy, Politics and Economics from the University of Oxford, an M.A. from Columbia University (New York) and a Ph.D. from the University of Kiel. He has been a staff member of the Institute of World Economics in Kiel, a Professor of Economics at Erasmus University Rotterdam and a Visiting Professor of International Economics at the University of Chicago (Graduate School of Business). His research interests focus on international finance, international organizations, the theory of public choice, and social policy.

JOHN WILLIAMSON is a Senior Fellow at the Institute for International Economics in Washington, D.C. His extensive career in international finance and monetary affairs includes service as an economic consultant to the UK Treasury from 1968–70, as an adviser to the International Monetary Fund (1972–74), and teaching posts at the Universities of York (1963–68) and Warwick (1970–77) in England, the Pontificia Universidade Catolica do Rio de Janeiro in Brazil (1978–81) and as a Visiting Professor at MIT (1967, 1980). His publications on international monetary affairs include *The Failure of World Monetary Reform 1971–74; IMF Conditionality; The Open Economy and the World Economy; The Exchange Rate System; Political Economy and International Money; Financial Intermediation Beyond the Debt Crisis; Capital Flight and Third World Debt;* and, most recently, *Voluntary Approaches to Debt Relief.* He was educated at the London School of Economics and received his Ph.D. from Princeton University.